DESIGNING PUBLIC DOCUMENTS

The Policy Studies Institute (PSI) is Britain's leading independent research organisation undertaking studies of economic, industrial and social policy, and the workings of political institutions.

PSI is a registered charity, run on a non-profit basis, and is not associated with any political party, pressure group or commercial interest.

PSI attaches great importance to covering a wide range of subject areas with its multi- disciplinary approach. The Institute's researchers are organised in groups which currently cover the following programmes:

Crime, Justice and Youth Studies – Employment and Society – Ethnic Equality and Diversity – European Industrial Development – Family Finances – Information and Citizenship – Information and Cultural Studies – Social Care and Health Studies – Work, Benefits and Social Participation

This publication arises from the Information and Cultural Studies group and is one of over 30 publications made available by the Institute each year.

Information about the work of PSI, and a catalogue of available books can be obtained from:

Marketing Department, PSI
100 Park Village East, London NW1 3SR

Designing Public Documents

A review of research

Elaine Kempson and Nick Moore

POLICY STUDIES INSTITUTE
London

8753

FG (KEM)

The publishing imprint of the independent
POLICY STUDIES INSTITUTE
100 Park Village East, London NW1 3SR
Telephone: 0171 387 2171   Fax: 0171 388 0914

ISBN 0 85374 536 0

PSI Research Report 732

A CIP catalogue record of this book is available from the British Library.

1 2 3 4 5 6 7 8 9

PSI publications are available from:
BEBC Distribution Ltd., P O Box 1496, Poole, Dorset, BH12 3YD

Books will normally be despatched within 24 hours. Cheques should be made payable to BEBC Distribution Ltd.

Credit card and telephone/fax orders may be placed on:
FREEPHONE   0800 262260 or FREEFAX   0800 262266

Booktrade representation (UK & Eire):
Broadcast Books, 24 De Montfort Road, London SW16 1LW
Tel. 0181 677 5129

PSI subscriptions are available from PSI's subscription agent:
Carfax Publishing Co. Ltd., P O Box 25, Abingdon, Oxford OX14 3UE

Laserset by Policy Studies Institute
Printed in Great Britain by BPC Books and Journals Ltd, Exeter

Contents

Acknowledgements

1   Introduction   1

PART ONE   THE DOCUMENT DESIGN PROCESS

2   The document design process   5

PART TWO   PLANNING PUBLIC DOCUMENTS

3   The use and users of public documents   9
4   Reading and comprehension   14

PART THREE   DESIGNING AND DRAFTING PUBLIC DOCUMENTS

5   Guidelines for document designers   25
6   Format of documents   27
7   Structure of text   31
8   Structure of forms   35
9   The language of forms and leaflets   41
10   Aspects of visual design   51

PART FOUR   TESTING AND REVISING PUBLIC DOCUMENTS

11   Testing and evaluating documents   65
12   Editing and revising documents   72

REVIEWS   75

Acknowledgements

This book is based on a series of five literature reviews and covers the period from 1979 to 1991. Three of these reviews were prepared by Elaine Kempson, the fourth was compiled by Ian Rowlands at PSI. These reviews were funded by the Department of Social Security. The fifth was funded by the British Library and compiled by David Lewis who is now based at the Information Design Unit, having previously worked for the Document Design Unit of the Department of Social Security. We are very grateful to David for allowing us access to his report.

The work of bringing the reviewed research together into this volume was funded by the Department of Social Security.

1 Introduction

For many years document design was a do-it-yourself task. Everyone knew how to write and design forms and leaflets, and many people tried to do so. As a consequence many public documents were poorly designed and difficult to use.

During the 1980s the Plain English Campaign drew this to public attention through their annual awards for the worst examples of gobbledegook. This provided a welcome boost to the small but growing group of professional information designers. Writers, graphic designers and psychologists were working together to introduce higher standards of design. They were, however, facing a monumental task.

Information design is about using language and design to produce documents that meet the needs of their intended audience. The primary concern of this book is its application to public documents that are intended either to convey information—such as leaflets or manuals; or to collect information—forms or questionnaires.

The research on which this book is based is drawn from a wide range of disciplines: linguistics; graphic design; information science; printing; ergonomics; psychology; marketing; education, and social research.

It is difficult to keep in touch with developments in all those subjects. The aim of this book is to help information designers overcome this problem. It brings together over 250 reports and articles that were published during the period from 1979 to 1991. The primary focus has been research relevant to information design in Britain.

These publications have been synthesised to produce an overview of research that is relevant to the design of public documents. No such undertaking can ever claim to include every relevant document. We hope, however, that we have covered all of the significant research.

The compilation of this review was commissioned by the Department of Social Security for the Document Design Unit of the Benefits Agency.

Part I

THE DOCUMENT DESIGN PROCESS

Part I – Contents

2   THE DOCUMENT DESIGN PROCESS   5

2   The document design process

Successful document design requires detailed planning before any attempt is made to produce a document at all. Before starting to write or rewrite a leaflet or form it is essential to have a clear understanding of:

- *Who* are the intended audience and what are their needs, knowledge and expectations.

- *Why* the document is being produced.

- *What* are its intended content and function.

- *How* it will be distributed and used.

Pat Wright has identified three key stages in the design process:

A planning stage, during which the important issues are: collecting information, including information about the intended users of the document; deciding on the organisation and sequence of the information, and deciding how to present the information.

A drafting stage, when the important issues are: developing your thinking as the writing unfolds; being open to design problems that were not apparent at the planning stage, and avoiding becoming pre-occupied with the drafting process to the exclusion of an overall concern for the document.

A revising stage, when the important issues are: possibility of revising the organisation of the document as well as its text; taking the needs of the user into account, and the need for pilot testing (Wright 1981 and 1988).

Many writers have stressed this need for an overall approach to document design (Burgess 1984; Cabinet Office 1984; Duffy 1981; Pakin 1984; Pruyn and Jonkers 1984; Redish 1981a; Redish and others 1981; Sless 1985; Wright 1981).

The structure of this book mirrors the design process, with sections covering planning; designing and drafting; and testing and revising public documents. This overview is accompanied by an extensive annotated bibliography for those who want further information about specific publications.

Part II

PLANNING PUBLIC DOCUMENTS

Part II – Contents

3   THE USE AND USERS OF PUBLIC DOCUMENTS   9

Extent of leaflet use   10

4   NATURE OF LEAFLET USE   14

Use of forms   16

Reading and comprehension   17

3   The use and users of public documents

The first step in the design of successful public documents should be to identify who the users of a document are; to establish what they need the information for, and to assess how they will use the document.

People generally have quite specific information needs. Users of public documents neither want nor need general explanations about overall systems such as those for social security or taxation.

Research at the United States Document Design Project tried to identify the extent and nature of the difficulties facing the general public when they use public documents. It showed that most problems were caused by a failure to consider the requirements of a document from the perspective of the audience (Rose 1981).

An example of this is that users of social security documents were far more interested in information that was specific to their own circumstances than they were in general information (Hedges and Ritchie 1988; Campbell Keagan Limited 1990). Interactive leaflets, which called for a response from the reader, were useful in focusing people's attention, engaging their interest and helping them find their way around a document. They did, however, run the risk of being mistaken for a form (Hedges and Ritchie 1986).

An extensive investigation of Health Education Council publications showed that the people producing them had been quite inaccurate in their assessment of the public's requirements for health education information. The document designers believed that they should sell health, with short and simple messages, along the lines of commercial advertising. They also thought that they should avoid discussing any conflicts or confusion in the medical evidence on heart disease. It seemed, however, that far from wanting short and simple health messages, the target audience wanted more detailed information.

Moreover, instead of simple, consensual advice, they wanted help in evaluating conflicting medical evidence (Farrant and Russell 1986).

Such findings emphasise the need for producers of public documents to identify the precise information needs of the target audience at the very outset of the design process.

It is equally important to identify clearly the intended audience for a document and to design it accordingly. All too often public documents relate more to an administrative system or piece of legislation than they do to user groups. The Department of Health and Social Security, for example, identified the client groups with which the users of their documents most closely identified. They have subsequently redesigned many of their leaflets so that they relate to specific groups of people, such as people who are sick or disabled, rather than describing particular welfare benefits (MIL Research Ltd 1986b).

Extent of leaflet use

A number of studies have shown that leaflets are not well used. When people need information they are far more likely to ask another person, usually a friend, relative or colleague, than they are to consult a printed document. For example, welfare benefit claimants were more likely to talk to other claimants than to refer to an official benefit document. One study found that only one in twenty claimants had used a leaflet (Behavioural Research Consultants 1985). Similarly, traders preferred to have their VAT questions answered in person (MORI 1985) and employers were more likely to ring the Department of Health and Social Security or Tax Office with National Insurance enquiries than they were to refer to the *Employers guide to National Insurance contributions* (MIL Research Ltd 1984b).

In a different context, care workers—social workers, home help organisers, district nurses, health visitors, health education officers and voluntary agencies—made little or no use of leaflets (Epstein 1981). Advice centre workers, too, seldom consulted leaflets and very rarely gave them to their clients (McGarvie 1982).

Research commissioned by the Inland Revenue focused on the extent to which solicitors and accountants used taxation publications. Nearly all said that they would consult a booklet or publication if they had a tax problem, although they were far more likely to use commercial publications than those produced by the Inland Revenue (FDS Ltd 1986).

In contrast, only about one in ten of recipients of an official energy efficiency leaflet had read it thoroughly, while three in ten had not read it at all. Of those who had *not* read the leaflet the majority were aged either under 25 or over 65 (British Market Research Bureau Ltd 1985).

The reasons for the low level of use were the focus of the study commissioned by the Department of Health and Social Security. The results showed that people, in general, had very low expectations of official documents. They expected them to be difficult to understand, uninteresting and unlikely to give answers to specific problems. People were not highly motivated to get and use documents. A number of reasons were identified, including stigma; sensitivity to claiming benefits; a state of confusion; anxiety, and the lack of skills or ability to read printed documents (Hedges and Ritchie 1986).

Research findings such as these have led to a recommendation that literature should be designed to reinforce the grapevines through which information is gathered (Hedges and Ritchie 1986).

Although leaflets are not used to a great extent, they seem to compare favourably with other forms of mass communications. An evaluation of a publicity campaign to encourage council tenants to buy their homes, for example, showed that leaflets were by far the most frequently mentioned aspect of the campaign. They also led to much higher levels of knowledge than either press or television advertising (Research Surveys of Great Britain 1985).

It is likely, therefore, that printed documents will continue to be an important means of communication between official bodies and the public. The challenge, therefore, is to identify ways of increasing the likelihood that such documents would be read.

The Department of Energy incorporated a competition to win a new, detached, energy efficient house into the text of a booklet to promote energy efficiency. People who entered the competition were more likely to recall the booklet; were more positive towards and better informed about energy efficiency, and were more likely to have made energy-efficient installations after having received the booklet (BJM Research Partners 1986a).

The Department of Health and Social Security has tested the effect of including information in more permanent documents. They compared the use made of leaflets with the extent to which the notes contained in benefit order books were used. This suggested that order books were, in fact, a major source of reference for the claimants interviewed. This finding led to a recommendation that documents which are a natural focus of interest to claimants, such as order books and entitlement notices, should be used in preference to leaflets as a means of conveying information (Hedges and Ritchie 1986).

One of the reasons for the low level of use may be simply that the leaflets do not reach the people for whom they are intended. Official information was only consulted when it was near to hand and easy to locate. Yet the display and distribution systems for Department of Health and Social Security publications were inadequate and even when such literature was supplied the relevant pieces of paper tended to be outnumbered by the irrelevant ones (Hedges and Ritchie 1986).

In a detailed and extensive study carried out for the Department of Health and Social Security, Joyce Epstein investigated the use of leaflets by one section of the public—elderly people. She showed that, whilst most agencies stocked large quantities of leaflets, very few elderly people had seen, let alone used them (Epstein 1981).

Many leaflets requested by organisations for redistribution do not reach the public. A telephone survey of agencies requesting free or inexpensive material from the Alcohol and Drug Information Clearinghouse showed that a third of more than 60,000 leaflets requested had been wasted (Newman and others 1983).

Generally, people were not opposed to the use of leaflets as a means of communication, but they did have views on the way that they should be advertised and distributed. VAT-registered traders preferred to have leaflets distributed with VAT returns, by VAT officer visits, or by making them available in a wider variety of places. There was little support for suggestions that leaflet reference libraries be created at VAT offices; that there should be more enquiry counters at VAT offices, or that audio or video cassettes should be produced instead of leaflets (Market and Opinion Research International 1985).

4 Nature of leaflet use

Leaflets seldom perform a single function. Income Support leaflets, for example, were used in different ways to satisfy different information needs:

- Most respondents tended to use leaflets on benefits as a *rough guide* —few expected to find detailed information, instead they preferred a quick, simple indication of whether or not it was relevant to them.

- Sometimes, detailed information in leaflets was used as *ammunition* before, or following, personal contact with Department of Social Security staff.

- Some respondents took leaflets home to consider them in *greater depth*, especially if an interview had been arranged at the Department of Social Security.

- Leaflets seemed to be of greater interest to *new benefit claimants* who wanted to know how a benefit was structured.

- Leaflets also provided guidance to *intermediaries*—people who were not claiming benefits themselves but advising a third party (Campbell Keagan Limited 1990).

In some cases it is important to know whether people will retain the leaflet for subsequent use. By far the most common behaviour was to keep papers for 'so long and then to have a clear-out'. Documents were kept if it was thought that they were likely to be relevant or of interest at a later stage or if they indicated that they had to be kept. However, even where documents were filed away, they were seldom consulted subsequently.

There were a number of reasons for this. The documents were not easy to use when seeking a specific piece of information. Furthermore, people were not certain which documents to look in and most people did not know where they had 'filed' the documents.

These findings led the researchers to make two recommendations. First, that folders or wallets, which would help people to locate their benefit documents easily, might lead to greater use of written communications. Secondly, that both the relevance of a document and the need to retain it should be immediately apparent (Hedges and Ritchie 1986).

The importance of these findings is reinforced by other research showing that there is a decay over time in people's awareness of printed documents they have received (British market Research Bureau Ltd 1985, Research Surveys of Great Britain 1985). A follow-up study showed that memory decay following the receipt of the booklet had, in fact, been compounded by an inefficient and incomplete distribution service by the commercial distributor (BJM Research Partners 1986b).

Clearly, a number of considerations affect the nature of leaflet use. One is the person's attitude towards the matter which is the subject of the leaflet.

Scott Kerr concluded that, for elderly people at least, attitudes are far more important barriers to claiming means tested welfare benefits than a lack of knowledge. In other words 'a certain level of awareness would appear to be *necessary* yet not sufficient to catalyse claiming' (Kerr 1983). Such negative attitudes to claiming need to be considered when the content and purpose of a leaflet is being discussed.

People frequently failed to understand the *purpose* of a form or leaflet (Charrow and others 1980; Warder and England 1981). It seemed that, when people were unable to understand either the purpose or the content of a document, they assumed that it was unimportant or irrelevant to them (Corden & Corden 1984; Firth 1980; Holland & Rose 1980; Warder and England 1981).

There are some indications from the health education field that leaflets may have a latent effect which is only triggered by some other stimulus. Use of leaflets about giving up smoking was activated by follow-up letters or by some powerful external persuasion—in this case a steep price rise for tobacco (Ledwith 1984).

It is important to recognise that written communications are not just information carriers. They are an important part of the corporate image of an organisation, and that people's reactions to them were coloured by their attitude to the organisation as a whole (Hedges and Ritchie 1986).

This conclusion received some support from a set of four related studies looking at the public's reaction to a leaflet dealing with public finance, which was produced by the Treasury. Some sections of the leaflet were interpreted by the public as being party political propaganda. This particularly applied to those which presented trend statistics. But it also included the word *government*, which was interpreted as the party in power and even the reason for the choice of the colour blue for the leaflet. The wording of some sections of the text was also criticised, for example, 'we can choose to spend our own money or let the government spend it for us in higher taxes' (Communication Research Ltd 1984b).

Joyce Epstein concludes that both the design and distribution will affect the final impact of a leaflet on its intended audience:

> Not only the quality of information, but the timing is very important. People with a need for information remember and use it more than people without a need, at that moment. Leaflets delivered at point of sale, ie. when needed, offer a better chance of impact (Epstein 1981).

This suggestion had, in fact, been tested in an earlier study carried out by Eric Briggs. A group of claimants were sent a statement of how their supplementary benefit payments had been calculated. The knowledge of this group was then compared with a control group. There was some indication that direct receipt of the leaflet did enhance knowledge of supplementary benefit. However it must be noted that, overall, knowledge levels were extremely low. Also, of those receiving the leaflet, only a half had actually read it (Briggs and Rees 1980).

Use of forms
Just as people exhibit a range of behaviour in the way they use leaflets, it is clear also that they employ widely differing strategies when it comes to filling-in forms.

At one extreme, some people left no stone unturned in their attempt to understand and get to grips with the task in hand. They tended to read everything – including the parts which did not apply to them – and approached the actual form-filling with a great deal of care and attention. At the other extreme people jumped straight into completing the form, often without reading any supporting notes or documentation. Between these two extremes, the logic which people used to complete a form often bore little resemblance to the logic of the document designer (Palmer and MacLeod 1989).

There has been considerable research into the ways in which forms can be made easier to use. This is covered in Chapter 8

Reading and comprehension

Re-analysis of the results of a large-scale literacy study identified a range of factors that contributed to comprehension difficulties. Multiple regression analysis showed that five of these were significant predictors of document difficulty. In order of significance these were:

- *Number of organising categories:* the extent to which a reader needed to decode the hierarchical structure of a document in order to perform a simple task.

- *Number of task specifics:* the number of separate pieces of information a reader needed to process in order to complete a simple task.

- *Degrees of correspondence:* the extent to which a reader needed to use higher-level inference or interpretation in order to follow an instruction and complete a task.

- *Type of information:* the amount of effort needed to locate or provide information requested in a document.

- *Number of document specifics:* the number of separate, explicit pieces of information contained in a document (Kirsch and Mosenthal 1990).

Pat Wright, reviewing psychology research into reading and writing, suggested that one of its deficiencies is the general assumption that the meaning is entirely within the text. She maintained that, in reality, readers go far beyond the text in deriving their interpretation (Wright 1980). Similarly, Schumacher says that the comprehension of text is an interactive process involving both the text and the knowledge and experience, or *schemata*, that the reader brings to it (Schumacher 1981). Using this interpretation it is possible to identify three reasons why readers might fail to comprehend a passage:

- They may not have the appropriate knowledge and experience to interpret it.

- They may have the correct schemata but the passage may fail to activate this knowledge.

- They may find an interpretation of the passage which handles the information, but which is different from that intended by the author.

Three further studies confirm the importance of background knowledge for the comprehension of a text (Koh 1985; Lee 1986; Levine and Haus 1985).

The general thesis is, then, that reading comprehension involves prior knowledge both of the content and context of the document and of the way that written text is organised. Both of these factors are in turn influenced by the reader's cultural background (Barnitz 1986; Carrell 1983). Different cultural experiences and background knowledge affected comprehension in different ways (Andersson and Barnitz 1984).

For example, adults learning English as a second language experienced difficulties not only because of a limited knowledge of English semantics and syntax, but also as a result of gaps in the background knowledge assumed by the author (Crandall 1985). Indeed it has been suggested that background knowledge has a greater effect than language level on the reading comprehension of second language learners (Hans and Levine 1985).

Differences in culture and language may be so deep-seated that they distort the information contained in public documents and cause inappropriate messages to be received. Studies have shown that readers whose second language was English were not able to comprehend culturally unfamiliar texts to the same extent as those with which they were familiar—even when factors, such as readability and vocabulary, were taken into account (Lasisi and others 1988). Again, non-native speakers of English tended to rely on words and syntax for their comprehension (Jonz 1989) and their reading was generally less efficient (Verhoeven 1990).

Such findings are not restricted to people learning English as a second language. Reading strategies adopted by adults with very limited literacy skills showed evidence of a highly restricted view of reading. Reading was seen simply as a series of almost mechanical operations on words. Without prompting, most adults drew spontaneously on their existing knowledge rather than on print-based cues as their first response to a basic document task (Malicky and Norman 1989). People suffering from pre-lingual deafness also seemed to have gaps in background knowledge that affected reading comprehension (Crandall 1985).

The importance of background information to form and leaflet design was demonstrated in a comparative study of Attendance Allowance leaflets. This showed that people would not go to great lengths to give accurate information when they did not understand why they were being asked for it (Behaviourial Research Consultants 1985). Similarly, research on a redesigned Inland Revenue PAYE guidance booklet showed that some users experienced difficulties because the text assumed too much prior knowledge (MIL Research Ltd 1986a).

The way that prior knowledge is used was shown by a research project carried out at the Document Design Project in the United States. The researchers tape-recorded people thinking aloud as they read and interpreted the meaning of government regulations—a technique known as protocol analysis. This showed that the readers made significant attempts to use prior knowledge in order to understand the text of the document.

The most notable result from the analysis, however, was the extent to which the readers expressed the meaning of parts of the text in the form of a concrete story or event. In other words, when interpreting the text the readers did not rephrase the original using shorter sentences or simpler words. Instead they made much more radical changes to the text, illustrating it with brief scenarios (Flower and others 1980).

A similar finding was reported in an observation study of the use of the United States Medicaid form. This showed that caseworkers frequently used examples and scenarios to translate sections that were not understood by their clients (Charrow and others 1980).

In another protocol analysis study, Melissa Holland and Janice Redish identified three types of strategy that were used by people filling in a job application form. These were:

- *Decoding strategies*, where the reader was devoting attention to the meaning of specific words or ambiguous statements.

- *Form-using strategies*, in which the reader attempted to relate items across the form or to draw on personal knowledge to clarify the meaning of passages.

- *Gglobal strategies*, where the reader put the document into a societal and institutional context. The reader was, for example, looking for the intention behind the questions or predicting how the answer would be interpreted.

They then compared the protocols of people who had completed successful application forms with those who had not. From this they found that the unsuccessful form-fillers concentrated primarily on decoding strategies whilst the successful ones employed all three types of strategy (Holland and Redish 1981).

The implications of these studies for form and leaflet designers are drawn out by Linda Flower. She suggests the following practical points.

First, forms and leaflets should be structured around the needs of the reader:

- *Organisation:* this should reflect the actions people need to take, not the regulations. Headings should be informative and reflect the questions users will ask.

- *Text:* this should be written in terms of concrete situations and the subsequent actions the reader will take. Wherever possible it should explain concepts in practical operational terms.

- *Grammatical structure:* wherever possible sentences should include human agents and actions.

Secondly, the form or leaflet should provide a context for the information it contains. This will involve giving extended examples or cases as well as using detail and specific cases to define the meaning of terms that will be unfamiliar to the reader (Flower and others 1980).

Other research has considered the effect on comprehension of the interaction between background knowledge and language skills. One such study showed that even when the words and syntax were familiar cultural differences blocked the understanding of a text (Bensoussan 1986).

A further piece of work investigated the relationship between vocabulary difficulty and prior knowledge on text comprehension. The results showed that both, individually, had an effect, but there was no significant indication of interaction between them. It should be pointed out, though, that this research did not focus on knowledge which was already possessed, but investigated the effects of pre-instruction (Stahl and Jacobson 1986).

A third study examined the relationships between background knowledge and the *register* and *cohesion* of a text. The term register refers to the style of language which is appropriate for a given situation, while cohesion refers to the linguistic relationships between different parts of a text. The results showed that background knowledge prevented ambiguous sections of the text being interpreted inappropriately, and that background knowledge and register together affected the ability of readers to process complex textual structures (Steffensen 1986).

Designers of public documents need to take account of the fact that most people use their documents to find a piece of information rather than read the document as a narrative. Pat Wright has suggested that the ability to search a document and to find information is one of the components of functional literacy (Wright 1988).

This is borne out by American research with young adults that showed that low levels of literacy were associated with poor performance in locating information in documents (Kirsch and Jugenblut 1986). Based on findings such as this, it has been suggested that more attention should be paid to locating information when measuring comprehension (Guthrie and Kirsch 1987).

The searching strategy adopted varied considerably between experts and those who were unfamiliar with the type of document. Experts were more likely to use features such as headings to get an overview of the document's contents (Lundeberg 1987).

Part III

DESIGNING AND DRAFTING
PUBLIC DOCUMENTS

Part III - Contents

5   GUIDELINES FOR DOCUMENT DESIGNERS   25

6   FORMAT OF DOCUMENTS   27
     Format   27
     Covers   28
     Titles and reference numbers   29

7   STRUCTURE OF TEXT   31
     Layout   31
     Headings   32
     Cross references   34

8   STRUCTURE OF FORMS   35
     Questions and answers   35
     Routings   36
     Presentation of text   38
     Notes and instructions   38
     Declarations   40

9   DIFFICULT WORDS AND PHRASES   41
     Difficult words and phrases   41
     Sentence construction   44
     Reader preferences   48

10   ASPECTS OF VISUAL DESIGN   51
     Typography   51
     Colour   54
     Illustrations   56
     Other graphics   59
     Algorithms and flowcharts   59

5   Guidelines for document designers

A number of authors have attempted to codify research into guidelines for form and leaflet designers. These vary considerably in length and sophistication. Some are simple *checklists,* often based on practical experience of rewriting one or more forms (Cutts and Maher 1980; Jansen and Steehouder 1984; Klare 1979; Lefrere and others 1983) while others are more extensive (Burgess 1984; Department of Health and Social Security 1984; Redish 1985).

Some have been developed for specific types of document or for forms (National Consumer Council 1984; Redish 1979); some concentrate on *a particular topic* such as *legibility and design* (Forms Information Centre 1984a; Shilling 1981; Simply Stated 1982) *colour* (Forms Information Centre 1983) and *simple words* (Department of Trade and Industry 1984; National Consumer Council 1984).

Other specific guidelines have been produced as a result of a study of people who were not fluent readers, either because English was not their native language or because of profound hearing losses since birth. These guidelines cover the provision of background knowledge as well as syntax, semantics and discourse organisation (Crandall 1985).

But the value of guidelines on form and leaflet design has been questioned on several counts. First, it has been claimed that there are invariably exceptions to almost every rule (Charrow 1979b). Secondly, it has been shown that lack of specific knowledge may not easily be remedied by written guidelines. An interesting and rigorous series of experiments focused on the editing process. These indicated that guidelines have a non-specific effect on writers and tend to increase the number of amendments overall. They were not, however, consulted for specific information (Wright 1985).

Thirdly, other researchers have shown that even generally-accepted guidelines are regularly broken even in good writing (Hukin and others 1986).

For these reasons, the most useful set of guidelines is probably that produced by the staff of the Document Design Centre. Not only is it comprehensive, providing real-life examples and summaries of relevant research, but the authors have tried to avoid simple rules about what to do and what not to do. Within each guideline there is a section discussing exceptions to the rule (Felker and others 1981).

Other useful guidelines include those published by the Canadian Law Information Council (1988) and a drafting manual produced by the Law Reform Commission of Victoria (1987). Although each of these focuses on legal information, they are relevant to other types of document. The Law Reform Commission document is particularly valuable as it includes examples of the rewriting of several legal documents. These are presented as dual texts, with the original and revised versions of the same document on facing pages.

The Communications Studies Department at Sheffield Polytechnic has developed a set of *design rules* linking features of the writer, reader and document to produce advice on writing style.

Pat Wright has argued in favour of the intelligent use of heuristics to identify possible trouble spots. In particular she advocates using heuristics that focus on the users of documents and consider what happens before, during and after their interaction with documents. More specifically, she identifies questions about:

- What readers may do or know before reading a document: the questions they will formulate and how they will approach finding the information they need.

- What happens *during* the reading process; what comprehension processes are involved and what might help or hinder them.

- What happens *after* they have read the document; how readers use their newly acquired knowledge.

6   Format of documents

Format

Relatively little research has focused particularly on the format of forms and leaflets. Even so, a good deal of information can be gathered from market research tests of specific documents. The format of a document needs to take into account the people who will be using it.

A test of a revised version of the Department of Health and Social Security leaflet *Cash Help* showed that the format—a four-sheet fold-out—caused considerable problems. Many people experienced difficulty in working out the order of the pages. Elderly and disabled people found it physically difficult to open the leaflet out further than the first fold (MIL Research Ltd 1982).

Similar difficulties with concertina folded leaflets have been reported in other tests (Behavioural Research Consultants 1983 and 1985; Lefrere and others 1983). In two cases a smaller book format was preferred by both the public and staff (Behavioural Research Consultants 1983; MIL Research Ltd 1982). Clearly a balance needs to be struck between layout and size.

Tests of a booklet aimed at women and dealing with violent crime showed that an A5 format was preferred because it was easy to handle (Campbell Kegan Ltd 1986).

On the other hand, two other documents, both aimed at employers, one covering National Insurance and the other PAYE, were preferred in an A4 format. The reasons given were that the documents looked less official and less daunting to use. They were also more convenient for filing with other documents (MIL Research Ltd 1984b; MIL Research Ltd 1986a).

Consumer testing of leaflets has shown that people found a broadsheet format difficult to follow (Communication Research Ltd 1984b and 1985). Another interesting point to note is that the redesign of a document which involved using more pages and heavier paper caused handling difficulties (Fisher 1986).

A test of two versions of a claim form for the Community Care Grant compared landscape and portrait formats and assessed how people reacted to the accompanying wrap-around leaflet. In general, people reacted much more positively to the landscape than to the portrait version of the claim form. Landscape format was felt to be more spacious and less visually cluttered and respondents welcomed the fact that there was more room to accommodate questions and answers. Also, the longer line lengths appeared to enhance readability.

The landscape version of the accompanying wrap-around leaflet was also well received: this format seemed to encourage claimants to open the pack more slowly and absorb information bit-by-bit. This confirmed earlier research which showed that wrap-around leaflets encouraged a 'slow release' of information and that people were more likely to read and absorb the leaflet information before trying to complete the form.

A disadvantage of the vertical wrap-around was that it was perceived as a cover for the enclosed form rather than as an integral part of the claim pack. This encouraged claimants to discard the leaflet without reading it first (Palmer and MacLeod 1990a and 1990b).

Covers

The visual impact of the cover of a document plays an important part in attracting people's attention.

People were more likely to retain and subsequently to use a document when they thought that it would be relevant or of interest to them. This suggests that the cover of a document should be used to convey certain important information about the document. In particular, people should be able to judge from a cover the contents of a document; its intended readership, and whether it should be retained (Andrew Irving Associates 1989; Hedges and Ritchie 1986; Palmer and MacLeod 1989; Research Business 1986).

There is, however, a danger of putting too much information on a cover. Consequently non-essential or detailed information should be relegated from the cover or front page to other parts of a form (Palmer and MacLeod 1989).

The use of colour on a cover had a significant impact on the effectiveness of leaflets. Covers printed in attractive colours were preferred to those in uniform dark colours such as dark blue or black (Epstein 1981; MIL Research Ltd 1984a; Research Business 1986). At the same time, there needed to be a minimum level of contrast between print and background. When reading at a distance there was a slight advantage in having light print set against a dark background (Wright 1979a).

Bold cover visuals and the imaginative use of colour reinforced initial interest in an Income Support leaflet. But some people reacted unfavourably to the use of glossy or expensive-looking materials for a leaflet about social security benefits. In fact, a more conservative house style helped to reinforce the formal relationship that most respondents expected to have with a government department such as the Department of Social Security (Campbell Keagan Limited 1990).

People were most likely to remember leaflets about Attendance Allowance when they had a concrete object on the cover. Colour and the title seemed to be of less importance (Behavioural Research Consultants 1985). Frequently, this involves the use of a symbol. The International Standards Organisation criteria for the development of public information symbols contain a good deal of useful information which is applicable to the design of covers of public documents. For example, it provides very useful formulae which can be used to calculate both the size of the symbol and the minimum dimension of significant details for every metre of viewing distance. It also recommends that symbols should be solid rather than outline forms, and should have left/right symmetry (International Standards Organisation 1984).

Titles and reference numbers

Short titles were generally better than long ones. Not only were they easier to remember but, with short titles, it was possible to use larger type sizes which were easier to see. Upper case letters were generally easier to read at a distance than lower case letters of the same point size but took up more horizontal space (Pat Wright 1979a).

Titles, like the overall cover design, needed to convey important information about the document and its intended audience. Those which included a 'call to action', such as 'Do you qualify?' or 'Do you need to apply?' were particularly effective (Andrew Irving Associates 1989).

Many public documents need to carry a reference number or some other form of identifier. Research suggests that it is better not to mix letters and numbers but where this is unavoidable, they should be kept in two separate groups. The use of mnemonics in identifiers makes them easier to remember. And where more than three digits are used they should be grouped into twos or threes (Wright 1979a).

Contents pages and indexes
Contents pages made long documents more usable. Even though the initial impression given by a detailed contents page was more off-putting than a simpler one, it made a revised guide easier to use (Don Preddy 1985; MIL Research Ltd 1986a). Similarly, comprehensive and easy-to-use indexes increased the use of public documents (MIL Research Ltd 1984b; MIL Research Ltd 1986a). In fact, the poor indexing of Inland Revenue publications was one of the reasons why solicitors and accountants preferred to use commercial publications (FDS Ltd 1986).

7 Structure of text

Layout

Poor readers tend to be unaware of the structure of a text. Any layout that makes the structure more obvious will, therefore, help readers to comprehend the text (Crandall 1985; Horowitz 1985).

There has been a great deal of work on the ways of organising text (Frase and Schwartz 1979; Hartley 1980; Hartley 1982). Much of the research has concentrated on the effect of printing text so that each line contains only one meaningful unit. This is generally referred to as 'chunking' a text. Although chunking had a positive effect on both comprehension and proof-reading tasks, the resultant high variation in line-length had a stronger negative effect (Keenan 1984).

An attempt to determine the optimum line length, so that as many lines as possible corresponded to a single chunk of information, showed that lengths between 40 and 60 characters lead to maximum comprehension. But line lengths were better determined by analysis of the language level of the text than by overall guidelines (Frase and others 1985).

Almost all of this research, however, relates to the design of textbooks or other educational texts. Its generalisability to leaflets and forms is questionable. Most of the studies have involved testing recall of information from educational texts; but we know that public leaflets are read primarily to retrieve specific pieces of information.

A case study of a Dutch rent-rebate leaflet suggested that fragmenting the text can also be of value when the purpose of a leaflet is to calculate entitlement. It showed that better results were achieved when text was divided so that users had to complete each instruction before they could move on to the next. The leaflet also needed to contain a form on to which the results of calculations and decisions could be noted in a convenient way (Jansen and Steehouder 1984).

Page layouts which include white space have been shown to have advantages. Users thought that it made a document easier to follow (Nova Research Ltd 1986). White space also made a document look more modern and friendly and was useful for making notes. The use of coloured margins was also thought to add visual appeal to the form (MIL Research Ltd 1986a). But inconsistent column widths led to sections of the text being missed by users when the postal claim form for supplementary benefit was evaluated (Lefrere and others 1983).

Instructional designers and researchers tend to recommend the use of visual cues to direct the readers' attention to the most relevant information. The effects of such cues on recall were measured in a study of instructional texts. This showed that when pictorial and textual cues were used together they led to significantly greater recall. Neither type of cue alone did so (Beck 1984).

On the other hand, a booklet which had a confusing layout, making it difficult to distinguish between headings, introductory paragraph and quotations, encouraged skip reading (Campbell Kegan Ltd 1986).

Headings

There is considerable evidence to show that the use of headings improves the ease with which text can be used (Stark 1988; Wright 1979a).

The use of headings in forms increased the speed of completion (Behavioural Research Consultants 1983). They were also important in leaflets where they helped readers to locate a specific piece of information (Behavioural Research Consultants 1985; Don Preddy 1985; Hartley and Trueman 1983).

In a test of warranties for consumer goods, however, it was found that headings did not lead to a statistically significant improvement in either the number of correct answers retrieved from the text or the time taken to respond. Warranties without standardised headings were read and understood just as easily as those with headings (Charrow and Redish 1980).

A subsequent study of insurance policies showed that clear prose generally outweighed misleading headings and overcame the lack of headings. The authors point out, however, that these findings, and those of Charrow and Redish, may not apply to all documents. The insurance policies they tested were all designed so that they would be easy to use. The study of warranties used only short passages of text. It seems, therefore, that the role that headings play depends on the length, style, purpose and degree of familiarity of a document (Swarts and other 1980).

Just as significant, however, was the finding that nine out of ten people showed a strong preference for the warranties with standardised headings. So, whilst the headings may not necessarily make a text easier to read, they could well increase the likelihood of it being read in the first place (Charrow and Redish 1980).

The value of headings depended on their position, their content and the way in which they are signalled (Wright 1979a). It appeared that neither the position (in the margin or embedded in the text) nor the nature of a heading (a statement as opposed to a question) had any effect on the retrieval of information (Hartley and Trueman 1985).

Inaccurate, incomplete or vague headings hindered people who were looking for specific information in a text. A study of insurance policies showed that ineffective headings were often vague and focused on broad concepts. Effective headings, on the other hand, were accurate, specific and focused on the reader's needs and goals (Swarts and others 1980). Certainly, this conclusion is supported by research which showed that readers understood documents by drawing on their prior knowledge (Flower and others 1980; Schumacher 1981; Wilhite 1989).

Occasionally it is important to indicate the sequence of headings. In one such case the use of numbers was found to be better than letters (Lefrere and others 1983).

Headings which were printed in the margin as white text in a black block made pages of text look easier to read, as well as making it simpler to locate specific sections of the text (Campbell Kegan Ltd 1986).

Similarly the use of coloured highlighting for paragraph headings and coloured print for sub-headings made it easier to scan a page for relevant information (MIL Research Ltd 1986a). But while the use of colour to signal headings attracted attention to them, the colour then interfered with the reading process. This effect was most marked with high chroma colours (Wheildon 1984). Colour change alone was not sufficient for a heading to be recognised as such (Wright 1979a).

Finally there is the choice of typeface. Headings printed in capital letters were less legible than those using a mixture of capitals and lower case (Wheildon 1984).

Cross references

Cross references made a contribution to the ease of use of public documents (FDS Ltd 1986, MIL Research Ltd 1984b), particularly when they were highlighted typographically (Hedges and Ritchie 1986). People were confused by a document which used both page and paragraph numbers when making cross references and generally preferred the use of paragraph numbers only (MIL Research Ltd 1986a).

8 Structure of forms

Questions and answers

The Forms Information Centre has prepared detailed guidelines on the different ways of setting out questions and answers. These are based on research, commonsense and principles of good design and are written to help writers select the most appropriate question and answer format for a particular group of users and particular type of document (Forms Information Centre 1985a and Wright 1981).

Inconsistency in the instructions on how to record replies caused problems for form fillers. Qualitative research prior to the redesign of the driving test application form showed that such inconsistency led to many mistakes and omissions (Business Decisions Ltd 1985).

Standard ways of recording answers need to be used throughout a form. Tick boxes were particularly effective on both driving test application forms and tax forms (Business Decisions Ltd 1985; Nova Research Ltd 1986; Sless 1987). Multiple answer options were rather better than checklists where form-fillers needed to indicate which of a range of options applied to them (Frohlich 1985b).

Questions which required respondents to write in answers needed at least two lines for the replies (Frohlich 1985b). The use of examples on forms to illustrate possible replies often led to difficulties. There was a very strong tendency for them to be interpreted as an exhaustive list of answer options (Frohlich 1985b).

Forms are used to collect a variety of types of information, some of which require particular design solutions. These include calculations, dates, signatures, addresses and personal identification numbers, such as National Insurance numbers.

Calculations The use of arithmetic symbols helped to clarify the calculations that needed to be made on a taxation form (Nova Research Ltd 1986).

Dates People generally wrote the day and the month as numbers, that is 7-7 for the seventh of July. The majority also wrote the year in its abbreviated form, that is 86 rather than 1986 (Department of Health and Social Security 1986b). Where dates were required in an all-figure format for computer processing, answer spaces consisting of boxes produced more accurate replies than those providing a line on which the date was to be written (Forms Information Centre 1987).

Signature space It is most important that the space allowed on a form should be large enough to allow the form-filler to sign with their normal signature. A review of 300 signatures of British names given on plain paper showed that 95 percent of them would fit into a space 60mm long and 20mm high (Forms Information Centre 1984b).

Addresses Forms that did not specifically ask for a full address, did not elicit accurate replies. Those which were most successful specified exactly which components of the address should be given and allocated one line to each (Frohlich 1985b; Mapes 1982; Sless 1987).

Personal identification numbers Forms which asked for personal numbers, like National Insurance numbers, needed a separate box for each letter or number (Department of Health and Social Security 1985b).

Where the answers on a form are to be input to a computer it is frequently necessary to use character separators so that the form-filler writes one letter in each allotted space. The most satisfactory format for these was a ruled line at the top of the response area, with small ticks to indicate the spaces for individual characters. This is illustrated below (Boag and others 1987).

Date   2 3 0 3 1 9 9 2

Routings
One problem that regularly faces form and leaflet designers is the need to design one document that can be used by various groups of the public. In such cases it will not be necessary for every user to read every section, and some means of routing the user through the document must be provided.

However, a detailed analysis of routing behaviour showed that, by and large, subjects followed a linear path through the form. If they could answer a question they would do so, even if the routing indicated that the questions was not relevant to them (Frohlich 1986b). Even where the text contained sufficient cues such as headings and underlining which indicated that they could skip these passages, the readers were afraid to do so (Jansen and Steehouder 1984). The usual result is that people will read all sections of a form or leaflet even though they may be irrelevant (Behavioural Research Consultants 1983; Jansen and Steehouder 1984; Lefrere and others 1983).

A detailed observational study of the reading and routing activities of people as they filled in a postal claim form for Supplementary Benefit showed that only about one third of routing instructions were read. Those most likely to be read were at locations on the form where the subsequent routing was most unclear. Those least read followed the answer areas and included instructions like 'go to next column'. In other words, people seemed to read the minimum necessary to complete the form quickly (Frohlich 1985b).

Part of the problem was that users frequently misunderstood routing conventions. Indented sub-questions following an affirmative answer were completed by people who had given a negative reply, whereas they should have ignored them (Frohlich 1986b). Confusion was also caused when subsequent questions were sited alongside the previous question's last answer area rather than below it (Frohlich 1985b).

Other problems arose where routing was indicated inconsistently. Users routed themselves incorrectly when routing instructions were given both from 'yes' and from 'no' responses. This led the researchers to recommend that routing instructions should be made from either one or the other, not from both (Frohlich 1985b).

The problem of routing through the form was also made more difficult where the form used both instructions and typographic conventions for routing guidance. While the use of routing instructions encouraged users to progress through the questions on the form unless told otherwise, the use of typographic conventions encouraged users to find their own routing paths using the layout of the questions as guidance (Frohlich 1986b).

A subsequent study looked at the way form-fillers adapted their behaviour when completing a simple electronic version of the same form. This showed that electronic forms were completed in rather a different way from paper forms. While paper form-filling followed a linear path, computer form-filling involved many more routing digressions. Some of these were initiated by the system itself, others by the user. It seemed that users were not entirely happy to trust the routing recommendations made by the computer system. Despite these digressions users were far less likely to consider irrelevant questions and they seldom provided answers to questions out of sequence (Frohlich 1986a; Frohlich 1986c).

Presentation of text

It would seem that unstructured text is normally the least satisfactory option. Users in one study found it both unattractive and difficult to use to pick out relevant information (Hedges and Ritchie 1986). Other studies have shown that a step-by-step presentation is preferred (MIL Research Ltd 1986a; Nova Research Ltd 1986). Similarly, the question and answer format used in two other documents was found more interesting and easier to handle than a series of statements in a block of text (Don Preddy 1985; Research Business 1986).

Notes and instructions

There is a great deal of research showing that notes and instructions accompanying forms are seldom read thoroughly and are frequently ignored by as many as two-thirds of users (Allison and others 1985; Behavioural Research Consultants 1985; Frohlich 1986a; Sless 1987; Wright 1979a).

Preliminary instructions on the P1 Income Tax form were often missed (Behavioural Research Consultants 1983). Similarly notes printed on tinted paper at the beginning of the Criminal Injuries Compensation Scheme form were not always read (Matthews and others 1982). Two-thirds of people using a Maternity Pay Rebate form claimed to have read the explanatory notes but only a third had read them all. Similarly only a third of the people had referred to the accompanying booklet at all when filling in the form (Communications Research Ltd 1983b).

Where the notes to a form are provided in a separate leaflet people expected the number of the form and leaflet to be related (Behavioural Research Consultants 1985). People found it easier to cope with Arabic numerals than with Roman ones. And while they coped with short alphabetic series, finding 'reference note 8' was easier than finding 'reference note H' (Wright 1979a).

Most of the research relates to general explanatory notes. Research carried out by the Document Design Unit of the Department of Health and Social Security focused on two specific areas: instructions to use capital letters and instructions to include the postcode with an address. This showed that seven out of ten people used capital letters, whether or not they were instructed to do so. Similarly the positioning of a prompt to include the postcode had no effect on the number of people who did so (Department of Health and Social Security 1986b).

Several projects have looked at ways of overcoming users' reluctance to read notes and instructions. A number of different solutions have been proposed on the basis of this research:

- Including material within the text rather than as separate notes (Wright 1979a).
- Using a step-by-step format with check-off boxes (Nova Research Ltd 1986).
- Highlighting important instructions typographically (Hedges and Ritchie 1986).
- Placing instructions immediately before the question to which they refer (Frohlich 1985b).
- Putting the explanations in places where people are likely to look— entitlement notices, order books or giros—not just in bulky leaflets which may neither be seen nor read (Hedges and Ritchie 1986).
- Using examples rather than instructions (Lefever and Dixon 1986).
- Giving information about the structure and organisation of a task before giving instructions about the steps which need to be taken to complete the task (Dixon 1982; Wright and Hull 1988).

The preparatory work for the Forms Helper computer system demonstrated that form-fillers actually read fewer than one third of the instructions contained on a paper form. When the first, prototype computer system was designed it was hoped that this failure to read instructions could be overcome. The results were, however, disappointing and showed that even fewer instructions were read on the computerised system. The reasons for this seemed to lie in the layout of instructions on the computer screen and in the automatic routing of the Forms Helper system. Because the system automatically routed users to the next appropriate question, no routing instructions had to be read by subjects. They appeared to recognise this redundancy and largely ignored displayed instructions and explanations. The problem seemed to be that the systems designers were attempting to replicate the format of a printed form (Frohlich 1986a; Frohlich 1986c).

Declarations

Many public forms end with a declaration which the form-filler must sign to say that they believe the information they have given is both complete and correct. People found it frightening to sign a declaration especially when it was complex (Kempson 1984). One such complex declaration appeared on the Inland Revenue PAYE form and included a number of separate statements. The format of this declaration was revised so that each statement was listed on a separate line and followed by a tick box. Subsequent testing showed a strong liking for this format (Nova Research Ltd 1986).

9 The language of forms and leaflets

It is sometimes asserted that documents which use lay language and a clear and straightforward presentation could be considered to be condescending. Inland Revenue research with owners of small businesses and Property Services Agency research with contractors and officials both indicated the reverse. The easier a document was to use, the more favourably it was received (MIL Research Ltd 1986a; Talkback Research 1985).

Furthermore, there is clear evidence that people read Plain English versions of a legal document more quickly than the original version with no loss of comprehension (Holmes 1987).

Difficult words and phrases

The most comprehensive analysis of difficult words and phrases is contained in a review of pre-1979 research, prepared for the Central Office of Information by Pat Wright. She showed that reading problems were caused by the use of:

- Unfamiliar words.

- Ambiguous words.

- Derived words.

- Negative words.

Ambiguities were caused by the use of the word *not* in sentences like 'To qualify you should *not* be over 65 and in full-time employment'. People found comparisons which used words like *more, bigger, heavier* easier to understand than those using their opposites—*less, smaller, lighter*.

The present and simple past tenses were most easily understood, and she identified a range of difficulties relating to the use of conditional and imperative forms of verbs.

Readers found certain phrases difficult. These included phrases using a string of qualifiers, like *industrial injuries compensation review tribunal*. They also included phrases where the relative pronoun had been left out (Wright 1979a).

Since Pat Wright's 1979 review there has been a considerable amount of research which has both confirmed and extended her conclusions.

Verb forms In her research on the editing process Pat Wright found that verb forms were both preferred and read more quickly than nominalisations (nouns created from verbs). This rule cannot, however, be applied too rigorously as some nominalisations seemed to function as lexical terms in their own right. *Reduction* and *investment* were given as examples (Wright 1985).

Negative words It is well established that negative words cause reading difficulties. The word *not* is especially problematic because it can also make the meaning of a sentence ambiguous. Laboratory research showed that performance was always better for instructions with *no* negatives but performance for instructions with two negatives was not necessarily worse than performance for instructions where there was only one. Indeed in some cases it was significantly better, as the readers seemed to reframe the double negative instruction as a positive one (Wright and Wilcox 1979).

Word type Research with undergraduates showed that word type was an important indicator of text difficulty. Reading times rose more steeply for nouns than for verbs, and for new nouns compared with repeated nouns. They also increased with the cumulative number of new arguments per sentence (Haberlandt and Graesser 1989).

Unfamiliar words The less often a word appears in print then the less likely it is to be known by a reader. The problem is especially acute for people with no other way of learning words. A study of pre-lingually deaf people showed just how much smaller their vocabulary was than that of hearing people. Hearing-impaired students knew 62 per cent of words only up to the 2,000th most frequently used word in print while hearing students knew the meaning of 63 per cent of words up to the 24,000th most frequently used word in print (Walter 1985).

Words with specific meanings There is a related problem where everyday words have very specific meanings within government rules or regulations. In 1984 the Department of Health and Social Security Forms Unit commissioned a study which looked at whether the public understood the meaning of a number of words and phrases commonly used in their forms and leaflets. A large proportion of them were misunderstood. These ranged from expressions such as *the person you live with as man and wife* or *boarder* which have a specific meaning within social security regulations to ones like *rates* or *tax year* which have a generally accepted meaning. Even everyday words like *savings* caused problems and were interpreted differently by different people (Department of Health and Social Security 1984).

Research into the postal claim form for Supplementary Benefit showed that people frequently thought that *savings* excluded both the cash they had in their pockets and the money held in the current bank accounts. And *income* was frequently understood not to include social benefits or pensions (Lefrere and others 1983). Exactly the same misunderstanding was identified during an evaluation of the Department of Health and Social Security leaflet *Cash help* (MIL Research Ltd 1982).

Tests carried out on Attendance Allowance leaflets identified further specific words and phrases that cause problems when used in a text. *Cash help* was taken to mean single payments rather than continuing cash benefits. *Disabled person* was not thought to include people with a mental illness or handicap. *In-patient* was believed to cover anyone attending a hospital, even as an out-patient. *Residential home* was interpreted as the home where they lived rather than the social services' term for a communal home for elderly or disabled people. Finally the word *allowance* was viewed by the public with less stigma than the term *benefit* (Behavioural Research Consultants 1985).

A study of some of the words, concepts and terms used on Department of Social Security forms revealed widespread misunderstanding of a number of concepts which are central to claiming benefits. Concepts like *qualify, entitled* and *can get* were sometimes interpreted by the public in a sense quite different to the narrow, technical sense intended by the Department of Social Security.

Concepts related to time, such as *backdate* and *arrears* seemed to pose considerable difficulty for some people—although this could largely be overcome by using more straightforward constructions such as *before* or *at the end of* (Parkinson 1990a).

Expressions of frequency Such expressions, which are often used on questionnaires or forms, can also cause difficulties. These include scales such as *always, often, occasionally, seldom and never*. Scales like these were interpreted inconsistently by different readers and the researchers conclude that they should be replaced by numerical quantifiers, such as 'half of the time' or '50 per cent of the time', wherever possible (Hartley and others 1984).

Quantifiers Words such as *several* and *a few* have also been studied to identify people's understanding of them (Newstead and others 1987). The research found that:

- *Most* was seen as more than *lots*.
- *Lots* was seen as the same as *many*.
- *Lots* was seen as more than *half*.
- *Several* was seen as the same as *some*.
- *Some* was seen as more than *a few*.
- *A few* was seen as the same as *few*.

A study of both quantifiers and indefinite pronouns showed that *some* was the easiest quantifier for readers to understand, whether alone or as part of an indefinite pronoun, whilst *every* was the most difficult. The easiest pronoun was *...thing*, the most difficult being *...body* (Wilbur and Goodhart 1985).

Sentence construction

Complex sentences cause difficulties for everyone and are particularly troublesome for people over 70 years of age. People in that age group had more difficulty than young adults with long, embedded clauses and with embedded clauses at the beginning of sentences. This was tentatively attributed to linguistic deterioration as a result of memory limitations in older age (Kemper 1986).

People learning a second language also seemed to face difficulties with complex sentence structures. They were unfamiliar with particular structures, simply because they were not used in their native language. Research showed that the organisation of written text is different in different cultures. Whereas English generally uses a linear pattern, other languages follow different conventions. Semitic and Arabic languages consist of a series of parallel structures; Oriental languages are circular and discuss a subject from a variety of tangentially related views; Romance languages are characterised by many digressions, while Indic languages have a spiral-like discourse pattern (Barnitz 1986).

Cultural differences in discourse patterns were thought to explain why students translating into Hebrew and Arabic had difficulties with logical connectors, such as, *since, while, however, nevertheless* and *whereas* (Benoussan 1986).

Pat Wright's 1979 review of research again provides a good starting point for considering the general problems with the structure of sentences. She found that sentences should be neither too short nor too long. But while many long sentences were difficult to understand, the real fault lay in the way the ideas were inter-related not in the length itself. Replacing a long sentence with a number of short ones was often no solution. Research has shown that people sometimes found it much easier to see the appropriate relationships when all the information was within a single sentence (Wright 1979a).

The skill lies in constructing a sentence so that the relationships are clearly understood. Sentences which included relative clauses were preferred and read more quickly than the same text written as two sentences (Wright 1985). Readers found it easier if the main clause came first and the subordinate qualifications followed (Wright 1979a); while adverbial clauses were best placed in the middle of a sentence rather than at the beginning or the end (Wright 1985).

In general, sentences were easier to understand if the information about what to do preceded the statement about when to do it. People encoded conditional statements by first working out an action plan and then attaching to this plan the relevant conditional information (Dixon 1982).

Earlier research on complicated sentences showed that readers understood those that were joined by *and* more easily than those joined by *but*. The word *or* was more difficult still. Among the most difficult of all were link words indicating causal relationships, such as *because, therefore* or *so*. (Wright 1979a).

Protocol analyses of form-fillers have shown that difficulties arose if multiple *or* clauses were used or if questions included qualifiers (Frohlich 1985b).

The Document Design Project has undertaken a series of experiments on the use of conditional sentences, which are very common on government leaflets and forms (Rose and Cox 1980; Holland and Rose 1980). The first of these looked at the relative difficulty of a range of conditional sentences which included the words *and*, *or* and *not*. The results showed that:

- *Or* took longer to process than *and*. So strings of *ors* should be avoided.

- Negative embedded clauses should be rephrased. For example *not male and not married* should be rephrased as *female and single*.

- Instructions which included *not both* or *not either* were especially difficult for readers.

- Care should be taken to avoid 'pseudo-ambiguous clauses'. For example it was not clear whether the instruction *If you are not male and single go to question 5* meant that single female should go to question 5 or not. To clear up the ambiguity the instruction should be rewritten as *If you are single and not male then go to question 5* (Rose and Cox 1980).

Many guidelines to writing suggest that more complex conditional sentences should not be presented as prose. The aim of the second Document Design Project investigation was to discover the level of complexity at which the alternatives should be considered. To do this they looked at the ease with which readers coped with a range of very complex instructions such as *If you are male or both married and not employed go to question 5*. They had hoped to identify whether there were thresholds of complexity beyond which comprehension deteriorated markedly. If fact, they found that each of the major sentence dimensions—number of categories (eg male, married, employed); sentence type; the connecting words (ie and-or), and negatives—seemed to contribute to the overall difficulty of the sentence. Furthermore, these dimensions seemed to be interactive in their effects. The results also showed that where readers had difficulty in understanding a complex series of categories they assumed that it did not apply to them.

In drawing out the practical implications of the detailed results of this work, the researchers concluded that the following sentence constructions are suitable for general use:

- Implicit strings of categories that are joined by *and*: eg *if A,B,C,D, and E.*

- Explicit strings of categories regardless of whether they are connected by *and* or *or* and regardless of the number of categories: eg *if A or B or C or D.*

- 'Two group hierarchical sentences' where the main connective word is *or*: eg *if A and B or C and D.*

- 'Three group hierarchical sentences' with more than four categories: eg *if A and B or C and D or E and F.*

They recommended that all other complex instructions should be tested experimentally before they are included in any document that is intended for public use (Holland and Rose 1980).

Conditional sentences are also well-known to cause problems. A minority of people using Department of Health and Social Security forms found the conditional *if... then...* instructions difficult to cope with (Hedges and Ritchie 1986).

Pat Wright has continued her work in this area by investigating whether the two negative conditionals *if not* and *unless* were processed in a similar way. In fact, they were processed rather differently, possibly due to different common usage of the terms. Subsequent research showed that *if not* and *unless* were not equivalent terms (Wright and Hull 1986 and 1988).

Learners of English as a second language were found to comprehend unreal conditional sentences—*if... would...*—better than real conditional sentences—*if... will...* The position of the *if clause* had no significant effect on comprehension (Berent 1985).

Other work has looked at the use of the word *this* to refer back to a preceding idea or clause in a sentence (the 'unattended anaphoric' use of *this*). The results showed that sentences were interpreted more easily if the *this* referred back to the main or focal topic of the sentence. In other circumstances *this* should be accompanied or 'attended' by a noun or noun phrase.

There are, however, occasions when either an attended or an unattended *this* can be used. The authors suggest that the clarity of such sentences should be assessed by writers asking themselves *this what?* If they cannot fill in the *what* easily, then either the referent needs to be added or the sentence needs redrafting (Geisler and others 1985).

The passive voice has been shown to cause difficulties (Wright 1979a). Research with deaf students showed particular difficulties with sentences using agentless passives such as *The child was loved* (LoMaglio 1985).

Research with a group of adolescents with learning disabilities showed that it was possible to enhance their reading comprehension by using the active voice rather than the passive. It was also possible to improve comprehension by re-stating key information; by reducing the past perfect to simple past tense, and by stating the subject of a sentence explicitly (Abrahamsen and Shelton 1989)

Reader preferences

All of these studies have concentrated on words or grammatical constructions which cause reading difficulties. Others have looked at reader preferences, since these too play a part in making a document acceptable and likely to be read.

Some of the terms and expressions used on public documents, such as *community charge* or *state pension*, are not necessarily the same as those used by people in their everyday lives. The distribution of preferred terms may be subject to regional and age differences (Parkinson 1990a; PPCR Market Research 1990a and b).

More generally, people seem to be tolerant of ungrammatical language when it follows the pattern that would be used in everyday speech. Research by Pat Wright has demonstrated that the public was much more prepared than technical writers to accept current vernacular, such as split infinitives. Older people were no more likely to reject current vernacular than young ones (Wright 1985).

Contracted verbs When asked for their views on the use of contracted verbs such as *aren't* or *can't*, a third of the people studied did not notice that contracted verbs had been used. They read the text as if the verb had been written out in full. Of those people who did notice, many more preferred the use of non-contracted verbs than preferred the contractions (Kempson 1984).

Pronouns The need to avoid sexist language poses writers with problems when they need to use a singular pronoun. A study to investigate people's preferences found that twice as many preferred *he/she* as preferred *they* to refer to a single person whose gender was not known (Kempson 1984).

Forms of address A National Opinion Poll was commissioned by the *Daily Mail* newspaper on the acceptability of *Ms* as the female form of address. Generally it was not well accepted. Only one in ten people said they liked it, and four in ten positively disliked it. Women were no more likely than men to like *Ms*. It was, however, more acceptable to people aged under 35 (National Opinion Polls 1981).

Forms of address were also studied in a project commissioned by the Department of Health and Social Security Forms Unit. In this case opinions were obtained on three versions of the same official letter, one addressed *Dear Sir or Madam*, one addressed personally and a third that had no salutation at all. The most striking finding was that two-thirds of the participants did not notice that the letters were addressed differently. When they did, they preferred the personalised letter (Kempson 1984).

When letters were enclosed with a postal questionnaire, there was no difference between the effects of personalised and form letters on the response rate (Worthen and Valcarce 1985). A follow-up study that reanalysed the same data suggested that, where questionnaires asked for personal information, a form letter tended to be preferred (Trice 1986).

Numbers Other than the number *one*, the majority of people both preferred numbers to be written in digits rather than words and thought that digits were clearer. Slightly more than half of them thought that figures over 1,000 should include a comma, while almost nine out of ten thought a comma should be included in figures of 10,000 or more (Department of Health and Social Security 1987).

Warnings and declarations It is often claimed that warnings and declarations deter people from completing forms. Group discussions, commissioned by the Department of Health and Social Security Forms Unit, explored this in some detail. Half the participants said that having to sign a declaration made them more careful when completing a form. A third said that declarations had no effect on them, and a quarter said they became frightened or anxious. They also expressed preferences for specific wordings of declarations (Kempson 1984).

Surprisingly, nine out of ten people thought that there should be a warning on a form. The most common reason, given by a half of the participants, was that if giving false information could lead to prosecution then they would just as soon know. However almost half the participants said that warnings had no effect on them at all—they had grown used to seeing them. Again, as with the declarations, discussions were held on the preferred wording for a warning (Kempson 1984).

10 Aspects of visual design

The overall appearance of a public document plays a critical part in its impact, acceptability and ease of use. This applies equally to leaflets and to forms. In this chapter we consider research into the visual aspects of document design; specifically, typography, colour and the use of illustration.

Typography

Two sets of guidelines on legibility and typography have been prepared for designers of public documents (Forms Information Centre 1984a; Reynolds 1988).

Upper and lower case It is generally accepted that text printed in lower case with a few initial capitals is easier to read than text printed using capital letters only. Lower case vertical typefaces with a few capital letters were easiest to read. The use of capitals for more than just a few words slowed readers down (Wright 1979a). Fewer than one in ten of adult volunteers found text printed in capital letters easy to read. In addition, headlines in capital letters were much less legible than those in lower case (Wheildon 1984).

There may be occasions when it is necessary to break the generally accepted rule about case. Some computer printers, for example, are not capable of switching between capitals and lower case. This led the Department of Health and Social Security Document Design Unit to investigate the relative merits of printing text entirely in capital letters and entirely in lower case. Whilst neither is desirable, they concluded that using capitals only is to be preferred to using lower case only (Department of Health and Social Security 1986a).

Type size For a general readership, the ideal size for type was between 6 and 12 point (x heights of between 2mm and 4mm). People's speed of reading tended to be slower outside this range, but speed was affected by other critical factors, such as the length of the line and spacing between the lines (Wright 1979a).

Elderly people's reading speed increased as the type size was increased. Participants were happiest with type size of 12 point or over, although there was no significant increase in reading speed over 14 point. The report of this project also considers the implications of the research findings for the design of printed materials for elderly people (Vanderplas and Vanderplas 1980).

Typeface The use of italics for more than a few words slowed readers down, leading to the conclusion that italics should not be used for large bodies of text (Wright 1979a). More recent research has showed that text set in italic type caused an initial reaction in adult readers but did not affect their comprehension levels (Wheildon 1984). The use of bold text type both reduced comprehension and caused fatigue (Wheildon 1986; Wright 1979a).

Sans serif typefaces led to lower levels of comprehensibility and made it difficult for readers to hold their attention, and were generally less satisfactory than serif typefaces (Wheildon 1984; Wright 1979a). However, under laboratory conditions, a sans serif font was slightly more legible than a serif one, although there was very little difference between them in readability (Suen and Komoda 1986). Elderly people read Roman styles of type more quickly than Gothic ones (Vanderplas and Vanderplas 1980).

With the increasing use of computers, the legibility and readability of dot matrix fonts has been compared with letter quality ones. Not surprisingly perhaps, the dot matrix fonts were found to be both less legible and less readable (Suen and Komoda 1986).

Kerning Type with proportional spacing was easier to read than material with non-proportional spacing, where each letter took up the same amount of space (Wright 1979a). Kerning, or reducing the space between letters, led to a reduction in the comprehension levels of adult readers (Wheildon 1984), although students read close-spaced type more quickly (Moriarty and Scheiner 1984).

Typographic variations In some documents, typographic variations were used to give visual cues to the structure of the text, or for other purposes. The use of too many typographic variations, however, made it difficult for the reader to keep track of what the variations meant (Wright 1979a).

Semantic qualities of type Legibility is only one consideration when choosing a typeface. The other is selecting the typeface which will create the desired effect. This is generally referred to as the 'semantic property' of the typeface as opposed to the 'functional properties' of size, boldness, contrast and aspects of form.

Studies of semantic properties are not new. One of the first was conducted by Anna Berliner in 1920. More recently, two projects evaluated a range of typefaces on scales which measured their semantic properties (Bartram 1982; Rowe 1982). Typefaces were shown to possess perceptual qualities (such as hard-soft or fast-slow) about which subjects generally agreed. Furthermore, the subjects' performance of a simple classification task was impaired when the meaning of a word and the qualities of the typeface were incongruent (Lewis and Walker 1989).

The semantic properties ascribed to typefaces by designers were not always the same as those ascribed by non-designers. Whilst there were general similarities, there were marked differences on certain factors for most of the typefaces. From this it was concluded that designers should be aware that their readers may not share their view of a typeface. The report suggested a method of testing such discrepancies (Bartram 1982).

Selecting the typeface which is the most appropriate for the audience of a document is seldom easy. Some interesting preliminary research looked at practical ways of achieving this. Although the results were tentative they suggested a way of comparing a profile of subjective ratings for the organisation producing a document with the profile for each of a number of alternative designs. Using the same technique, graphic designers could identify from their clients the corporate personality they wished to have created (Walker and others 1986).

Justification of text Research has suggested that generally people were faster when reading unjustified text than they were reading paragraphs where the right-hand edge had been aligned vertically (Wright 1979a). However, the opposite was found for adult readers of public documents, where text was better justified at both margins (Wheildon 1984).

Line length There is a good deal of evidence to show that a line length of between 40 and 60 characters is easiest to read and to comprehend. Text set wider than 60 characters and narrower than 20 characters was particularly hard to read (Frase and others 1985; Wheildon 1984; Wright 1979a).

Text is most comprehensible if it is presented as chunks, or meaningful units (see page 31). However the effects of the variable line length that result from such chunking tended to counteract the increases in comprehension (Keenan 1984).

It follows, therefore, that text will be most comprehensible if a line length is selected that allows the maximum number of lines of text to consist of one chunk of information. This has led a team of researchers to develop a method of computer analysis of text to determine the optimum line length. Whilst they found that line lengths of between 40 and 60 characters were generally most comprehensible, it was far better to ascertain the optimum line length for each piece of text (Frase and others 1985).

Vertical space between lines also influenced the ease of reading. Longer lines needed more space between them to be read easily (Wright 1979a).

Colour
Again there are sets of guidelines prepared for designers of public documents on the use of colour. The Forms Information Centre has distilled both practice and research into a topic sheet on the use of colour in forms and leaflets (Forms Information Centre 1983). Guidelines on when to use a second colour have also been compiled by the Open University Textual Communication Research Group (Waller and others 1982).

There are two main considerations in deciding what colours to use: the effect on legibility and ease of use; and the psychological impact.

Legibility The most important factor is the effect of colour contrast on the legibility of text. A minimum contrast of 30% was necessary for easy reading. Yellow on white seldom achieved this; orange on white was borderline (Wright 1979a). Yellow generally seemed to cause problems. Use of a bright yellow colour on a form caused eye strain and processing difficulties for social security staff (Firth 1980). Reversed out yellow lettering on a black background was difficult to read according to consumer testing of the cover of a booklet (MIL Research Ltd 1984a).

Similar difficulties arose with the use of red type. Red print used in a booklet on export services for businesses was difficult for many people to read (MIL Research Ltd 1984a).

The strong contrast provided by a dark blue type on a white background improved clarity, when compared with black on white. But it did not contribute significantly to the ease of completion of the form (Nova Research Ltd 1986).

The use of coloured type, and high chroma colours in particular, for headings attracted attention to the page but interfered with the reading process (Wheildon 1984).

A follow-up study looked at the effects of printing text in a range of colours, including black, and also at the effects of printing on white and tinted paper. Texts printed in black, and colours closest to black, were found to be easiest to read and to result in the highest levels of comprehension. Most effective, however, was black type printed on a light (10%) tint. This gave relatively high levels of comprehensibility and was, at the same time, more attractive to readers. Reversing out the print so that, say, the text was white on black dramatically reduced the levels of comprehension (Wheildon 1986).

Psychology There has been a considerable amount of general research into the psychological effects of colour but little of it has been related to public documents.

Although most redesigned forms and leaflets use a second colour, very few of the case study reports comment on its use. Where they do, it is often to say only that users felt that the colour made the document 'more friendly' or 'more approachable' (Firth 1980; MIL Research Ltd 1982).

It is possible, however, to build up some useful information by collating the results of consumer tests of public documents.

- Brown print, used on a National Insurance employers' booklet, was not generally liked, because it was more difficult to read in poor lighting. Some people, however, thought that brown was a more 'modern' colour than blue (MIL Research Ltd 1984b).

- Blue print on a white background was thought to be both more friendly and less bureaucratic than black and white when it was used for a taxation form. However, while some people thought that this would encourage users to complete the form, others felt that the unofficial appearance might lead people to be less conscientious when completing it (Nova Research Ltd 1986).

- Red print used in a booklet on export services for businesses was liked by most people although some found it difficult to read (MIL Research Ltd 1984a). When a taxation form was tested with consumers there were spontaneous comments that red type would be both undesirable and inappropriate for this type of form (Nova Research Ltd 1986).

- Orange, bright yellow and pink were also felt to be undesirable colours for the type on a tax form (Nova Research Ltd 1986).

- Black was considered to be too sombre a colour for the cover of a booklet (MIL Research Ltd 1984a).

The use of colour can, in some circumstances, have a positive effect. For example, the use of coloured margins was liked, as was the use of coloured highlighting for paragraph headings (MIL Research Ltd 1986a). In contrast the vast majority of people were annoyed by the use of special screening effects on illustrations (Wheildon 1984).

Illustrations

The functions which illustrations and graphics play in information design in general are complex and much of the research comes from the field of educational psychology. Not surprisingly, it focuses on the role of illustrations in educational materials where they are largely used to complement and extend prose-based information. Two independent reviews of this research have drawn together the main findings of recent research into illustrations and have outlined some of their implications for designers of public documents. They conclude that pictures and illustrations can have a positive effect on text comprehension, especially with simple texts and people with limited reading ability (Lewis 1988; Parkinson 1990b).

Most illustration research has focused on people's perception of pictures rather than on their function within a text. More specifically it has focused on the perception of pictures and the acquisition of visual literacy by children and on cross cultural studies. Where studies have addressed themselves to the function of illustrations they have tended to focus on whether they enhance the levels of comprehension of texts (Brody 1981;, Duchastel 1980; Goldsmith 1984).

Research suggests that illustrations reinforced the primary reading strategy of adult non-readers, which was to rely on experience and knowledge rather than print-based text cues (Malicky and Norman 1989). But there was also a danger of illustrations interfering with the reading process, causing errors and slowing down or distracting readers (Lewis 1988; Parkinson 1990b). Children with different reading abilities employed quite different approaches when reading illustrated texts; those with more limited reading abilities tended to rely on illustrations to a far greater extent than those who were able to read more fluently (Reid and Beveridge 1990).

It has been argued that use of pictorial material can help to communicate with readers from different cultural backgrounds and especially with those for whom English is not their first language. But pictorial representations involved conventions just as writing did (Wright 1979a).

The Health Education Authority explored the information needs of minority ethnic groups and their response to an English language *Pregnancy Book*. As expected, the fundamental determining factor of the book's usefulness was the reader's level of literacy in English. But in instances where the level of literacy was low, the book's photographs and diagrams were shown to be fairly instructive on their own (McGuire 1989).

Research with semi-literate African communities showed that graphics needed to be context-based. This meant that the use of such graphics needed to be preceded by in-depth research of the target readership and their interpretative patterns (Tomaselli and Tomaselli 1984).

Culturally-related barriers also existed for non-picture visuals used in health learning manuals. A key finding was that learners with little or no experience of visuals may well find them incomprehensible (Cripwell 1989).

This research is complemented by consumer tests of specific documents which provide some circumstantial evidence. Illustrations helped to make a text look more attractive and usable, but only if they were relevant and useful (Campbell Kegan Ltd 1986; Communication Research Ltd 1984b and 1985; Cragg, Ross and Dawson 1983; Firth 1980; Harris Research Centre 1985; MIL Research Ltd 1982 and 1986a; Research Business 1986). However, it seemed that straight graphics were preferred to cartoons, which were seen as 'childish', 'flippant' and 'amateur in the extreme' (Communication Research Ltd 1984b; Harris Research Centre 1985).

Illustrations can be used either to capture attention or to enhance comprehension. So far as the former is concerned, research suggests that most people looked first at the graphics and, if the message conveyed by them was understandable and interesting, they would then scan or read the text. Few people read a text from beginning to end, using the graphics to support their understanding (Communication Research Ltd 1984b). Where, however, the attention of the audience was already engaged, leaflets were equally effective whether or not they included illustrations: this was found to be the case, for example, with leaflets designed to encourage motorists to wear seatbelts (Wright 1979a).

Comprehension can be assisted in different ways. For instance, people generally welcomed the use of illustrations in leaflets about Community Charge Benefit because they were felt to break up the monotony of long texts and were also useful in reinforcing signposting and routing (PPCR Market Research 1990a).

It has also been argued that pictures and illustrations can also enhance public documents by helping to foster a sense of identification among intended users. A Community Care Grant claim pack that used photographs of 'typical' claimants on the front cover was preferred to one which did not. Sample target groups felt that the photographs softened the 'official' image they had expected (Palmer and MacLeod 1990b).

Conversely, there was a danger that photographs reinforced stereotypes and suggested, inadvertently, that the information might be relevant only to certain types of people. This possibility might be reduced by using faceless drawings or cartoons (PPCR Market Research 1990a).

Other graphics

Many information designers use *symbols* on public documents, particularly on their covers. The International Standards Organisation has produced a very useful set of visual design criteria for the development of public information symbols. This includes guidance on the size, proportions, symmetry, directional characteristics, and detail of information symbols (International Standards Organisation 1984). The effectiveness of symbols has been shown to be related to their design: the presence of a well-designed hazard symbol on a product significantly improved the chances of consumers reading and complying with written instructions (Friedmann 1988).

An evaluation procedure has been developed to identify good and bad symbols at an early stage of development and to predict their likely acceptability by the intended audience (Zwaga 1989).

The Department of Health and Social Security Document Design Unit has experimented with the use of *speech balloons*, containing questions that many people wanted answered, as a way of providing an indication of the contents of a document. While more research is needed to test alternatives, the initial results showed that this can be an acceptable way of organising text (Hedges and Ritchie 1986).

A number of different types of graphics were used in a leaflet on public finance. The *sliced horizontal charts* were the easiest to interpret, though a minority of people preferred the information to be presented as tables (Communication Research Ltd 1984b).

Algorithms and flowcharts

We saw (pages 36 - 38) that users of forms and leaflets have considerable difficulties with routing devices. The use of complex instructions added to that difficulty. As a result researchers have investigated lists and flowcharts as alternatives to prose (Holland and Rose 1981; Jansen and Steehouder 1984; Wright 1982).

A full review of research up to 1981 is included in an article by Pat Wright. She concluded that it was not possible to summarise the findings of the research into a neat set of guidelines. Instead she offered some general principles which designers might bear in mind.

- The ease with which alternatives to prose were used depended on more than legibility and layout. It was necessary to be aware of how readers interacted with printed materials.

- Eliminating redundancy could be a false economy. It may have saved space, but it often created problems for users of a table.

- Designers needed to provide the users of tables and flowcharts with a decision structure and to use space to help readers perceive the functional groupings within the material (Wright 1982).

The proposed use of diagrams and flowcharts in a leaflet about National Insurance was popular with employers (Andrew Irving Associates 1989); and recommendations for improving a leaflet about Income Support included a suggestion that flowcharts be used to explain the overall structure of the benefit (Campbell Keagan Limited 1990).

Again, consumer testing of three different leaflets has suggested that flowcharts were both liked and very efficient—but only for those people who understood them. A minority of people could not cope with them at all (Hedges and Ritchie 1986; MIL Research Ltd 1984b; MIL Research Ltd 1986a). Further, the haphazard use of flowcharts made the page appear cluttered (Research Business 1986).

A minority of people also found matrices difficult to cope with, while others could not handle indented lists following a colon (Hedges and Ritchie 1986).

Two research studies have looked at the value of algorithms in the specific context of forms and leaflets. The first of these tested four versions of a Dutch government rent-rebate leaflet. Three of these were written in prose and one was composed of flowcharts. The research showed that users were unlikely to calculate the right rebate entitlement using any of the leaflets, although the flowchart format proved to be significantly better than any of the three prose leaflets (Jansen and Steehouder 1984).

Researchers at the Document Design Project followed up their earlier studies on conditional instructions (Rose and Cox 1980; Holland and Rose 1981) with a project that tested whether such instructions were better understood when they were presented as either lists or flowcharts. The research showed that both types of algorithm were processed more easily and more accurately than prose, except where users were unfamiliar with the format. In those cases, both lists and flowcharts were processed more slowly than prose.

Of the two types of algorithm, flowcharts seemed to be processed more quickly than lists. There was no difference in the accuracy except that inexperienced users were much more likely to misinterpret the flowcharts (Holland and Rose 1981). Even so, users soon learned how to cope with the new format and came to prefer them to prose.

The findings of the Dutch rent rebate study offer some explanation for the improved performance with algorithms. They showed that readers of the prose versions did not read the precise information in the text until they had failed several times to calculate the rebate entitlement. They also showed that the readers would postpone making decisions or calculations until they reached a passage where they needed them. They then reconstructed the instructions from memory. Moreover, readers were reluctant to skip passages of text that were irrelevant to them even though they were instructed to do so (Jansen and Steehouder 1984).

This seems to suggest that algorithms, especially flowcharts, should in the long term help users to cope with complex conditional sentences. However, until users become familiar with the format, flowcharts should be accompanied by brief explanatory notes.

Part IV

TESTING AND REVISING
PUBLIC DOCUMENTS

Part IV - Contents

11 **TESTING AND EVALUATING DOCUMENTS**   65
    Readability formulae   65
    Checklists and guidelines   67
    Error rates   68
    Cloze tests and paraphrase testing   68
    Surveys   68
    Protocol analysis   70

12 **EDITING AND REVISING DOCUMENTS**   72

11 Testing and evaluating documents

Once a form or leaflet has been designed it is important that it should be tested and revised until it is shown to achieve its purpose. The growing emphasis on this stage of the design process of public documents is reflected in a large number of research techniques. Some of these are based on an analysis of the document, others involve testing the document with users. There have been a number of reviews of the research methods that can be used to test public documents (Lynton 1985; Schumacher and Waller 1985; Sless 1985; Wright 1979b).

Pat Wright reviewed field studies, interviews, surveys and laboratory experiments as techniques for testing public documents and considered the usefulness of each of them for assessing the content, presentation and usability of documents (Wright 1979b). The figure below summarises her conclusions.

Research techniques	Three quality control checks		
	Content	Presentation	Usability
Field studies	•	•	•
Interviews	•		•
Surveys	•	•	•
Laboratory experiments		•	•

In their review, Schumacher and Waller developed a checklist of characteristics against which testing methods can be assessed. They then applied this to a range of methods, indicating the situations in which each was likely to be most useful. This showed that protocol analysis was probably the most useful established technique for testing public documents (Schumacher and Waller 1985).

Readability formulae
One of the earliest techniques for testing documents was the use of readability formulae. These are usually based on counts of the length of words and the length of sentences, although more recent formulae

attempt more sophisticated measures. There has been a considerable amount of research on the validity and usefulness of readability formulae as a means of testing public documents. A number of authors have reviewed the research evidence and have generally reached the same conclusions.

- The statistical validity of most formulae for public leaflets is questionable. Most have been validated against educational tests, using schoolchildren.

- They are incapable of distinguishing between sense and nonsense texts.

- They do not measure a wide range of other factors that are known to affect comprehension. These include grammatical constructions; organisation of the text; and graphics and typography.

- They cannot measure a text against the knowledge and needs of an intended audience.

- Different formulae lead to widely different reading ages for the same document.

Most writers on the subject also point out the dangers of requiring texts to be written to a particular readability level. This, it is claimed, focuses attention on meeting the score requirement rather than looking at the document as a whole and organising the material to meet the needs of the users (Bentley 1985; Campbell and Holland 1982; Canadian Law Information Council 1985; Charrow 1979a; Drury 1985; Felker 1980; Firth 1980; Forms Information Centre 1985b; Hartley and others 1988; Hartley and others 1980b; Holland 1981; Kern 1980; Readability formulas... 1981; Redish and others 1981; Smith and Smith 1984; Wright 1979b).

As examples of this, readability scores on the Flesch scale did not correlate with levels of comprehension for antenatal leaflets (Owen and others 1984) or for jury instructions (Charrow and Charrow 1979); and leaflets for elderly people that were written to the Dale Chall readability formula did not lead to higher levels of comprehension (Walmsley and others 1981).

A British team of consultants has attempted to overcome some of the deficiencies of the existing readability formulae. The resulting British

Index of Reading Difficulty is, in fact, a set of formulae which have been evolved for different applications. Some of these add little to the existing formulae. Others are based on a great deal of development work, chiefly identifying the words that are difficult for or unfamiliar to a large proportion of the public. This work has led to the generation of a set of rules that are based on good practice and sound commonsense. However, these rules are so complex that the formulae take skill and a good deal of time to apply. In addition, they do not cover the grammar of the text (Communication Research Ltd 1984a). Other attempts to develop better formulae have concentrated on devising a test for short pieces of text (Fry 1989 and 1990) and on trying to take account of the meaning of words (Mali and Sykes 1985).

Despite their limitations, it is still argued that readability formulae have their place and are useful, providing that those using the tests are aware of the limitations (Wagenaar and others 1987). But because of the serious doubts that have been raised about their use to evaluate public documents, attempts have been made to find alternative tests that are easy to apply.

Checklists and guidelines
In one such attempt, the Document Design Centre staff evolved a set of design guidelines that can be used to evaluate forms and leaflets. These were based in part on a detailed analysis of the problems that people face when using public documents (Rose 1981).

Others have provided checklists for assessing public documents (Canadian Law Information Council 1985; Redish 1985).

As part of her study of editing processes, Pat Wright, too, suggested a method of assessing a form and identifying where revision is necessary. This method involved a number of stages, including assessments of the ease of understanding specific sections of the form; assessments of specific design and presentation factors; and an overall judgement of the design of the form (Wright 1985).

More recently, multiple regression analysis has been used to identify five key variables that influence the readability and useability of documents (Kirsch and Mosenthal 1990).

Error rates

A rather different approach was taken by research commissioned by the Document Design Unit of the Department of Health and Social Security. The main focus of this research was an analysis of the errors made when people filled in forms. The researchers produced several formulae by which it is possible to work out the expected error rate for a given form. It is possible, by comparing these figures with the actual error rate, to show both the scope and the need for improvement to a form. The researchers also made suggestions on costing the difference between the actual and the expected error rates (Coopers and Lybrand 1986).

Cloze tests and paraphrase testing

Another controversial technique is the cloze test. In this test, a passage of the text is selected and every, say, fifth word deleted. Subjects are then asked to read the text and fill in the missing words. Such tests are a fairly common way of testing the comprehension of school pupils. It is questionable whether they are valuable for evaluating public documents. They have been used for this purpose but were not found to be especially useful (Ashby-Davis 1985; Canadian Law Information Council 1985; Firth 1980; Hartley and others 1980b). The effectiveness of cloze tests depends to a great extent on their design and on the context in which the tests are administered (Hartley others 1980b).

Paraphrase testing has been developed as a technique to evaluate public documents. It was used successfully to pinpoint the difficulties people had with jury instructions. The paraphrases were analysed linguistically to identify the grammar and vocabulary that caused comprehension difficulties (Charrow and Charrow 1979).

Surveys

In a lengthy study, employing a wide range of techniques, Diana Firth concluded that text-based techniques were no substitute for actually trying out documents.

The only way to find out in detail about a document (its impact, appeal, design and comprehensibility) is to study it in use and ascertain users' reactions to and comprehension of it. This does not need to be carried out on a grand scale with a wealth of quantitative data. The most meaningful approach is a qualitative/interpretive one, for example, depth interviews, group discussions and observations (Firth 1980).

Many others have echoed these views (Hartley and others 1980b; Hill and Mayon-White 1987; Redish and others 1981; Rose 1981; Wright 1979b). Experience at the Document Design Centre in the USA led to the conclusion that non-research trained document designers can plan and conduct a useful empirical evaluation of a public document (Redish and others 1981).

Questionnaire surveys are by far the most commonly used technique. A critical incident study of the problems people reported when reading public documents evolved a very useful checklist of items to be covered in such surveys (Rose 1981).

The Department of Employment assessed three different survey methods in their comparison study of two versions of the Maternity Pay Rebate form. They compared face-to-face interviews with telephone interviewing and postal questionnaires. There was little different between the methods in the information provided either on the ease of completion of the form, or on suggestions for improvement. Postal surveys were the most-cost effective—they cost only half as much as face-to-face interviews—but they led to the largest proportion of outright refusals. Telephone research did not provide reliable information on response rates (Department of Employment 1983).

In a study of the Medicaid form, researchers observed staff in a local Medical Assistance Office helping members of the public interpret the form. This was shown to be a useful technique not only for pinpointing difficulties but also for showing how they needed to be overcome (Charrow and others 1980).

A related technique was used in the testing of the Family Income Supplement form. Volunteers in a Family Services Unit were given a copy of the form to complete and then asked to describe how they had done so and what difficulties they had. This proved to give a great deal of useful information both about the specific aspects of form design and about people's feelings in general. It was noted, however, that it put the volunteers in a vulnerable position. Not only were they revealing their difficulties with form-filling but also their personal financial situation (Corden and Corden 1984). To avoid this, it has been suggested that it is better to ask people to indicate the areas which they feel could cause *other* people difficulty (Hartley and others 1980b).

Protocol analysis

The USA Document Design Centre developed a protocol analysis technique to identify how people read and interpreted government regulations. Participants were asked to 'think aloud' as they read the regulations and were tape-recorded as they did so. The tape-recorded 'protocols' were then analysed. The most notable result from the analysis was the extent to which readers expressed the meaning of a line or section in the form of a concrete story or event. From this the researchers devised a measure of the extent to which documents reflected this process. When this technique was tested on actual documents, it was found that the scores for sections within each document were consistent (Flower and others 1980).

The protocol analysis technique has been further developed by the staff of the Document Design Centre. They showed that it can be enhanced by asking the participants specific questions afterwards to probe areas they may not have identified in their protocols (Swaney and others 1981; Flower and others 1980). Subsequently, they have shown that protocols, supplemented by accuracy tests, were also a good way of testing forms (Charney 1984) and the results could be used as an aid to revision (Duffy and others 1989).

An interactive software package, SHAPA, has been developed for analysing recorded protocols. This offers a number of advantages over traditional methods, both in the speed of coding the protocols and in providing easy access to summary data (Sanderson and others 1989).

Another technique that is closely related to protocol analysis is the macro-eye movement procedure. There are a number of variants on this procedure but the one best suited to detailed design questions is the 'light pen procedure'. In this, subjects in a darkened room are given a text to read using a light pen. The pen is linked to a computer which records how the text was read onto a page grid. Sections of text that distort the normal reading pattern can be detected in this way. It is especially useful for investigating page layout and the usefulness of certain access structures (Schumacher and Waller 1985).

12 Editing and revising documents

There are four basic ways in which documents can be revised and edited (Siegel 1979):

- Revising the content.

- Simplifying the organisation of the document.

- Simplifying its language.

- Reducing its length.

Research with government regulations has shown that changing a single feature, or a few features, in a document did not lead to significant differences in comprehension. Such changes did, however, lead people to express a preference for the simplified document (Redish and others 1981).

It has also been shown to be important, when revising a document, to go beyond the existing text. A case study using an apartment lease tested two fundamentally different editing techniques. The first used the existing document as a base and 'translated' its contents. The other created an entirely new document based on the needs of the users. This involved revising the content as well as the language and design of the document. The second technique was more appropriate for documents which covered complex legislation (Siegel and Glasgoff 1981).

An interesting study of editing techniques involved a protocol analysis of experienced writers as they edited a legal document. The resulting texts were then assessed for comprehensibility. The researchers identified the characteristics of the editors who produced the most and the least comprehensible revisions and from these evolved a set of guidelines (Bond and others 1980):

- Revision should be broad in scope and cover the generation and organisation of material, as well as grammar, syntax and punctuation.

- Attention to, and an understanding of, the needs of the audience is of major importance.

- Good revisions need good structure as well as good content.

- A good revision strategy involves reading and re-reading.

- Revisions should be evaluated.

In an attempt to provide a deeper understanding of editing processes, Pat Wright carried out a series of five inter-related experiments. The research revealed considerable differences in both the number and nature of editorial decisions made by different people. This was possibly because of lack of knowledge of editing. It seemed that this lack of knowledge may not easily be remedied by the provision of written guidelines. Finally, there was some evidence that the editorial decisions of professional writers were different from those of the general public (Wright 1985).

The early 1980s saw the development of a number of computer-based text-editing systems. These can be used to check spelling; identify punctuation and grammatical errors; identify constructions, such as passives and abstract words, that cause difficulties to users; and indicate sexist or racist phrases that can cause offence. They can also be used to apply readability formulae, to count sentence length and to analyse the frequency of simple and complex sentences (Anderson 1983; Frase and others 1985).

Five of these systems—Grammatik II, Right Writer, Electric Webster, Punctuation and Style and PC Style—were tested on three documents. The tests showed both the strengths and weaknesses of each program (Raskin 1986).

The computer-based text-editing systems have been compared with comments made by writers' colleagues. This showed that text-editing programs were more thorough and systematic than humans, but that they covered a much narrower range of activities. Humans offered a much wider range and included suggestions for improvements to the content (Hartley 1984).

Text-editing systems would, therefore, seem to be a useful means of checking certain aspects of the text. For the present, at least, they need to be supplemented by comments from human editors.

REVIEWS

Reviews

Abrahamsen and Shelton (1989)

Eileen P Abrahamsen and Kathleen C Shelton. 'Reading comprehension in adolescents with learning disabilities: semantic and syntactic effects'. *Journal of Learning Disabilities* 22(9), 1989, 569-571.

A report of work on a group of adolescents with learning disabilities (average age 14 years) in which the researchers investigated the effects of syntax and semantic complexity on the comprehension of selected passages from a social studies text.

When certain modifications were made to these passages, students were shown to retain significantly more information (as measured by accurate responses to subsequent questioning), although in all cases the modifications and the original text were rated at the same level of difficulty using the Fry Readability Formula. This indicated that increased comprehension had been achieved without lowering the reading level.

The specific interventions which were shown to significantly enhance reading comprehension were:

- Stating the subject of a sentence explicitly.

- Using the active voice rather than the passive.

- Reducing the past perfect tense to the simple past.

- Repeating key information.

Allison and others (1985)

Frances Allison, Simon James and Alan Lewis. *The comprehensibility of Inland Revenue literature: with special reference to the problems of the elderly and recently retired.*
Inland Revenue, 1985.

Part 1 describes the UK tax system and the way it is administered, while Part 2 analyses the difficulties tax payers face in dealing with their tax affairs, focusing particularly on elderly and more recently retired tax payers. These difficulties were identified using a number of methodologies:

- A nation-wide survey of tax payers.

- Interviews and discussions with Inland Revenue officials.

- A survey of the errors made by pensioners in completing their P1 tax returns.

- An analysis of enquiries made at Inland Revenue enquiry stands.

- A review of tax assistance provided by other agencies, including a survey of letters about tax problems written to newspapers, questions raised on a local radio phone-in programme and enquiries made at citizens' advice bureaux.

The main findings of Part 2 are that tax payers often do not read the explanatory notes. Instead they plough through the entire form, when they could go directly to those sections relevant to them. As many as 80-90 per cent of tax-paying pensioners do not complete the forms they receive correctly.

The report discusses the implications of the types of assistance sought from other agencies for the design of the tax return form.

Part 3 reviews the research into public documents and attempts in the UK and elsewhere to improve tax forms and leaflets.

Anderson (1983)

Jonathan Anderson. 'Research note: readability in the classroom revisited: amendments and additions to the STAR readability program'. *Journal of Research in Reading* 6(1), 1983, 57-61.

Describes modifications to STAR (simple test approach for readability), a computer programme which provides a series of routine indices of text reading difficulty.

These modifications include:

- The provision of the Fry readability graph and Fry grade levels of difficulty.

- The inclusion of an index of reading difficulty called Lix as well as a new index Rix which, it is claimed, is the quickest of all the formulae to apply.

Anderson (1989)

Dorothy Anderson. *A guide to information sources for the preparation, editing and production of documents.*
Gower, 1989.

A guide to established published sources of information for those called upon to write articles, prepare reports, or present conference papers in the course of their professional lives.

Anderson provides a systematic guide to the range of dictionaries, standards, manuals, year books and pocket guides aimed at authors and editors planning for publication. The book's highly practical bias, with extensive guidance on how to produce and publish documents, will be of interest to document designers as well as a more general audience.

Andersson and Barnitz (1984)

Billie V Andersson and John G Barnitz. 'Cross-cultural schemata and reading comprehension instruction'.
Journal of Reading 28(2), 1984, 102-108.

Language and cultural factors affect reading comprehension at many levels, as a result of sometimes profound differences in orthography, morphology, syntax, and patterns of discourse. This article addresses two issues. First how do cultural differences in background knowledge influence reading comprehension? Secondly, how can teachers improve English reading comprehension among students from different cultures?

Andersson and Barnitz show that readers use prior knowledge extensively to help understand text. This knowledge is organised in the form of topical clusters or schemata. Different culturally-induced schemata can affect understanding in different ways. The authors suggest the following guidelines for developing reading comprehension in students from other cultures:

• Select appropriate materials for reading instruction.

- Develop cross-cultural vocabulary wherever possible.

- Use methods and approaches which are sensitive to the readers' own cultural schemata.

Andrew Irving Associates (1989)

Communications with employers.
Andrew Irving Associates for the Department of Social Security, 1989.

The Department of Social Security (DSS) requires employers to administer National Insurance (NI) and other employee contributions on its behalf. This study reports on research commissioned by the Department to find out the views of employers on the recently revised booklets and other guidance materials provided for them by the DSS, and to see how these could be modified to maximise their effectiveness.

The researchers adopted a qualitative approach and their findings are based on a series of 60 depth interviews and group discussions with employers and DSS inspectors. The broad objectives of the research were to develop a typology of users; to establish indications of consumer satisfaction with the new and revised information materials; to evaluate the effectiveness of DSS press advertising associated with the changes; and to make specific recommendations where appropriate.

On the whole, users reacted positively to the changes:

- The redesigned materials were generally appreciated by users as a step in the right direction.

- Attempts to simplify the contents were widely noticed and appreciated.

- The use of bold, primary colours was well-liked.

In such a large and important area as National Insurance, there are inevitably tensions between providing simple instructions while covering the its full complexity of the scheme. The research pointed to a number of areas where further improvements in communication could be made:

- The idea of more diagrams and possibly a visual step-by-step guide (flowcharts) was warmly received.

- Users were keen on the idea of a telephone helpline service, although they recognised the need for manual reference tools.

One of the key findings of the researchers was their uncovering of widespread confusion about the roles and functions of the new materials:

- In particular, users felt that booklets and other materials should carry a note about their *purpose* on the cover—it is not sufficient to simply indicate this information in a covering letter.

- There should be more stress on titles rather than numeric codes in the document design.

- Official documents should carry a clearer indication of the time period they are intended to cover.

The DSS press advertising campaign to promote awareness of the changes was poorly recalled, possibly because of the confusion about the roles and functions of the new materials. The advertisement had used an unengaging visual and lacked clear DSS branding or indication of the subject matter. However, users still appreciated the idea of being given advance warning about the changes.

Ashby-Davis (1985)

Claire Ashby-Davis. 'Cloze and comprehension:
a qualitative analysis and critique'.
Journal of Reading 28(7), 1985, 585-590.

Ashby-Davis argues that in cloze tests the person taking the test has to perform as a writer and as a reader and that for this reason the test is biased in favour of those who can both read and write well. Therefore the test is not a valid instrument for measuring reading comprehension and is biased in favour of those who can read and write well.

Bagley and Maxfield (1986)

M Bagley and MS Maxfield. 'After-image color perception
for designers'.
Perceptual and Motor Skills 63, 1986, 995-1007.

After-image is an experience that occurs most vividly when the focus
of the eyes is shifted to a white surface after focusing for 15-30 seconds
on a well-lit coloured object.

Following a pilot study to refine a methodology, 125 students
participated in an experimental study. Of these, 100 were design
students and the rest non-design students who were unfamiliar with
the discrimination of after-images. The subjects were given ten colour
chips mounted on white index cards, and the chips were viewed in the
sequence the pilot study had shown caused least eye fatigue, that is, in
alternating contrasting hues. Each subject was asked to look at a chip
for 10-20 seconds, followed by a second period of 30 seconds. Then
they transferred their focus to a plain white index card and used
pre-prepared colour comparison cards to record the colour of their
after-image.

The results for the design and non-design students were so similar that
they were combined. Generally there was a high degree of consistency
in the after-image colours reported, with the majority falling within a
single hue family. Some colours, however, led to larger ranges of hues
than others.

The research also tried to identify whether the stimulus colours and
colours of after-images were reversible. In other words, if subjects
report that a red stimulus generates a blue-green after-image, do they
also report that a blue-green stimulus generates a red after-image?
The results showed that such reversibility is not exact. For example,
red and blue-green are a pair that reverse, whilst yellow and
purple-blue are not as consistent.

The author concludes with three practical applications of the results
for information designers:

• Simple experiments can be used to identify the colours that will
lead to the greatest discrepancies in the perceived after-images.

- Designers can use the method to survey their own vision and discover regularities in their own perception.

- After-image pairs may be combined in a creative colour circle or other design.

Barnett (1988)

L Barnett. *Forms for the general public: do they really work?*
Business Forms Management Association Inc., Toronto, Canada, 1988.

An excellent summary overview of the key information design issues associated with the production of effective public documents. While the main focus of the article is on forms, a great many of the points covered apply equally well to other types of document.

Barnett argues for the use of the Sless model of communication, which proposes that information designers should consider the basic message of a document in relation to both the author's intentions and to the audience's needs.

Barnitz (1986)

JG Barnitz. 'Toward understanding the effects of cross-cultural schemata and discourse structure on second language reading comprehension'.
Journal of Reading Behaviour 18(2), 1986, 95-116.

It is well documented that reading comprehension depends to some extent on prior knowledge of not only of content and context (schemata) but also a knowledge of text structure. In this article, Barnitz reviews research spanning a 55 year period into the factors which influence reading comprehension in a second language or culture.

Cultural schemata – much of this research has used folk tales as the text and it is doubtful whether the results can be generalised to public documents. There have, however, been studies using letters about a wedding and stories about medical beliefs that would be more directly applicable. These have shown that people:

- Read information about an unfamiliar culture more slowly.

- Recall less of the information.

- Often distort the information content.

Cultural schemata and language – studies in this area have demonstrated that schemata, context and language ability all interact during second language learning.

Linguistic or formal schemata – research shows quite clearly that different cultures may vary considerably in their thought patterns and in the way written text is organised.

There is little research on how culturally-specific discourse patterns affect reading comprehension, but interest in this area has increased. Research so far seems to indicate that these patterns play an important role in both comprehension and recall of text. Where the text is written in an unfamiliar discourse pattern, both comprehension and recall may be reduced. For example, people from an Arab culture tend to find text organised as a collection of descriptions most easy to process, yet this is very difficult for people from an Oriental culture to comprehend.

Bartram (1982)

David Bartram. 'The perception of semantic quality in type: differences between designers and non-designers'.
Information Design Journal 3(1), 1982, 38-50.

When designers select a typeface for a piece of design work they are making value judgments about its appropriateness. The judgments are based on an assessment of two sets of properties: functional and semantic. *Functional properties* are those concerned directly with legibility, such as type size, boldness, contrast and other aspects of form. Once a range of legible typefaces has been identified, the designer then selects one which will create the desired effect—such effects are attributed to the *semantic properties* of the typeface.

This paper describes a study which was devised both to test the *generality* of designers' assumptions about the semantic properties of different typefaces and to provide a tool for measuring these properties. Twelve typefaces were selected which covered a wide range of semantic properties (these were Univers 67, Future Medium,

Grotesque 9 Italic, Arnold Bocklin, Old English, Ringlet, Palace Script, Brush Script, and Lazybones). Each of these typefaces was assessed according to 13 different subjective scales: beautiful – ugly / pleasant – unpleasant / good – bad /expensive – cheap / interesting – uninteresting / bold – delicate / strong – weak / heavy – light / happy – sad / hot – cold / relaxed – tense / fast – slow / active – passive.

Two groups of people were used in the evaluation: one consisting of 38 design students and the other of 52 university students on social science and science courses (non-specialists).

Analysis of the data revealed four major semantic factors:

- A general measure of *evaluation* (five scales: beautiful – ugly / pleasant – unpleasant / good – bad / expensive – cheap / interesting – uninteresting.

- A measure of strength or *potency* (three scales: bold – delicate / strong – weak / heavy – light.

- A measure of happiness of *mood* (three scales: happy – sad / hot – cold / relaxed – tense.

- A measure of vitality of *activity* (two scales: fast – slow / active – passive.

The scores obtained on any one of these factors were uncorrelated with those obtained on any other. Comparisons between the factor scores for the two groups of people showed general similarities. At the same time there were marked differences on certain factors for most of the typefaces. From this it is concluded that designers must be aware that their audience may not share their view of semantic qualities of the typeface. A 'rough and ready' method of testing for such discrepancies is described.

Baumann and others (1989)

Adrian E Baumann and others. 'Asthma information: can it be understood?'
Health Education Research 4(3), 1989, 377-382.

Asthma is an important public health issue in Australia, often going unrecognised or inadequately self-managed. This empirical study is an evaluation of public written information about asthma available through major Australian newspapers, self-help organisations and education programmes. The researchers focused on the readability of these materials, defined in terms of Gunning's FOG reading age scores.

The results suggest that many attempts to inform the general reader about asthma are unlikely to succeed—because the materials used are often aimed at a reading age which is well above that of the general community. For example, some of the leaflets produced by the National Asthma Campaign correspond to a reading level consistent with nearly eleven years of schooling.

Beach (1987)

Richard J Beach. 'Tabular typography'. In: J C van Vliet (ed.)
Text processing and document manipulation.
Cambridge University Press on behalf of the British Computer Society, 1986, 18-33.

This paper reviews the principal typographic issues for presenting information in the form of two-dimensional tables. These issues include table structure, the alignment of rows and columns, the treatment of whitespace within tables, readability, and the problem of breaking up large tables.

Beach argues for the reinstatement of vertical rules in tables (against current fashion) and the use of dotted leaders between columns 'to help the reader capture the content and meaning of the table'.

Beck (1984)

Charles R Beck. 'Visual cueing strategies: pictorial, textual and combinational effects'.
Educational Communication and Technology Journal 32(4), 1984, 207-216.

Instructional designers and researchers tend to recommend the use of visual cues for directing students' attention to specific points, on the grounds that readers need assistance in locating the most important information. This study attempted to assess different ways of visual cueing by first separating and then combining pictorial and textual cues. The emphasis was on elementary school students.

As part of the assessment the study compared the instructional value of cued with non-cued pictures; compared the effectiveness of cued text where words were underlined or printed in different colours; and assessed whether a combination of pictorial and textual cues would prove to be the most effective strategy. The project compared the performance of average and low reading ability students.

The study used 256 fourth grade students divided into three groups that received identical sets of pictures and texts and were then tested for recall of the test. These groups varied according to the nature of the cues in the text. Some were given no cues at all, while others had either pictorial or textual cues (or both).

The main finding was that the students who received both pictorial and textual cues recalled significantly more than either of the other two groups. Neither pictorial nor textual cues alone led to increased levels of recall over uncued text. Perhaps not surprisingly, the students with average reading abilities achieved higher recall scores on all counts than those with low reading abilities.

Behavioural Research Consultants (1983)

Research into two redesigned versions of the P1 tax form.
Behavioural Research Consultants for the Central Office of Information Research Unit and the Inland Revenue Forms Unit, January 1983.

This qualitative study was based on 44 depth interviews with potential users of the P1 tax form. The aim was to test alternative formats of both the form itself and the accompanying guidance notes. In addition, the views of Inland Revenue Officers were sought through two group discussions.

The study showed that *visual appeal* is an important factor in 'setting the scene for completion', but the notion of 'visual appeal' is a complex one. The use of colour to highlight forms often adds to their visual appeal, but the choice of colour and its interaction with other features of design may be a disadvantage both in terms of completion and subsequent processing.

Respondents said that smaller forms were easier to handle and tended to be preferred by staff and tax payers. But the indications were that layout should not be sacrificed to size: a short but cramped and complex form should be avoided, as should small print. The size and concertina folding system for the notes was found to be hard to handle and to find the relevant section: many respondents said they would have preferred a booklet.

With regard to *ease of use*, it was noted that preliminary instructions were often missed and that as a routing device, 'cross boxes' headings and sections were shown to be insufficient since users read all sections regardless of whether or not they applied to them. Reorganisation of the form into sections with headings did, however, increase the speed of completion.

The double centre spread used in one version was reported to be difficult to complete, often leading to confusion and errors.

Other problems encountered were related to comprehension difficulties attributable to language, vocabulary and syntax.

Behavioural Research Consultants (1985)

Research into the Attendance Allowance leaflet and form.
Behaviourial Research Consultants for the Central Office of Information, 1985.

The overall aim of this project was to provide guidelines for the preparation of future editions of an Attendance Allowance form and leaflet and other documents for disabled people.

To do this three different versions of the form and leaflet were tested— the existing form and two revised versions. The work was carried out in a number of stages. Stage One focused on the original forms and leaflet and the research consisted of depth interviews with 16 recent claimants. Stage Two focused on the two revised versions, using a number of research techniques:

- Depth interviews with 50 people, split into two groups.
- Hall tests with 312 people.
- A group discussion with six health care staff.

- A group discussion with six DHSS staff who process the completed forms.

The report gives the results of each of these research techniques then subdivides them into sections dealing in turn with each revised form and leaflet. It is, therefore, difficult to assess the relative importance of the various points made. Nevertheless it is possible to identify some findings which could be generalised to the design of other forms and leaflets. In the main, these conform with the findings from other studies.

One of the main points identified is the importance of being clear about the audience being addressed in the form or leaflet. In the case of Attendance Allowance this is especially important since although the claimant of the allowance is the disabled person, it is frequently the carer who completes the form. This led to considerable confusion when information such as address and national insurance numbers were required.

All three versions of the form and leaflet had complex folding arrangements. The depth interviews showed that this was a source of problems and stress for users, confirming other research findings.

The depth interviews also emphasised the point that users do not generally read instructions at the top of the form, and that where separate notes are provided in a leaflet they expect the numbering of the form and leaflet to be related. It was also cler that form-fillers will not go to great lengths to give accurate information, when they do not understand why they are being asked for it. One such example from this particular study was the request for the address of the local post office.

Bennett and others (1990)

Rex Bennett, Douglas Durand and Sam Betty. 'Managerial ratings of written compositions: impact of information technology on the persuasiveness of compositions'.
Information and Management 19(1), 1990, 1-6.

This empirical study investigated the suggestion that documents composed directly at a keyboard (KC) differ structurally and stylistically from traditional communications (TC) composed with pen or pencil and then typed up. The working hypothesis developed the notion that composing text at a word processor reduces writing efficiency but provides gains in communication effectiveness.

The results of the study revealed that senior executives rate KC-documents much more positively than TC-documents and tend to place more confidence in them. The study provides further evidence to suggest that the use of word processing technology itself leads to important changes in managerial perceptions of written communications.

Bensoussan (1986)

M Bensoussan. 'Beyond vocabulary: pragmatic factors in reading comprehension – culture, convention, coherence and cohesion'. *Foreign Language Annals* 19(5), 1986, 399-407.

Bensoussan describes two studies with students translating from English into Hebrew. In the first, 60 students were asked to translate 70 words, first from a word list, and a week later from the same list together with a long text from which the words were obtained (in context). On average, students were shown to be able to guess 17 of the 70 words purely from the context.

In a follow-up study 62 students were asked to translate, either into Hebrew or into Arabic, specific words taken from a narrative text (a passage from an F Scott Fitzgerald short story). The mistranslations identified two areas of difficulty beyond difficulties with vocabulary.

The first was related to cultural differences. In fact, cultural differences sometimes blocked understanding even when the words and syntax were familiar.

The second area of difficulty arose arose from cultural differences in discourse patterns. For example, Hebrew contains mostly clauses connected by simple additive conjunctions, whereas English has many subordinate clauses. The research identified specific difficulties with translating both logical connectors (such as since, while, however, nevertheless, and whereas) and with modifiers (adjectives and adverbs).

Logical connectors and modifiers were also found to cause difficulties
in a third study in which students were asked to translate specific
words from an English language text into Hebrew.

Bentley (1985)

Diana Bentley. *How and why of readability*.
Centre for the Teaching of Reading, University of Reading, 1985.

In this review of some of the formulas available to measure readability
Bentley starts with a cautionary section pointing out some of the many
factors that cannot be measured by means of readability formulas.
Twelve different measures are described. These are: cloze procedure;
Elley noun count; Flesch score and FJP index; FOG index; Forecast; Fry
readability test; Johnson method for helping children to choose books;
Mugford; Powers – Summer – Kearle; SMOG index; Spache; syntactic
complexity.

Bentley's review also includes brief details of three software products
which have been developed to test readability: 'Readability';
'Readlevel'; and 'Textgrader'.

Berent (1985)

G P Berent. 'Markedness considerations in the acquisition of conditional
sentences'.
Language Learning 35(3), 1985, 337-372.

This study involved two experiments which were designed to assess
the abilities of learners of English as a second language to produce and
comprehend English conditional sentences.

The subjects were 55 people studying English as a second language,
28 of them at the highest of four proficiency levels and 27 at the third
highest of the levels.

In both experiments the sentences included examples of three major
conditional types:

- *Real conditions* eg if you jump out of the window you will break
  your leg.

- *Unreal conditions* eg if you jumped out of the window you would break your leg.
- *Past unreal conditions* eg if you had jumped out of the window you would have broken your leg.

In the first experiment, the subjects had to complete 24 conditional sentences by supplying the appropriate verb forms.

This showed that real conditions were most easily produced, followed by unreal and past unreal conditions. There was little significant difference between the unreal and past unreal conditionals. This was however affected by the position of the 'if clause' and depended on whether it preceded or followed the main clause. There was some indication that subjects were more able to produce unreal conditional verbs when the 'if clause' followed the main clause. In this case they were more easily produced than the past unreal conditional verbs.

In the second experiment, the subjects had to indicate the meaning of the conditional sentences by selecting from a series of four possible meanings.

The results were the exact opposite of those in the first experiment. In general the students were better at comprehending the unreal and past unreal conditional sentences than they were at comprehending the real conditional sentences. There was little significant difference between the unreal and the past unreal conditionals. The position of the 'if clause' had no effect on the comprehension of the conditional sentence.

In both experiments the higher proficiency students achieved higher scores than the lower proficiency ones.

Beveridge and Griffiths (1987)

Michael Beveridge and Valerie Griffiths. 'The effect of pictures on the reading processes of less able readers: a miscue analysis approach'. *Journal of Research in Reading* 10(1), 1987, 29-42.

Research into the influence of illustrations has moved on from the question of whther they facilitate learning to trying to specify more precisely the conditions under which the 'picture superiority effect' occurs.

This paper reports on research examining the impact of illustrations on the reading performance of 19 eleven year-old children with reading difficulties. Reading performance was assessed using Reading Miscue Analysis – a highly ecologically valid technique measuring observable processing – and the results were analysed by applying two-way analysis of variance (ANOVA). Four indicators of reading performance were employed:

- Total number of errors.

- Time taken to read passages.

- Overall level of comprehension.

- Understanding of grammatical relations.

The findings of this study show that, in the majority of these aspects of the reading process, a statistically significant interaction could be observed between the use of illustrations and reading levels. The results suggest that differences in the influence of pictures on the reading process are associated with text difficulty. At the lower level of text difficulty, performance with illustrated texts was shown to be better, but for more difficult texts the reverse was true. One possible explanation for this is that, at the highest level, reading speed and fluency suffers because attention is distracted by the need to process the graphic information.

BJM Research Partners (1986a)

Energy booklet door-to-door distribution research.
BJM Research Partners for the Department of Energy, 1986.

The Department of Energy was concerned by an earlier research report (British Market Research Bureau 1985) which showed that only 20 per cent of people interviewed were able to recall a booklet that had been distributed direct to households. The Department commissioned this research study to assess whether the low level of recall was due to inefficient and incomplete distribution or to memory decay following receipt of the booklet.

The findings of this study showed some evidence of decay in memory. After four days around 70 to 80 per cent could recall the booklet, whereas after 26 days only about half of recipients could do so. This was, however, still considerably higher than the 20 per cent level of recall reported after a similar time period in the earlier report.

BJM Research Partners (1986b)

Monergy booklet: follow-up research report.
BJM Research Partners for the Department of Energy, 1986.

This study focused on the effects of including a competition (to win a new detached, energy-efficient house) in the text of a booklet intended to promote the idea of energy efficiency.

Telephone interviews were held with 500 people who had entered the competition. This was followed by more detailed personal interviews with 100 entrants and 200 non-entrants from the same neighbourhoods. All had received the booklet through a general household distribution.

The findings revealed significant differences between entrants and non-entrants. Entrants were more likely to recall the booklet and were both more positive towards and better informed about energy efficiency. Entrants were more likely than non-entrants to have made energy-efficient installations after having received the booklet.

BJM Research Partners (1991)

Department of Social Security – information needs.
BJM Research Partners for the Department of Social Security, 1991
(in three volumes).

The Department of Social Security provides a range of benefits for people in need. In most cases, the payment of benefit is dependent upon the entitled person actually claiming it. This means that potential claimants need information about eligibility and how and when to claim.

Currently, there exists a 'passive' system for communicating this information to potential claimants, mainly in the form of the leaflets which are available from the DSS or from Post Offices. Sometimes, these may be supported by posters or telephone— although it is thought that awareness of the latter is very low. This 'passive' system requires potential claimants to want to find the information for themselves rather than the DSS itself actively seeking out potential claimants.

This study began with a literature review, supplemented by interviews with a number of people who had previously carried out work in this area. This was followed up by extended interviews with 20 people in each of ten DSS target groups in order to explore their information needs, the routes they use to gather information, and the homogeneity of the groups and their attitudes towards the DSS and the benefits system. The project is reported in three volumes, containing the findings of the preliminary information audit exercise; the findings from each of the ten client groups; and an overall summary which develops a model for marketing DSS information.

The conclusions of the report on desk research focus mainly on the barriers that discourage people from taking up the means-tested benefits to which they may be entitled. These barriers are described in terms of thresholds which must be crossed before a claim is pursued. These include:

- Perceived need for benefit.
- Basic knowledge of the benefits system.
- Perceived eligibility for benefit.
- Perceived utility of benefit.
- Feelings and beliefs about the application procedure.
- A belief by the client that their problem is temporary.

The first volume then summarises some of the recent research which has looked at the problem of improving the take-up of means-tested benefits and also at people's attitudes towards the DSS. These research findings suggest that, given the complexity of the underlying issues, a broadly-based multimedia campaign is the only effective way to communicate information about benefits and eligibility criteria to potential claimants.

The second volume of the report presents a more detailed investigation into the information needs and information-seeking behaviour of a number of client groups. Each of the ten DSS target groups identified for the purposes of the study were selected so as to include people whose lives were experiencing, or who were about to be affected by, major changes or upheavals.

These groups included:

- School leavers.
- People having children.
- People separated from their partners.
- People unemployed or suffering loss of income.
- Approaching retirement.
- People in long term care (and their carers).
- The recently bereaved.
- People setting up a new household.
- People with chronic debt problems.

This volume of the report concludes that, in general, the system for disseminating information about potential benefit eligibility works well where the target group is easily defined (eg school leavers) and therefore easy to identify. However, for more difficult to identify groups, the system works less well. It does not work well, for instance, for people in later retirement who do not make themselves known to the system and are often reluctant to claim. Nor does it work well for people who are recently separated and for whom the need for knowledge comes suddenly. Often these people do not know where to go initially.

In the final volume of the report, the researchers identify a need for improved information systems to target four particularly difficult groups: people recently separated from their partners; those who are unemployed or on reduced incomes; people in long-term care; and those in later retirement. The report argues that each of these groups needs an information 'safety net' to compensate for the fact that they are so difficult for the DSS to identify and target with precision. Any new arrangements should make it possible for potential claimants to know where to turn immediately for help and then to feel confident about the advice they can expect to receive.

In view of the generally negative perceptions of people towards the

DSS, one possible solution could be to have a high profile 'Benefits Advice Centre' on every high street. Such agencies would operate at arms length from the formal DSS system and restrict the role of the local DSS office to claims-processing only.

Boag and others (1987)

Andrew Boag and others. *Proposals for the re-design of Yellow Pages forms.*
University of Reading, Department of Typography and Graphic Communication, 1987.

Most of this report comprises comments on layout that are based on earlier research. It does, however, include the results of a small-scale test of four different ways of printing character separators where the form filler is constrained to write one letter in each allotted space. These were:

(1) F O R M A T 1

(2) F O R M A T 2

(3) F O R M A T 3

(4) F O R M A T 4

Of these format 3, which used ruled lines with ticks at the top of the response area, was the most satisfactory. With this format people seemed to write smaller and so write completely under the character separators.

The two formats where the character separators were above the space for response (formats 1 and 3) were completed slightly faster than those (formats 2 and 4) where the separators were printed beneath the response area.

Bond and others (1980)

Sandra J Bond and others. *Translating the law into common language: a protocol study.*
American Institutes for Research, technical report 8, 1980.

Experienced government writers—four lawyers and four non- lawyers — were invited to rewrite a portion of a government regulation for a general audience. They were asked to think aloud and were audio-recorded while they revised the document, in order to identify the protocols they were using as they worked. Their revisions were then ranked for comprehensibility.

The aim of the study was to determine whether the people who draft legal documents are equally able to rewrite them so they can be understood by the general public.

The characteristics of the two writers whose revisions were ranked as the most comprehensible were that both were lawyers and were the only participants who were confident that they had both understood the document and produced a satisfactory revision. These were the only two who read the entire passage before attempting any revision. More than the others, they were very concerned with the appearance of the regulation and suggested a number of changes to the typeface and layout. Both interpreted the task of revision broadly and their protocols contained many references to writing rules. They understood the needs of their audience and referred to them often in their protocols. They were also the only participants to reread their revisions.

In contrast the writers whose revisions were the least comprehensible had clearly not appreciated the needs of their audience. They misunderstood important parts of regulation and tended to interpret the process of revision in a very narrow sense.

As a result of this study the authors suggest a number of guidelines for revising public documents:

- Revision should be broad in scope and cover the generation and organisation of material as well as grammar, syntax and punctuation.

- Attention to the needs of the audience is of major importance.

- Revisions should always be evaluated.

- A clear sense of the document's structure should be conveyed.

- Examples can help understanding.

- A good revision strategy involves reading and rereading.

Briggs and Rees (1980)

Eric Briggs and Anthony Rees. *Supplementary benefits and the consumer.*
Bedford Square Press, 1980.

This study took place between December 1974 and May 1975 at three Department of Health and Social Security offices: one in a totally urban area in the West Midlands; one in a mixed industrial area in the north of England; and one in a semi-rural area in the south of England.

The chief purpose of the research was to evaluate the impact of providing claimants with a detailed explanation of how their benefit entitlement had been calculated (Form A124). A total of 1,419 cases were selected at random, of which 690 resulted in successful interviews. 316 of these formed a control group who were not sent the A124.

Briggs and Rees found that local DHSS offices were the most important overall source of initial information. Posters and leaflets and information from Post Offices were hardly mentioned at all in this context, but they did contribute to the overall stock of knowledge, along with television and contacts with friends.

The impact which Form A124 made on the experimental group was disappointing—only 70 per cent recalled receiving it and only 52 per cent of the group actually read it.

Overall, it was found that knowledge of means-tested benefits was extremely low, although there was some limited indication that the Form A124 did enhance claimants' knowledge.

British Market Research Bureau (1985)

Energy efficiency booklet recall survey.
British Market Research Bureau for the Central Office of Information, 1985.

This report presents the results of an Omnibus survey of 993 people to assess the effectiveness of a booklet on energy efficiency which had been distributed direct to people's homes on behalf of the Department of Energy.

Fewer than a fifth of those surveyed were able to recall the booklet. Of those who did, 12 per cent said they had read it thoroughly, 59 per cent had glanced through it, while 30 per cent had not read it at all. Older groups were significantly more likely to have read the booklet (19 per cent of those aged over 45 compared with 7 per cent of those aged under 45). Most of those who had not read the booklet at all were either aged under 25 or over 65.

Brody (1981)

Philip Brody. 'Research on pictures in instructional texts: the need for a broadened perspective'.
Educational Communication and Technology Journal 29(2), 1981, 93-100.

This review concentrates on research which relates to instructional textbooks, by which the author means textbooks that are 'designed and used primarily for the purpose of direct instruction in a specific academic discipline or subject and for a specific audience'.

He suggests, like other researchers, that there are major shortcomings in most published research (see Duchastel 1980): in general, it has failed to discriminate between the role of illustrations on learning from reading and their effect on learning to read; in particular, research has tended to use simple illustrations—like line drawings—which are not representative of those found in instructional texts.

Brody argues for a more functional approach to research, concentrating on the precise mechanisms by which illustrations assist learning.

Burgess (1984)

John H Burgess. *Human factors in forms design.*
Nelson-Hall, 1984.

The author applies the human factors principles used by military and industrial equipment designers to the design of 'accurate money-saving and time-efficient' forms.

Burgess adopts a formal systems approach to forms design. Before design begins, forms should be assessed against other methods of data collection, and factors such as their reliability and accuracy weighed against time- and cost-effectiveness. Once the decision to use forms has been made, designers should choose content and design elements in the light of the data required and the form in which it is required. Designers also need to consider who will use the form; what skills they will need to complete it; and how the data will be processed.

The book offers guidance on tailoring the verbal content and style to the reading level of respondents and ensuring that instructions and questions are as clear as possible. It also shows how to select visual design elements so that the form is easy to read and understand. Suggestions for type size and style, proper use of headings and colour shape and size coding, colour and weight of paper, print contrast and sectionalising and configurational arrangements are included.

Business Decisions Ltd (1985)

A report on qualitative research into DL26.
Business Decisions Ltd for the Department of Transport, 1985.

This report covers research that was commissioned by the Department of Transport to provide guidance for the redesign of a driving test application form.

A total of 42 semi-structured interviews were held—36 with potential driving test applicants and 6 with professional driving instructors. The study revealed a number of inconsistencies in the design of the then current form which contributed directly to mistakes and omissions when it was completed. The main problem related to the different methods by which replies were invited. These included 'cross out', 'tick', and 'write in NONE'—all on the same form.

Suggestions for improvement made by the respondents themselves included

- More and better headlines, signposting and routing.

- Bold print for instructions.

- Consistency in type size and style.

- Standard recording methods, with tick boxes wherever possible.

Cabinet Office (1984)

Forms design: administrative forms — guidelines for managers of forms units.
Cabinet Office, 1984.

A set of guidelines which apply to forms, standard letters and leaflets and are based on the experience gained from forms design in a wider range of government departments. Topics covered include:

- Allocating responsibility for designing a form.

- Defining the purpose.

- Assessing the current performance.

- Agreeing the target performance.

- Testing the performance of the new form.

- The language.

- The layout.

Campbell and Holland (1982)

Leo J Campbell and V Melissa Holland. 'Understanding the language of documents because readability formulas don't'.
Linguistics and the Professional 8, 1982, 157-171.

The main thesis of this article is that readability formulas are, at best, imprecise instruments which attempt to measure how difficult written material might be to a reader. The authors trace the development of readability measures and show that, since almost all of them have been validated against educational materials using school children, they are of limited applicability to public docuuments. Campbell and

Holland demonstrate that the principles underlying the formulas often conflict with other guidelines for writing comprehensible English that have been generated from psycholinguistic research. They also point out that there are other factors which have been shown to affect readers' comprehension of text, including:

- The abilities, needs and knowledge of the intended.

- Audience.

- The purpose of the document.

- The organisation of the text.

- Graphics.

The authors conclude that as none of these factors are taken into account by existing readability formulas the predictive value of any single formula should probably be viewed with pessimism—especially in the case of public documents. Instead they recommend that the 'scenario principle' should be used (see Flower and others 1980).

Campbell Keagan Ltd (1986)

Violence against women booklets research report.
Prepared for the COI, Campbell Kegan Ltd, 1986.

Describes the results of eight group discussions and eight depth interviews held to assess two booklets; one produced by the Home Office, the other by the Metropolitan Police. Both booklets dealt with violence against women.

Much of the report is specific to the particular leaflets being tested. The more general findings included:

- The A5 format of one booklet made it easy to handle

- The format used for the headings made one booklet especially easy to use. These were placed in the margin and were printed as white text in a block of black. They made it easier to locate specific sections of text and made the page of text look easier to read.

- In contrast the second booklet was criticised for its confusing layout, making it difficult to distinguish between headings, introductory paragraph and quotations. This encouraged skip reading.

- The photographs used in one booklet were felt to have impact, and to be both relevant and useful. The line drawings, however, were criticised for being irrelevant.

- The inclusion of a summary section led to unnecessary repetition.

Campbell Keagan Ltd (1990)

Income Support: new brochure development.
Campbell Keagan Ltd for the Department of Social Security, 1990.

An A5 leaflet (IS1) which had been used by the Department of Social Security (DSS) to explain Income Support to potential claimants was due to be replaced from April 1990. The Department developed two alternative replacement versions and commissioned Campbell Keagan Ltd to evaluate the new leaflets, with a view to helping it select the best option. Version 1 was a slimmer booklet with similar appearance to other DSS leaflets. It had similar content to the original, but in amended order. Version 2 was another A5 leaflet with relatively few changes (notably the exclusion of some illustrations).

The research objectives were to explore the proposed leaflets in terms of their ease of use; how they conveyed understanding of eligibility and of any actions required of the reader. The qualitative study was conducted amongst a small sample (15), and is best regarded as an exploratory study of the target market.

Most respondents preferred the layout and order of Version 1 with its logical sequence of steps towards applying for help. Version 2 was not easy to use although it was described as being more approachable and 'friendly-looking'. The appearance of Version 1 was more in keeping with other DSS leaflets, and reinforced the formal relationship most respondents expected to have with the DSS (some respondents were perturbed by the more 'commercial' approach of Version 2).

A number of specific recommendations for improving the information design of leaflet IS1 emerged out of the research. These included:

- Incorporating a 'call to action' in the title (such as 'Do you qualify?' or 'Do you need to reapply?').

- Creating bolder cover visuals with more impact and greater use of colour.

- Improving layout by emboldening and enlarging print.

- Using illustrations, possibly a flow diagram, to explain the structure of Income Support.

- Indicating the *types of people* for whom Income Support might be relevant on the front cover (to encourage take-up).

Canadian Law Information Council (1985)

Small claims court materials. Can they be read? Can they be understood?
CLIC, 1985.

Describes two tests of small claims court materials: the application of readability formulae and cloze tests.

As with earlier studies the results from the two tests were at variance. And, as a consequence, the author questions the validity of applying a readability formula to public legal information documents.

In the second half of the report the author describes a method of assessing such documents by producing annotations based on the following questions:

- Who is the intended reader?

- How is the information organised?

- How is legal language used?

- Are sample cases given?

- Is the design clear?

- Overall, how difficult is the text?

Canadian Law Information Council (1986)

Preparing information on the law? Guidelines for writing, editing and designing.
CLIC, 1986.

A useful set of guidelines, many of which are applicable to other types of information as well as that about the law.

Carrell (1983)

P L Carrell. 'Some issues in studying the role of schemata, or background knowledge and second language comprehension'.
Reading in a Foreign Language 1(2), 1983, 81-92.

According to proponents of schema theory, we comprehend something when we can relate it to something we already know. Text comprehension is therefore an interactive process between the reader's background knowledge and the content and structure and the text itself. It therefore involves much more than linguistic competence.

In the first part of this article, Carrell reviews studies which have investigated the role of formal schemata (those involving knowledge of the structure or form of a document) and content schemata in text comprehension. Much evidence has been produced to show that both play a major role, but the author was unable to identify any research which specifically investigated the relative contributions of the two types of schemata.

The second part of the article covers cross-cultural research and the question of the cultural specificity of schemata. Research on formal schemata has mainly been restricted to folk tales and is unlikely to be generalisable to public documents. Research on content schemata has shown there to be some cultural specificity. The results are complicated by those from similar studies which show that subjects from a similar cultural background differ in their content schemata. However, it is clear that schema theory offers some useful insights into language comprehension in general and in second language comprehension in particular.

Charney (1984)

Davida Charney. 'Redesigning and testing a work order form'.
Information Design Journal 4(2), 1984, 131-146.

An account of the evaluation, redesign, and testing of an order form used in the Carnegie-Mellon University printing office. The first step in the evaluation was to review the form's content, identify trouble spots on the form, and anticipate the consequences of eliminating or changing particular parts of the form. This was researched in three ways:

- Interviewing the staff who extract information from the form.

- Surveying back-files of completed forms.

- Analysing earlier research findings that relate to form design.

The method employed to test the revised form is of particular interest. Twelve subjects were used in the test: six had previously used the old version of the form and six had never used the form before. Within these two groups the subjects were randomly assigned to the old version or the new version of the form. All the subjects were given four tasks, each of which involved completing the order form. As they did so they were asked to think aloud, following a set of instructions for giving a thinking-aloud protocol. These protocols were tape-recorded and were subsequently analysed to identify areas that had caused difficulties for the subjects. This qualitative data was supplemented with measures of the time taken by subjects to complete the form and the accuracy with which it was completed.

Charrow claims that by pairing these two methods it is possible to use a very small sample population and so reduce the costs of testing forms.

Charrow (1979a)

Veda Charrow. *Let the rewriter beware.*
American Institutes for Research, 1979

In this assessment of the value of readability formulas, Charrow claims that it is a dubious premise that shorter sentences and words in a passage, make it more readable. In fact, it is not the length of a sentence that affects its readability but its complexity. Compare, for example:

The man embarrassed the girl who kissed the boy who eats oatmeal (12 words).

The boy who the girl who the man embarrassed kissed eats oatmeal (12 words).

Sometimes a longer sentence is easier to understand, and makes more sense than a shorter one:

The happening of the accident creates the presumption of defendant's negligence (10 words).

The very fact that the accident happened allows us to presume that the defendant was negligent (16 words).

Similarly, word length is not always indicative of comprehension. Not all short words are common and well known, and many longer words might be. Finally, it is not possible with a readability formula to distinguish between nonsense sentences and those which are clearly written. A sentence will have the same score even when the order of its words has been scrambled, making it nonsense.

The author then goes on to look at some of the other factors that affect the comprehensibility of written text, including:

- Grammar.
- Semantics and context.
- Word frequency.
- Personalisation.

Charrow concludes that it takes more than a set of rigid rules, a thesaurus, a frequency dictionary, and a readability formula to make a document comprehensible. Writers should understand the limitations of these tools and know when not to use them. They should also be able to devise and employ valid tests to measure real people's comprehension of the original and rewritten documents.

Charrow (1979b)

Veda Charrow. *What is 'Plain English' anyway?*
American Institutes for Research, 1979.

The author analyses some of the more frequently-used guidelines and demonstrates that they should not be taken as hard and fast rules, and also considers the value of readability formulae. His findings include:

- Everyday use of language does not consist of short sentences containing only short words.

- By removing relative clauses it is also possible to increase the complexity of the text, since readers are forced to make their own logical connections.

- Advice to avoid the use of the passive voice should not be taken too literally.

- Readability formulae are not reliable measures of comprehensibility.

- Readability formulae are only index measures measuring the symptoms—not the causes—of complex writing.

- They ignore syntactic and semantic structures, which are thought to be major causes of difficulty.

Charrow and Charrow (1979)

Robert P Charrow and Veda Charrow. 'Making legal language understandable: a psychologistic study of jury instructions'.
Columbia Law Review 79, 1979, 1306-1374.

This study had two main objectives. First, to test the hypothesis that legal language in general, and standard jury insturctions in particular, are not understood by the average juror; that the incomprehensibility is due to difficult language constructions; and that these constructions could be rewritten and do not necessarily arise from the legal complexity of the subject. Secondly, to develop a reliable and workable methodology which will provide guidance on how the comprehensibility of legal language can be improved.

The methodology selected was paraphrase testing in which the instructions to jurors were given orally and the subjects asked to paraphrase them orally. All the subjects were people who had been called for jury service. In the first experiment 35 jurors were asked to paraphrase each of 14 standard civil jury instructions. The paraphrases were then analysed linguistically. This analysis revealed the existence of numerous grammatical constructions, phrases and words that appear to typify legal language and to affect juror comprehension adversely. Examples of the constructions that were consistently not well understood and were poorly paraphrased by subjects are: subordinate clause passive; use of nouns derived from verbs in place of verb phrases; negatives; misplaced phrases; vague prepositional phrases (often beginning with 'as to'); unusual subordinate clause embeddings; unusual discourse conventions (such as restating entire passages in different words); and strings of synonyms.

For the second experiment the instructions were rewritten to overcome these textual difficulties. They were then tested again, using paraphrase testing, on 48 people who had been called for jury service. Each person was given seven instructions in both their original and rewritten forms. The results showed that the overall performance was significantly better on the rewritten instructions than on the original ones.

In addition to using paraphrase testing as a measure of comprehension, the authors applied the Flesch readability formula to each of the original and rewritten instructions. There was no correlation between comprehensibility and readability scores. For half the rewritten instructions the improved comprehensibility was reflected in improved readability scores. However, for two of the rewritten instructions that showed large improvements over the originals in comprehensibility, the Flesch readability scores were worse than those for the originals, and for one it was the same. Conversely four rewritten instructions showed no significant increase in comprehensibility over the originals, but had readability scores that were significantly better.

Charrow and others (1980)

Veda Charrow and others. *Revising a Medicaid recertification form: a case study in the document design process.*
American Institutes for Research, 1980.

Working through local offices, researchers were able to observe the problems that both staff and public had in understanding and using a medical insurance form, the District of Columbia Medicaid recertification form. The study showed that the public had considerable problems in understanding or interpreting technical terminology. In addition to difficulties at the text level, many people appeared not to understand the purpose of the form. It was observed that caseworkers frequently used examples and scenarios to 'translate' sections that were not understood when they were helping their clients to complete the form.

As part of the research the form was redesigned to try to overcome some of the problems observed during the field research.

Charrow and Redish (1980)

Veda Charrow and Janice C Redish. *A study of standardised headings for warranties.*
American Institutes for Research (Technical Report 6), 1980.

The researchers set out to discover if standardised headings increase or decrease people's speed of reading and accuracy in understanding the terms of consumer prediction guarantees and warranties, and the effect of such headings on people's general attitudes.

The subjects were 48 adult consumers who read groups of four warranties for television sets and then responded to questionnaires about the warranties. Each group of warranties had two with headings and two without. All were written in clear and simple English.

The results showed that there were no statistically significant differences in either the number of correct responses or the time taken to respond. That is, the subjects appeared to read and understand the warranties *without* standardised headings, just as easily as they did those *with* headings.

Nevertheless, approximately 90 per cent of the subjects showed a strong *preference* for the warranties with standardised headings. So, while headings may not make a text easier to read, they may well increase the motivation of people to read it in the first place.

Communication Research Ltd (1983a)

The readability of two Inland Revenue income tax return guides.
Communication Research Ltd, 1983.

An assessment of "Tax return guide" and "How to fill in your P1 tax return" by applying the British Index of Reading Difficulty (see Communication Research Ltd 1984).

Communication Research Ltd (1983b)

Maternity pay rebate form MP1: report on results of a face-to-face interview study.
Communication Research Ltd. Prepared for the COI/Department of Employment, 1983.

A study testing the redesigned maternity pay rebate form by means of 124 personal interviews. Again, many of the findings are specific to the form being tested, but two were of more general applicability.

Two thirds of people claimed to have read the explanatory notes on the new form, but only one third read them all. Most read them before filling the form in.

Only a third of people referred to the booklet "Employment rights for the expectant mother" at all when filling in the form.

Communication Research Ltd (1984a)

The British Index of Reading Difficulty.
Communication Research Ltd, 1984.

This brochure describes the British Index of Reading Difficulty—a series of six readability formulae 'developed for particular applications'. In general, these formulae fall into two categories: simple or complex. Simple formulae are liable to the same criticisms as other readability measures, but are easy to apply. The more complex formulae are based on considerable developmental work.

The British Index of Reading Difficulty has concentrated primarily on identifying which words are difficult or unfamiliar to a large section of the population. It has led to the generation of a complex set of rules based on good practice and commonsense. These do not, however, cover grammatical complexity. Because these formulae *are* complex they require skill and a good deal of time to apply.

Communication Research Ltd (1984b)

Public finance leaflet: report on a qualitative pre-test.
Communication Research Ltd for HM Treasury, 1984.

The methods described in this report of four related studies on a leaflet dealing with public finance include group discussions covering basic attitudes and reactions to the leaflet; a readability test (using the British Index of Reading Difficulty); hall-test interviews; and a subjective appraisal of a revised version of the leaflet.

Most of the findings are specific to the leaflet being studied, but some are more generally applicable. Few people read the text from beginning to end, using the graphics to support their understanding of the text. Most looked first at the graphics and, if the message conveyed by them was understandable and interesting, they then scanned or read the text. These findings are consistent with extensive COI research on other government publications.

In general, 'straight' graphics were preferred to cartoons. In fact, the cartoons were universally rejected as 'childish', 'flippant' and 'amateur in the extreme'. Of the 'straight' graphics, the sliced horizontal charts were seen as being the easiest to interpret, though a minority of people preferred the information to be presented in tables.

Some elements of the leaflet were interpreted as party political propaganda. These included the word 'government', which was interpreted as being the party in power; the presentation of trend data; the choice of text (eg 'we can choose to spend out own money or let the government spend it for us in higher taxes'); and even the choice of the colour blue for the leaflet.

Communication Research (1984 & 1985)

RN ratings: recruitment literature studies.. v.1 The reports v.2 Quantified study tabulations.
Communication Research Ltd, 1984.
RN ratings: Recruitment Literature: a quantitative study among potential recruits.
Communication Research Ltd, 1985.

The objective of this research was to assess the effectiveness of Royal Navy recruitment literature in terms of both its information content and its motivating ability. The booklets were tested using four different research techniques.

- 6 group discussions with potential naval ratings.

- Quantitative interviews with 194 potential naval ratings.

- 20 depth interviews with careers advisers.

- Readability analyses of the literature using the British Index of Reading Difficulty.

Most of the findings were specific to the booklets being researched. There were, however, some points of more general interest. These were:

- The use of a broadsheet format was criticised by a third of the quantitative sample as 'awkward to find your way round'.

- Some of the photographs used in the booklets were criticised as looking 'posed' and 'uninteresting'.

- Photographs on a blue background were thought to be particularly uninteresting.

Constable and others (1988)

Hilary Constable, Bob Campbell and Ron Brown. 'Sectional drawings from science textbooks: an experimental investigation into pupils' understanding'.
British Journal of Educational Psychology 58(1), 1988, 89-102.

The authors argue that although picture perception is an area that has been well researched, and there have been many studies concerning possible links between pictures and learning, the two fields are still not well articulated. Their empirical study examined various aspects of children's understanding of illustrations used as an adjunct to learning. The experiments were designed to find out if first-year secondary pupils could identify the anterior (back) surfaces of a series of biological objects (using six illustrations from standard textbooks).

While the results indicate that few of the children were able to perform this particular task correctly, some of the illustrations were found to be less difficult than others. Further analysis showed that a significant factor in picture perception in children relates to the number and the type of the pictorial conventions used. The authors concluded that these findings have implications for the role which illustrations play in reading, and further suggest the need to teach children explicitly about the conventions used in biological illustration.

Coopers & Lybrand (1986)

The cost of errors on forms.
Coopers & Lybrand for the Department of Health and Social Security, 1986.

As part of its drive to improve forms, the Department of Health and Social Security (DHSS) commissioned management consultants from Coopers & Lybrand to carry out research on the effectiveness of forms. The main focus of this research was the cost—to DHSS, form fillers, and employers—of errors made when people fill in forms.

A total of 4,416 completed forms were examined for errors. The examination revealed 611 forms with at least one error, and a total of 1,037 errors of which:

- 57 per cent were missing or incomplete answers.

- 22 per cent were failures to send documents.

- 6 per cent were failures to sign or date the form.

Not surprisingly, the number of errors per form increased with the length of the form. There were more errors on questions asking for employment details and income than on questions asking for other income and expenditure or asking for personal, family and domestic details. Irrespective of the length of the form, however, the report contains a number of formulae to estimate the expected error rate for a given form.

The actions taken by the Department to correct or overcome the errors were also examined. This produced a total of 710 remedial actions, of which:

- 27 per cent involved returning the form.
- 25 per cent involved sending a further form.
- 22 per cent involved helping the claimant to fill in the form.
- 12 per cent involved phone calls.
- 10 per cent involved writing letters.

The costs of these remedial actions to DHSS were estimated, based on average salary costs plus postage, stationery, travel and subsistence costs.

Corden and Corden (1984)

Ann Corden and John Corden. 'Testing the new FIS form with the help of FSU clients'.
FSU Quarterly 34(4), 1984, 29-35.

This article describes the testing of a revised Family Income Supplement Form with 10 volunteers from the Leeds Family Services Unit. Volunteers were given a copy of the form to complete and then immediately after asked to describe how they had done it and what difficulties they had had.

The volunteers were able to explain clearly why they had given particular answers and how they had interpreted particular instructions.

In general, the reseach showed that people found it difficult to fit their own circumstances to the administrative terms used if these differed from the terms they used colloquially. Their response tended to be to omit sections, to assume they were misprints, or to become irritated and anxious. It also demonstrated that strong emotions can be aroused when people tackle administrative forms. Where the form provokes irritation or anxiety, it contributes to an overall negative image of the agency involved.

The authors conclude that this is a useful methodology for analysing forms and leaflets, but that it does raise certain ethical issues. The people completing the forms were exposed – both in terms of their personal details being made available for others to see, and in terms of displaying their own difficulties with form filling.

Cragg, Ross and Dawson Ltd (1983)

Handy hints Leaflets: summary report on qualitative research.
Cragg Ross and Dawson Ltd, 1983

Six group discussions were held with lower income housewives, to assess the effectiveness of a leaflet containing 'handy hints' on the economical use of energy in the home.

The only finding that is of general applicability is that the illustrations were welcomed, for lightening an otherwise sober document. They did, however, run the risk of blurring the message of the leaflet because they were not used consistently. Sometimes they illustrated actions to be avoided while, on other occasions, they illustrated actions to be followed.

Cragg Ross & Dawson Ltd (1990)

Income Support leaflet for 16/17 year olds: report on qualitative research (debrief document).
Cragg Ross & Dawson Ltd for the Central Office of Information, 1990.

The Central Office of Information commissioned a qualitative research study to help it decide which was the more effective of two drafts of a leaflet aimed at 16/17 year olds who might qualify for Income Support. The drafts were evaluated in terms of the clarity of the text; relevance; tone of voice; and ease of comprehension. More specifically, the research was intended to provide guidance on the layout and design of the leaflet and its cover and to investigate possible methods and points of distribution.

Two target groups were included in the research sample: the young people themselves and professional carers. These latter were included to provide a broader perspective and to comment on the suitability of material for the client group. Depth interviews were conducted with 30 young people who were all living away from home and were either unemployed or working on YTS schemes. A further six interviews were conducted with professionals in personal (rather than administrative) contact with 16/17 year olds. The stimulus materials used were two slightly different draft texts produced by the Department of Social Security, and an alternative leaflet (plus poster) developed by students of St Martin's College of Art.

Among the main findings of the research were:

- Positive statements about the DSS or a successful claim were immediately countered by several negative ones.

- Attitudes towards the DSS were deeply cynical across the whole sample, and especially in London.

- Knowledge of the benefits system was highly variable, but the respondents were generally confused about their entitlements.

Initially, the respondents did not expect the DSS draft texts to be any more helpful than those they had already seen from the DSS. Leaflets were thought by this client group to be overused and to lack impact. Both the DSS texts were criticised for being discouraging in tone and for using difficult vocabulary and official terms; essentially, both failed the acid test since, even after reading, none of the respondents was able to make a firm judgement as to whether or not they were eligible. But the research revealed that the leaflets were felt to be more useful than expected and were relatively accessible and easy to negotiate.

Observation of the way in which the leaflets were used showed that very few respondents read the whole text, referring instead to the index—a feature which was well-liked. Typically, the only sections read thoroughly were those which had been identified as 'highly relevant' from the index. This finding emphasised the need for extensive cross-referencing if an index approach is used.

The most effective outlets to display the leaflets were found to include hostels; short-term accommodation; squats; street sites for those sleeping rough; and day care agencies. A further suggestion was to target places where young people might become eligible, such as residential homes and youth custody centre.

The research findings also pointed to the need for a more comprehensive leaflet to be used as a follow-up by advisers and, in some cases, by some of the client group themselves.

The conclusion was that, on present evidence, any conventional leaflet is likely to be ineffective in reaching and communicating with this particular target group.

Crandall (1985)

Kathleen E Crandall. 'Writing for English language learners'.
IEEE Transactions on Professional Communication 28(4), 1985, 3-10.

This article focuses on adults who are not fluent readers either because English is not their native language or because of profound hearing losses since birth.

In the first section, Crandall identifies the skills needed for successful reading, focusing on the following aspects of language:

- *Phonemes* – the smallest distinctive units of sound.

- *Morphemes* – the smallest distinctive units of meaning.

- *Syntax* – the arrangement of words, phrases and clauses in sentences.

- *Semantics* – the awareness of what constitutes a word, meanings of words used in the language, multiple meanings for single words and the functions of words in context.

- *Discourse* organisation – the methods used to organise ideas.

- *World knowledge* – the general background knowledge possessed by members of the culture using the language.

Adults learning English as a second language and deaf adults encounter difficulties because of weaknesses in their knowledge of the semantics and syntax of English. They may experience additional difficulties due to gaps between the background knowledge they possess and that assumed by the author. Finally, they may have reading difficulties because they are not familiar with discourse organisation techniques that are often present in the types of materials they are attempting to read.

On the basis of this analysis, Crandall proposes the following guidelines to help adult language learners, either those learning English as a second language or those who are deaf, to understand written materials:

Syntax guidelines

- Do not separate a subject from its verb.
- Do not delete optional parts of sentences.
- Put words and ideas in a logical order.

Semantic guidelines

- Use difficult words only when they are needed.
- Use needed difficult words in context and provide cues to their meaning.
- Where possible, use the most common meaning of multiple-definition word.
- Use negatives and implied negatives with caution.
- Place pronouns after and close to their referents.

Discourse organisation guidelines

- Inform the reader how you have organised a lengthy document.
- Provide topic headings and subheadings in a lengthy document.
- Provide a concise summary of the critical information in the document.
- Use tables, figures, illustrations, maps etc to support the text.

World knowledge guidelines

- Identify the audience for whom your document is intended and the skills they should possess.
- Only use specialised or technical information when it is important for comprehension and explain that information.

- Provide comprehension checks that allow readers to evaluate their comprehension of new information.

Cripwell (1989)

Kenneth R Cripwell. 'Non-picture visuals for communication in health learning manuals'.
Health Education Research 4 (3), 1989, 297-304.

This paper focuses on the application of non-picture visuals in health education materials targeted at professional health workers.

Pictures and diagrams are widely used to enhance the information impact of training materials, but while there has been considerable research into the use of pictures and illustrations, little is known of non-picture visual literacy, the main reason being the lack of valid and reliable tests.

The author relates some of his experiences developing health learning materials in South East Asia while acting as a consultant to the World Health Organisation, and discusses a number of problems associated with the interpretation of:

- Outcome flow charts.

- Life cycle diagrams.

- Pie charts and bar graphs.

- Instructional flowcharts.

- Instructional diagrams.

- Plotted graphs.

He argues that often the barriers to an understanding of these non-visual forms are culturally-determined and learners with little or no experience of their use may well find them incomprehensible. However, learners can be trained to use them effectively, as has been shown where replication studies of visual literacy have taken place.

Cutts and Maher (1980)

Martin Cutts and Chrissie Maher. *Writing Plain English.*
Plain English Campaign, 1980.

This report is based on the general experience of the Plain English Campaign. It reviews the extent of the problem and makes out a strong case for plain English.

The report concludes with some basic guidelines covering typography, layout and the use of language.

Davey and Kapinus (1985)

Beth Davey and Barbara A Kapinus. 'Prior knowledge and recall of unfamiliar information: reader and text factors'.
Journal of Educational Research 78(3), 1985, 147-151.

This study, using school children, attempted to measure the effects of prior subject knowledge, and the order in which information appears, on the recall of unfamiliar information.

Students were pre-tested to assess their base of existing knowledge. They were then presented with two types of text. In the first, familiar information preceded unfamiliar information. In the second, the order was reversed. The students were tested for recall immediately and one week after reading the passage.

The results of the study showed that the order in which familiar and unfamiliar information appeared affected the recall differently depending on the level of prior knowledge. Students with high prior knowledge recalled unfamiliar information best when it was presented first, but information order did not appear to affect recall for those with low prior knowledge. The effect of the order was much less marked when recall was tested one week after the passage was read.

Department of Employment (1983)

A study of a proposed new version of Form MP1 (Maternity Pay Rebate form): three research techniques compared.
Department of Employment / Central Office of Information, 1983.

The overall study of the Form MP1 had three objectives:

- To provide a comparative assessment of the old and new versions.

- To provide recommendations about how to further improve the new MP1, in order to make it more intelligible and easier to fill in.

- To provide an assessment of three different research techniques that could be used in a study of this kind.

The first of these two objectives was covered by research carried out by Communication Research Ltd (Communication Research Ltd 1983(b)). This report is concerned solely with the assessment of face-to-face interviews as compared with telephone interviewing and postal questionnaires. It was decided that face-to-face interviewing would provide the most detailed information. The results from this study were therefore used as the basis for evaluating the telephone and postal techniques. Comparisons were made for response rates, information yielded and cost. 120 interviews were held for each technique.

Response rates. Unfortunately the study did not provide statistics that were directly comparable. This was because there was a much longer period between the last despatch date and the 'closure date' for the face-to-face study than for the others. This factor was especially important for the postal survey where much more time was needed. It seemed, however, that despite these reservations on comparability, the postal technique elicited a far higher rate of outright refusals than either of the other two techniques.

Information yielded – comparative assessment of the old and new versions of MP1. The 3 methods gave broadly similar results on preference, which form was quicker to complete and (to a lesser extent) which form was easier to understand.

All techniques also reported that a significant minority did not read the notes on the new form and that about a half did not read them before starting to fill in the form.

Similarly all techniques reported that only a third of users referred to the booklet when filling in the form.

Thus on all these criteria it does not seem as if any of the research techniques had a clear advantage over the others.

Information yielded – suggestions for improvements to the new MP1. The highest volume of response was generated by face to face interviews (46%). This was closely followed by the postal survey (35%). By comparison, telephone interviews achieved a very low response rate (17%). The overall patterns of response, however, were really very similar. All the main categories of response were picked up by all the studies.

Cost. The difference in the cost of the three techniques are considerable. The telephone study cost less than three-quarters of the cost of the face-to-face study and the postal survey cost well under a half. The *relative* cost of the three techniques, however, will depend on the complexity of the study. For more complex studies, the relative costs will be similar.

On the basis of these results it must be concluded that postal surveying is a more cost-effective way of evaluating documents than either face-to-face or telephone interviewing.

Department of Health and Social Security (1980)

Committee on a multi-purpose claim form. Report on the studies of claiming means-tested benefits.
Department of Health and Social Security, 1980.

The Department of Health and Social Security set up a committee which looked into the technical feasibility of a multi-purpose claim form for social security claims. Department of Health and Social Security research staff then conducted a series of trials of a prototype multi-purpose claim form. They concluded that:

> (The form) generated no significant increase in the incidence of multiple claiming and it seems unlikely that large sectors of the population were encouraged by the scheme to entering the claiming network for the first time. Further, the form itself gave rise to some problems for the claimant who had to complete it and the complexities of the inter-office claiming procedure proved both cumbersome and inefficient for administrators.

> The prime objective of the scheme—to encourage the thereby to increase multiple claiming by families—was not achieved to significant degree in either trial.

Department of Health and Social Security (1984)

Words project.
Department of Health and Social Security, 1984.

An extensive study carried out by the Social Research Branch for the DHSS Forms Unit.

Participants, selected to represent a range of claimant groups, were given questionnaires which asked them to select, from a short list of alternatives, the precise meanings of 40 words and phrases commonly found in DHSS forms and leaflets (the words were given out of context). The words and phrases misunderstood by more than a quarter of the sample included: tax year; gross pay; basic pay; net pay; insurance premium; household; housekeeping; cash; earnings; savings; rates; tenant; lodger; boarder; dependants; and 'the person you live with as man and wife'.

Participants were also asked to indicate the precise meanings of 20 abbreviations used in DHSS forms and leaflets. In this case no alternatives were supplied. Abbreviations misunderstood by more than a quarter of respondents included: p.w.e.; LO; SSP; ACT; and i.e.

Department of Health and Social Security (1986a)

Capital letters versus lower case.
Department of Health and Social Security, 1986. An unpublished summary of research carried out by the Document Design Unit on behalf of the National Unemployment Office.

The research centred on the problem that the National Unemployment Officer computer printer can either print capital letters only or lower case letters only. The aim of the study was to see which of these two options 'people would find easier to read, process and understand'.

The text used in the study was part of a letter sent to Supplementary Benefit claimants. It was tested on 60 people. Half of the subjects were shown the document typed only in capital letters, the other half were shown the document typed only in lower case letters.

There were three stages to the study, which produced the following findings:

- Interviews to find out people's first impressions of the two documents were inconclusive—few people commented that the text had been printed in one case only.

- Timing subjects as they read revealed no difference in the time taken to read the two text— subjects who had read the document in lower case were more likely to be critical than those who read it in capitals only.

- Interviews to test levels of understanding showed that there was no significant difference in levels according to whether the documents were in upper or lower case.

It was concluded that printing in one case only is not to be recommended. Where it cannot be avoided, it seems that using capitals only is better than using lower case only.

Department of Health and Social Security (1986b)

A report discussing the results of how the public fill in DHSS forms and the effectiveness of the prompts used on these forms.
Department of Health and Social Security, 1986.

Five forms were selected to illustrate a variety of prompts to help users to complete them accurately, and 800 copies, taken from DHSS files, were analysed to see how the public had actually filled them in. The study looked particularly at:

- The effect of prompts to encourage people to write in capital letters.

- The effect of prompts to include postcodes with addresses.

- How people write dates.

- Alternative layouts of boxes for National Insurance numbers.

Capital letter prompts
Seven out of ten people filled in the forms using capital letters only, regardless of whether they had been prompted to do so. From this the Document Design Unit recommends that forms should use 'Please write clearly' rather than ask people to write in capitals.

Postcodes

Similarly seven out of ten people gave their postcode regardless of where the prompt was located in relation to the address box. This suggests that knowledge of one's postcode is more important than the presence of a prompt near the address box. The Document Design Unit recommend that forms give a separate line and prompt for the postcode.

Dates

Nine out of ten people wrote just a number for the day. Nine out of ten people wrote the month as a number instead of writing the name of the month. When the BDI claimants were excluded, eight out of ten people wrote the year as '86' even when there was enough space for it to be written in full. The BD1 claimants, a large proportion of whom would be elderly, were far more likely to write the year in full.

In general, then, the most common way for people to write the date was 3.7.86.

National Insurance Numbers

It seemed that people were more likely to fill in their National Insurance numbers correctly if one box was provided for each character.

Department of Health and Social Security (1986c)

Decimal points in answer boxes.
DHSS Document Design Unit, 1986 (unpublished).

Report of survey that looked at the effect of using a decimal point in answer boxes for sums of money.

The results suggest that the presence of a decimal point in the answer box increases the chances of the form fillers giving the amount in pounds and pence rather than in just pounds:

- 68 per cent of the sample presented with a decimal point gave pounds and pence.

- 26 per cent of the sample presented with just a pound sign gave pounds and pence.

When there was a decimal point, there was also an increased likelihood of the form fillers writing in two noughts when the amount that they were putting down was a whole number of pounds.

Department of Health and Social Security (1987)

People's understanding of concepts associated with numbers presently being used on forms, and their preferences for the expression of numbers in words or figures on forms.
DHSS Document Design Unit, 1987 (unpublished).

This study investigated the views of a random sample of 72 people on topics related to the use of numbers and concepts associated with numbers. It was concluded that people prefer numbers to be expressed in figures (eg 4, 70), rather than words (eg four, seventy). Commas and spaces were commonly used when writing both four and five digit numbers (eg 10,000). The majority of those sampled were able to demonstrate a clear understanding of the concepts 'more than', 'less than', 'under', 'over' and 'between' when they were used in conjunction with numbers on forms.

Department of Trade and Industry (1984)

Straight to the point: a guide to the use of simpler English.
Department of Trade and Industry , 1984.

A glossary of about 150 words and phrases giving the plain English equivalents.

Dixon (1982)

P Dixon. 'Plans and written directions for complex tasks'.
Journal of Verbal Learning and Verbal Behaviour 21(1), 1982.

Dixon builds on the theory that, in reacting to written instructions, people construct a plan of what they have to do. His research set out to discover whether these plans were constructed beginning with actions or with conditions. In this sense, 'Turn the knob' would be an example of an action statement. A 'condition' governs or influences the action, and so '... until the dial indicates zero' is a condition statement.

The research set out to test reading speeds and found that sentences were read faster when the action statement was placed before the condition statement.

Don Preddy (1985)
Royal Navy recruitment brochures: office's report on qualitative research.
Don Preddy, 1985.

A research study to assess the effectiveness of recruitment literature for Royal Navy officers. Thirteen group discussions and 12 personal depth interviews were held with potential recruits.

The more general findings of the research were:

Diagrams and illustrations

- The use of colour photographs and diagrams added clarity and interest to the text and were thought to make the booklets more attractive.

- The use of faces (particularly the large single faces) was disliked both on the covers and on the inside pages.

- Comments were made on the absence of racial minorities in the illustrations. This was taken to imply that applications from members of these groups were not welcome.

- Diagrams with technical examples, in one booklet, helped understanding. However, in a second booklet, the diagrams were eye catching, but confusing, and the information would have been better presented as a table.

- The use of too many monochrome photographs made one booklet look dull and boring.

Layout

- The broadsheet format of two of the leaflets was especially disliked.
- All but one of the seven leaflets were criticised for having insufficient clear headings.
- A contents page in each booklet would have been useful.

- Respondents particularly like the format of questions followed by answers used in one booklet.

Dorney (1988)

Jacqueline M Dorney. 'The plain English movement'.
English Journal 77(3), 1988, 49-51.

This paper reviews the recent history of the plain English movement in the United States, a movement conceived by consumer advocacy groups in the 1960s to ensure that government and private business produce documents that the public can read and understand.

Many of the aims of the plain English movement had been expressed in the form of federal and state legislation. Seven states had passed laws to regulate the comprehensibility of consumer contracts, while another fifteen had legislation pending. These 'Plain English laws' focus primarily on controlling the word and sentence lengths found in contracts, and also take into consideration factors such as readability formulas and the legibility of particular typefaces.

Dorney concludes with a review of US information sources on the use of plain English in government and business.

Drury (1985)

Alinda Drury. 'Evaluating readability'.
IEEE Transactions on Professional Communication 28(4), 1985, 11-14.

The author maintains that readability formulas provide misleading and inappropriate measures of text difficulty, especially for people who are non-fluent users of English. Instead, Drury proposes a qualitative readability evaluation based on four sets of issues:

- Vocabulary difficulty.

- Sentence structure.

- Text cohesion (clarity of writing).

- Layout and visual presentation of text.

The article includes fuller consideration of the specific factors which need to be considered under each of these headings.

Duchastel (1980)

Phillipe Duchastel. 'Research on illustrations in text: issues and perspectives'.
Educational Communication and Technology Journal 28(4), 1980, 283-287.

The author reviews research on the use of illustrations in educational and instructional texts and concludes that 'the state of the art is certainly a confused one' and little can be learned from the research. In general, research has tried to find out if illustrations can enhance learning. Little recognition has been made of the fact that the term 'illustration' is a generic one covering a wide range of formats such as photographs, schematic drawings, diagrams and maps. Similarly little of the research has taken account of the purpose of including illustrations in a text (for example, to interest and motivate a reader, to help explain a point made in the prose, or to enhance long-term recall of the prose). There is a great deal of market research by publishing firms which supports the intuition that illustrations make books more attractive, more appealing and more marketable. There are, however, no educational studies that have examined this issue directly. Although a few studies have shown that illustrations facilitate comprehension, a large number have not. The author believes that this apparent contradiction arises because the research has not taken into account the fact that some materials do not need illustrations to be understood. A number of studies have shown that illustrations can enhance recall. Most, however, have concentrated on immediate recall, few have tested the more likely effect, that of better long-term retention of illustrated texts.

The author concludes by arguing for a shift in the focus for pictorial research. He believes that more attention needs to be given to the functional approach—that is what a picture does in a particular context—rather than the morphological approach, where the prime concern is what a picture looks like.

Duffy (1981)

Thomas Duffy. 'Organising and utilizing document design options'.
Information Design Journal 2(3/4), 1981, 256-266.

The author synthesies the contributions in a special issue of *Information Design Journal* which is devoted to the design of forms and official information.

Duffy proposes an overall systems-analytic approach to document preparation, based on five phases:

- Analysis of the problem.

- Designing or planning the proposed solution.

- Developing the product.

- Implementing the product.

- Evaluating its effectiveness.

From this framework he evolves an analytic model of the document design process.

Duffy and others (1989)

Thomas M Duffy and others. 'Models for the design of instructional text'.
Reading Research Quarterly 24(4), 1989, 434-455.

The results of previous research (and popular opinion) would suggest that vividness and liveliness should be the most important considerations in textbook design.

This review article suggests that the traditional approach of providing textbook writers with a series of text-independent guidelines may be less effective than alternative strategies such as protocol-aided revision.

Epstein (1981)

Joyce Epstein. 'Informing the elderly'.
Information Design Journal 2(3/4), 1981, 215-235.

This study of the provision of information on social benefits and services to the elderly included a detailed look at the production, quality and distribution of eleven leaflets. These included four DHSS leaflets, two DoE leaflets, one Age Concern leaflet and five local leaflets. The research methods employed included interviews with the people who produced them and with 905 elderly people and 60 care workers (social workers, home help organisers, district nurses, health visitors, area health education officers and voluntary agency workers).

Depite the fact that most agencies in the field relied heavily on leafelts, few elderly people had seen, much less used any of them.

Few of the elderly people questioned had ever seen a leaflet on financial aid, keeping warm, or mobility.

On the whole, the more elderly and those living in rural areas were the least well informed.

The most common sources of help included family and other personal contacts, rather than written information.

People who needed information to read leaflets more often than people who did not.

Epstein concluded, with respect to leaflets from the DHSS that

> ... it is their ubiquity, perhaps as much as their civil service blue which makes them most likely, among the recognised leaflets to remain unread.

In contrast, the design of the DoE leaflets was praised, as was their highly targeted distribution.

The care workers seemed to make little or no use of leaflets:

- They seldom gave them to their clients.
- They perceived the leaflets as being too complicated for their clients to understand.
- They tended to refer to their own 'administration officers' rather than consult leaflets when faced with a question that were unable to answer.

The study concludes that leaflets should be attractive, easy-to-read, aggressively distributed, and leaflet presented at the 'point of sale' if they are to stand any chance of being well-used.

Farrant and Russell (1986)

Wendy Farrant and Jill Russell. *The politics of health information: a case study of Health Education Council publications* (Bedford Way Papers 28), Institute of Education, 1986.

The research on which this paper is based was conducted as part of a three-year action research project funded by the Health Education Council (HEC). The aim of the project was to evaluate the Council's publications and to gain an understanding of the institutional and organisational constraints within which they are produced. It also explored some of the ways in which production decisions influence the content and style of health education materials. This report focuses on the process of initiation and production of one such publication, 'Beating heart disease'.

The research involved:

- Interviews with staff of the HEC and BBC who were responsible for the initiation and production of the booklet.

- Observations of consultations between the HEC Publications Division and Medical Division.

- Monitoring of communications between the HEC and external consultants who were asked to comment on the booklet.

- Observations of consultations between the HEC and graphic designers, plus interviews with the designers.

- Monitoring of HEC Management Team and Council meetings at which the booklet and the corresponding programme were discussed.

- Depth interviews with 21 adults, ranging in age from 16 to 61.

Farrant and Russell's analysis shows that the booklet was essentially a top-down production. Its target audience was not canvassed during its drafting and, as a consequence, the authors claim that the Council's thinking about the booklet's target audience was riddled with middle-class assumptions about working-class life. The Council believed it should 'sell' health with short and simple messages, along the lines of commercial advertising. It also thought it wise to avoid the sometimes conflicting medical evidence surrounding heart disease.

When the booklet was tested on a sample of users, it was found that, far from wanting short and simple health messages, the target audience wanted more information. Furthermore, instead of the simple, consensual advice offered in the booklet, the audience wanted help in evaluating the conflicting medical evidence on heart disease. They were cynical of expert knowledge, and were suspicious of attempts to sell them a particular health message. In simple terms, the health educators had totally misjudged both the amount and the level of information required by the general public.

FDS Market Research LTD (1986)

Inland Revenue Publications Survey.
FDS (Market Research) Ltd, 1986.

The main objective of this research was to find out the extent to which solicitors and accountants use Inland Revenue publications and how useful they find them. A total of 612 telephone interviews were held, and respondents were not told that the survey was being carried out on behalf of the Inland Revenue until the end of the interview.

Nearly all respondents (96 per cent) said that if they had a tax problems they would consult a booklet or publication. Whereas only 13 per cent of the total sample mentioned Inland Revenue publications without prompting, 59 per cent mentioned specific commercial publications, like Tolleys Tax Guide. Users of Inland Revenue publications were asked to rate specific aspects of them. Generally they received low scores for indexing and cross referencing, but better scores for depth of coverage and clarity.

Felker (1980)

Daniel B Felker (ed.) *Document design: a review of the relevant research.*
American Institutes for Research, 1980.

This report, by members of the US Document Design Project team, reviews the literature in five areas relevant to document design. These include psycholinguistics; cognitive psychology; instructional research; readability; human factors; and typography. Almost all the research covered pre-dates 1979.

Felker and others (1981)

Daniel B Felker and others. *Guidelines for document designers.*
American Institutes for Research, 1981.

This report sets out 25 principles for clear writing and presentation, targeted at compilers of public documents. Each of the design principles is stated and illustrated with many examples drawn from real life. Key research is also summarised where it bears directly on information design practice.

For each guideline there is a 'qualifications' section where exceptions to the rule are discussed.

It is undoubtedly the most comprehensive, and probably the most useful, set of guidelines available for the compilers of public documents.

Firth (1980)

Diane Firth. *An assessment of a re-design exercise using supplementary benefits documents.*
Research Institute for Consumer Affairs for the Department of Health and Social Security, 1980.

This report is an assessment of 13 documents rewritten and redesigned by the Salford Form Market for the Department of Health and Social Security. Firth considered that few of the research findings were transferable to other public documents. The usefulness of the report lies in the general comments on the various assessment techniques employed. These fall into two categories: non-use techniques and in-use techniques.

Non-use techniques
Readability scores These were considered to be the most useful techniques for comparative testing of documents. But the scores derived from individual tests, were suspect since different tests led to widely different assessments of reading ages for the same document. However, as a practical technique, readability measures are easy to apply and the results are quick.

Cloze procedures Cloze tests were judged to be very time-consuming for the amount of data produced.

Underlining The purpose of this test was not understood by participants and the results were, therefore, invalid.

The overall conclusion for the non-use techniques other than the readability scores was

> the fieldwork time and analysis time spent... does not justify using them in future as results can, at best, be used to supplement other findings only.

In-use techniques

Depth interviews and group discussions. Here, Firth concurs with Pat Wright (Wright 1979b) that there is no substitute for actually trying out documents on users. The only way to find out about the impact, appeal, design, and comprehensibility of a document is to study it in use and discover users' reactions to and understanding of it. This does not need to be carried out on a grand scale with a large amount of quantitative data. It is also suggested that both the administrators of the documents and the consumers should be questioned. A revised document should be better for both these groups if it is to be considered an improvement.

Assessments of mistakes and user statistics. These techniques can be used only for certain categories of document. But they can be useful techniques if sufficient of the right kinds of document are available for analysis. Unfortunately, such assessments are time-consuming and costly, and are not considered essential. It was also clear from the study that often a revised document may be preferred to the original, both by staff and claimants, but perform no better in use.

Firth recommends depth interviews, group discussions and readability scores as the most effective evaluation tools for future use.

Fisher (1986)

Phil Fisher. 'Tax Form S project'.
CARE Newsletter 2, 1986, 3.

A short description of the redesign and testing of the Australian

Taxation Office's *Tax Form S*. One unexpected design flaw was that the new form, which had more pages and was printed on heavier paper than the old one, caused handling difficulties.

Flower and others (1980)

Linda S Flower and others. *Revising functional documents: the scenario principle* (Technical Report 10). American Institutes for Research, 1980.

The problem addressed in this report is 'can we define a set of powerful principles which would allow writers to revise public documents so that they meet the needs of the readers who use them?'

The most obvious candidates for such principles are readability measures and the report considers how well they meet these criteria. The authors conclude that they offer an easy to use principle for revising prose but fail to meet some of the most important needs of readers. To illustrate this the authors refer to the various reports that demonstrate the shortcomings of such formulae. Readability formulae can help, but they need to be complemented by a means of structural revision 'which can organise the information and a document around the larger comprehension needs of the reader and the function of the document'.

The report describes a research project intended to uncover some of the things readers need in order to process or comprehend a functional document. Tape-recordings were made of subjects reading and interpreting the meaning of Federal Regulations as they read (Protocol analysis)and a detailed analysis was made of the reading protocols of three representative readers of a Small Business Administration regulation.

The comments of the readers fell into two categories:

General statements and *content statements* General statements were those which did not relate specifically to the regulation, for example, 'This is going to be hard'. Content statements included, 'Alright, they want to keep all this money separate' and direct attempts to 'translate' the meaning of a phrase sentence or group of sentences. Further analysis showed that there were three distinct kinds of content statement: those referring to the structure of the document (*structure statements*); those drawing on the reader's prior knowledge (*retrieval statements*); and those in which the reader creates a scenario to explain a phrase, for example, a reader, considering the phrase 'ineligible concerns', saying 'suppose a fellow has a bar and he's selling moonshine which isn't taxed...' (*scenario statements*).

The results demonstrate that readers frequently use the structure merely to read the document. This was especially evident with one subject who attempted to discover whether she was, herself, eligible for the program.

Similarly all three readers showed significant attempts to use prior knowledge in order to understand the text of the document.

The most notable result from the analysis was the extent to which the readers expressed the meaning of a line or section in the form of a concrete story or event. For two of the subjects such 'scenario statements' accounted for more than half of their total statements on content, in particular for the translation statements. That is when interpreting the text the readers did not rephrase the original using shorter sentences and simpler words. Instead they made much more radical changes to the text, illustrating it with brief scenarios.

In the final part of the report the authors suggest practical revision strategies for public documents deriving from their research. They argue that it is desirable to structure information around the reader, reflecting the intended use of public documents as sources of information. The structure should, therefore, reflect the actions people need to take. In particular, headings should be informative and reflect the questions users will ask. The text should be written in terms of concrete situations and the subsequent actions people take. Wherever possible it should describe concepts in practical and operational terms, and sentences should be written with agents (preferably human agents) and actions: 'failure to pursue' should be rewritten, 'if you fail to pursue'.

The authors also argue that public documents should provide a context for the information they include. They suggest giving extended examples or cases, and using detail and specific cases to define the meaning of difficult terms.

Forms Information Centre (1983)

Colour in forms: a brief guide.
Forms Information Centre, 1983.

This guide provides a brief outline of the main issues to be considered when using colour in forms. Since there has been relatively little research on the use of colour in public documents, this guide is written chiefly from practical experience. Guidance offered includes:

- When to use colour.

- Choosing a coloured ink.

- Using coloured paper.

- some problems of using colour.

Forms Information Centre (1984a)

Legibility (Topic Sheet 1).
Forms Information Centre, 1984.

This is a set of guidelines, based on research and practical experience, that are relevant to both forms and leaflets. The guidelines cover:

- Choice of typeface (there is little difference in the legibility of the most commonly available ones).

- User of lower and capital letters.

- Type weight (medium weight is usually best, with sparing use of bold headings and emphasis).

- Type size (the optimum is probably 9 or 10 point, possibly 11 if the document is likely to be used by large numbers of elderly people).

- Line length (the optimum is 60 characters).

- Letter and word spacing (unjustified setting is easier and cheaper to produce and may be more legible).

- Justification (unjustified text may be more readable than justified text).

- Margins and page size affect line length.

- Contrast (at least 70 per cent contrast is recommended).

Forms Information Centre (1984b)

Signature Space (Topic Sheet 2).
Forms Information Centre, 1984.

This single sheet discusses the amount of space that should be provided for signatures. The guidance is based on an investigation by Paul Beard of the space requirements of a typical signature. This was determined by analysing 300 signatures of British names written on blank paper. The signatures were measured by being fitted into 30 templates of varying sizes, ranging from 30mm by 10mm to 70mm by 25mm. He found that a space 60mm long and 20mm deep was sufficient for 94 per cent of signatures.

Forms Information Centre (1985a)

Questions and Answers (Topic Sheet 3).
Forms Information Centre, 1985.

This Topic Sheet offers general guidance for the design of questions and answers on public forms and covers the following areas:

- Factors which influence the effectiveness of questions and answers.
- Ways of asking and answering questions.
- Choosing the most appropriate way of asking a question.
- Positioning question and answer spaces on a form.
- Indicating who is expected to fill in which answer—staff or public.

The advice given is based on practical experience and research evidence.

Forms Information Centre (1985b)

Readability and Readability Formulas.
Forms Information Centre, 1985.

A critique of the general users of readability formulae including some of the problems in their application, validity and accuracy. The information sheet described four of the most popular formulae that are used for testing adult prose texts: Flesch, Fog, Forecast and Smog.

A number of misuses of readability formulae are discussed and alternative methods of assessing readability are proposed. The author concludes that the best method of testing for readability is to use guidelines on writing clearly and then test documents on the intended audience.

Forms Information Centre (1987)

Dates as Answers on Forms (News Sheet 4).
Forms Information Centre, 1987.

Where the information from forms has to be input to a computer system, it is often necessary to have any dates written as numbers and in a particular position. The aim of this study was to identify the optimum way of designing answer spaces for the recording of dates on forms.

The study was based on an analysis of about 200 forms that had been completed in a normal rather than a test situation. Each form included four questions which required a date for an answer. Two of these used a box format, with central subdivisions for the digits in the day and year spaces, but not in the month space. The other two involved entering the date on a horizontal line.

The box format was more likely to result in the date being given entirely in numbers (98 per cent compared with 87 per cent). Of the two box formats, those with a central subdivision were far more likely to result in single digit answers being written on the right-hand side of the box (80 per cent compared with 29 per cent). This would be important where it is necessary to precede a single digit with a zero for computer input.

Frase and others (1985)

Lawrence T Frase, Nina H MacDonald and Stacey A Keenan. 'Intuitions, algorithms and a science of text design'. In: Thomas Duffy and Robert Waller (eds), *Designing Usable Texts*.
Academic Press, 1985.

This article explores the potential use of computers as an aid to the design and writing of public documents and discusses the findings of an experiment using computer analysis to determine the optimum line length for a piece of text.

Cognitive psychology research has shown that comprehension of a text is increased if the text is presented with one meaningful unit of information, or chunk, to a line. Yet traditionally text is printed in uniform line lengths. The aim of this study was, therefore, to determine the optimum line length to ensure that as many lines of a text as possible comprise exactly one chunk.

The experiment used 60 text passages of easy, medium and difficult readability levels. Each passage was segmented into meaningful chunks of information by a human and subsequently checked by five further people and a computer program for text segmentation. After segmentation, each passage was divided by computer into 15 different line lengths, anging from 5 to 75 characters. The computer then analysed each of the 60 passages, at each of the 15 line-length formats, to determine the best line length for each text passage.

The mean best line lengths for passages of different readability levels were significantly different: 44, 50 and 56 characters for the easy, medium and difficult texts respectively. Even these lengths gave only 25 per cent of lines containing exactly one chunk. In addition there was a great deal of variability in the scores for texts within any one of the readability levels. It was concluded that line lengths between 40 and 60 characters are suitable for most texts. However, for maximum comprehensibility, it seems that line lengths are best determined by the language characteristics of the text rather than by overall guidelines.

It would seem that other text features, such as point size, font, type style and hyphenation could also be explored in studies such as this. If so it could be possible to carry out computer-aided text design.

Frase & Schwartz (1979)

LT Frase and BJ Schwartz. 'Typographical cues that facilitate comprehension'.
Journal of Educational Psychology 71(2), 1979.

Written sentences often contain several meaningful components, such as causes and effects or events in a sequence. The authors report the results of five experiments investigating whether phrase segmentation and indentation can be used to facilitate comprehension. The subjects were college graduate technical aides from Bell Labs. The subjects were given eight test sentences, half of which were true and half false.

They discovered that both meaningful segmentation and indenting the text influenced performance and resulted in faster response times. However, once a text had been meaningfully segmented, the addition of indentation did not significantly affect response time.

Based on their research the authors conclude that neither length of line not justified margins are important to the ease with which a document is understood. They suggest that a format which presents the text in easily encoded units is more important than the line length or neatness of margins.

This research has, however, been criticised, both for its method of segmenting the text and its experimental design. An attempt to replicate the results using a revised experimental design found no significant differences in the times taken to retrieve information from standard texts, meaningfully intended texts and vertically spaced texts. (James Hartley. 'Spatial cues in text: some comments on the paper by Frase and Schwartz (1979)'. *Visible Language* 14(1), 1980, 62-79.)

Friedmann (1988)

Keyla Friedmann. 'The effect of adding symbols to written warning labels on user behaviour and recall'.
Human Factors 30(4), 1988, 507-515.

Millions of people are injured each year as a result of poorly designed or manufactured products. As more of them turn to the courts for compensation, product liability is becoming an increasingly important area, with the effectiveness of product warning labels assuming legal and commercial importance.

Research has shown that the design aspects of a warning label contribute to the warning being noticed and understood. Yet, despite their potential for being universally understood, little attention has been paid to the role of symbols.

The research presented here is an investigation of some of the complex information-design issues that influence whether or not people notice, read and comply with a product warning. Friedmann emphasises the need for extensive testing of warning symbols before they are used on consumer products.

Frohlich (1985a)

David Frohlich. *Human Factors in Form Design* (Alvey Demonstrator at Surrey Report).
University of Surrey, 1985.

Frohlich reviews some of the previous research into forms and form-filling as background to the Alvey DHSS Forms Helper Project at Surrey University.

He describes form-filling problems that have been identified in previous studies. Typical examples include:

- The form looks intimidating.
- The form asks apparently irrelevant questions.
- I don't know the answers.
- Where does the answer go?
- There isn't enough room to write the answer.
- The sequence of items doesn't make sense.
- How do I change a wrong answer.

Frohlich then reviews the extent to which research has addressed human factors issues in form design such as legibility; comprehensibility and readability; question and answer formats; organisation of questions and routing instructions.

Frohlich (1985b)

David Frohlich. *Summary of Form-filling Findings Relating to the B1*
(Alvey Demonstrator at Surrey Report).
University of Surrey, 1985.

This research report describes the results of a study of protocols recorded during a form-filling exercise, using the DHSS postal claims form for Supplementary Benefit (Form B1).

The results of the protocol analysis led Frohlich to make the following general recommendations relating to form design:

- Design the form to accommodate form-fillers who often fail to read general instructions.

- Make all routing instructions consistently from either 'Yes' or 'No' responses.

- Award multiple 'or' clauses wherever possible.

- Exercise caution in the use of examples because they may be interpreted as an exhaustive list of answer options.

- Do not ask questions with qualifiers.

- Use multiple answer options rather than checklists where the form-filler needs to indicate which of a range of options applies to them (for example, which social security benefits they are currently receiving).

- Site explanatory material *before* a question to increase its likelihood of being read.

Frohlich (1986a)

David Frohlich. *Human Factors Evaluation of the Forms Helper*
(Alvey Demonstrator at Surrey Report).
University of Surrey, 1985.

This paper draws together the results of earlier research carried out by David Frohlich in an attempt to evaluate the effectiveness of a prototype computer system, Forms Helper, designed with a variety of on-line facilities to help users complete the form. An earlier review of research on paper form-filling (see Frohlich 1985a) highlighted a number of form-filling problems that could potentially be solved if an electronic medium were used instead of a form. The three main problems were:

- Difficulties faced by paper form-fillers in finding their way through a form, answering all those questions relevant to them and routing away from irrelevant questions.

- Failure to understand the meaning of individual questions because printed explanatory notes are not read.

- Failure to provide satisfactory answers to questions because of the difficulty of writing inside limited answer spaces or of amending incorrect answers.

This study assesses the effectiveness of the Forms Helper computer system in overcoming these problems.

Form navigation

There was a significant variation between users in the extent to which they determined routing through the form themselves rather than following the routing recommendation of Forms Helper. Some users determined as few as 15 per cent of routing decisions themselves while others determined as many as 63 per cent. While paper form-filling followed a linear path, computer form-filling involved many more routing digressions. Some of these digressions were initiated by the system itself others were user initiatives. It seemed that users were not entirely happy to trust the routing recommendations made by the Forms Helper. Despite these digressions users were far less likely to bother with irrelevant questions on the Forms Helper and they seldom provided answers to questions out of sequence.

Understanding questions

The reading patterns of subjects using the Forms Helper were found to be broadly similar to those of subjects using the paper form. Both tended to overlook more than half the relevant titles, explanations and instructions. Although the pattern was the same, consistently more titles, explanations and instructions were overlooked by the users of the Forms Helper. There seemed to be a number of reasons for this. Subjects were often unaware of the availability of an explanation for questions which were located at the bottom of the screen page in Forms Helper. Once an explanation was located, there was sometimes confusion over which question it related to, especially if pre- and post-answer explanations were displayed together. Finally, the layout of explanations to the left of the screen-displayed form meant that users often read an explanation before or during reading the question itself. This clearly affected subjects' interpretation of the question.

Answering questions
Users of the Forms Helper system who had access to examples of completed answers for certain questions did not seem to be helped by having this facility. Most failed to use it, or if they did, failed to find the examples helpful. Similarly, the system help facility was rarely used and was found to be disappointing by those who did so. Using a keyboard or mouse to complete the electronic form led to a higher incidence of input errors than on the paper form.

In conclusion, Frohlich notes that the evaluation had demonstrated the feasibility of using computer software to support form-filling activities but it needed considerable enhancement to realise its full potential. Forms Helper was shown to be particularly effective in directing the course of a form-filling dialogue, while at the same time allowing users complete freedom to make their own decisions. However, Frohlich admits that its failure lay in the weakness of the support provided both for individual questions and the operation of the system itself.

Frohlich (1986b)

David Frohlich. 'On the organisation of form-filling behaviour'. *Information Design Journal* 5(1), 1986, 43-59.

This paper reports a detailed observational study of the reading and routing activities of subjects as they filled in a DHSS postal claim form for Supplementary Benefit (B1).

A total of eight subjects, aged between 19 and 56, took part in the study: four were unemployed and already claiming Supplementary Benefit, the other four were in employment. Only two had previous experience of completing form B1, but not of the version being tested.

All eight subjects were asked to read and think aloud as they filled in the form. Their protocols were tape-recorded and supplemented by an analysis of the completed forms and notes made by the researcher while observing the form-filling. The protocols were analysed in three different ways

- A copy of each completed form was annotated with information from the protocol, and the cassette tape counter number noted so that the route taken through the form could be reconstructed. Observation notes were also added to the form.

- A 'question path table' was constructed for each subject, showing the sequence with which questions were consulted.

- An 'event path table' was then compiled for each protocol. This used a 'dictionary' of terms so that the form filling behaviour could be described fairly specifically. The dictionary included seven events, depicting the various actions taken during the form filling (such as 'scan', 'answer', or 'diversion') and eleven descriptors used to qualify the events (such as 'disoriented' or 'inconsistent').

Frohlich's results showed that while three-quarters of questions visited were read aloud, this applied to less than half the section titles and to only about one third of question explanations and routing instructions. Evidence from observation and discussion suggested that this was a realistic indication of the extent to which these items were read at all.

The explanations most frequently read were those most necessary to an understanding of the question to which they referred. Those least likely to be read followed question answer areas and usually referred to the consequences of certain answers for the success of the claim.

A similar pattern applied to the routing instructions on the form: those most likely to be read were at locations on the form where the subsequent routing was most unclear. Those least read followed the answer areas and included instructions like 'go to next column'.

It appears therefore, that people read only what they think they have to read in order to complete the form quickly.

The analysis of routing behaviour showed that, by and large, subjects followed a linear path through the form. Where digressions did occur, they often corresponded to expressions of perceived confusion in the protocols. Routing accuracy was also measured and expressed as the number of incorrect choices of alternative routes expressed as a percentage of all such choices. The mean for all subjects was 20 per cent, representing a total of 50 incorrect choices. In all but one of these the choice led the form-fillers to consider additional irrelevant question. Reasons for the incorrect routing were that routing instructions were not read, or that routing conventions were misunderstood. For example, indented sub-questions following an affirmative answer that should have been ignored by subjects giving a negative reply. Also, if people could answer a question they would do so, even if the routing was intended to indicate that the DHSS did not require the information.

It was concluded that the problem of routing through the form appeared to have been made more difficult because of the use of both routing instructions and typographic conventions for guidance. This encouraged opposing routing strategies. Routing instructions tend to encourage users to progress through the questions on the form until told otherwise. On the other hand, typographic conventions encourage users to navigate their own paths, using the layout of the questions for guidance.

Frohlich (1986c)

David Frohlich. *On the reorganisation of form-filling behaviour in an electronic medium.*
University of Surrey, Alvey DHSS Demonstrator Project, 1986

This report builds on the earlier study of verbal protocols of formifilling behaviour, published in the *Information Design Journal* (Frohlich 1986 b). Whilst the earlier study focussed on the hard-copy, paper version of the form B1, this report looks at the way form-fillers adapted their behaviour when completing a simple electronic version of the same form. The initial versions of the Forms Helper provided a variety of on-line help facilities to help users complete the form. For this study, however, these were suppressed to ensure that subjects did not interact with any textual material that was not printed on the B1 paper form. As in the earlier study data from observational notes, verbal protocols and completed forms were combined in an analysis of the reading and routing activities of subjects on the Forms Helper. In this case, though, the researcher kept a log of the interaction between the user and the computer system.

The results were broadly similar to those obtained using the paper version of the form. Far more questions were vocalised than titles, explanations, or instructions. There were, however, some important differences. The routing recommendations made by the Forms Helper improved the accuracy of oriented progressions through the form and so reduced the proportion of irrelevant answers provided by form-fillers. At the same time, however, digressions from a linear path through the form were both more common and more complex on the electronic than on the paper form.

The author concludes that electronic form-filling behaviour seemed to be organised quite differently to the form-filling behaviour observed in the earlier study. In essence, when completing the paper form, subjects tended not to route away from questions on their own initiative. Those completing the electronic form, on the other hand, tended to resist the initiative of the Forms Helper in routing them to other parts of the form.

These findings have a number of implications for the design of electronic forms in general. First, they show that the active part played by the form in the interaction contributed significantly to the form-filling behaviour of the users. Electronic form designers need to take account of this and design an interaction rather than an interactive device. Secondly the use of an electronic medium offered far greater freedom for the design of froms, which is often difficult to exploit. For example, it becomes possible to build in dynamic information display. This was explored with the display of explanatory material in the study, and the results showed hoe difficult it can be to control the introduction of information into form-filling activity. The final implication of the findings for electronic form design allows from the other two. That is, that paper forms need to be re-designed for presentation on an interactive computer system.

The author notes that it is quite legitimate to question the value of the study since it merely replicated existing paper forms in a medium which is capable of far more. A better strategy might have been to explore the potential and limitations of the new medium in its own right. He justifies the approach by demonstrating that there are so many possibilities for designing a computer form that it is hard to know where to begin. He believes, however that studies like this help to reveal the dimensions along which changes in design of computer forms are most necessary and desirable.

Frohlich and others (1985)

David Frohlich and others. 'Requirements for an intelligent form-filling interface'. In: P Johnson and S Cook (eds), *People and computers: designing the interface.*
Cambridge University Press, 1985.

This paper describes preliminary work carried at the University of Surrey as part of the Alvey DHSS Demonstrator project, examining the kinds of support likely to be required by members of the public when filling in welfare benefit forms.

It reviews earlier published research on form design and then considers the implications of those findings for the design of an intelligent form-filling interface. It is proposes that these requirements can best be met using an Intelligent Knowledge-Based System.

Fry (1989)

Edward B Fry. 'Reading formulas – maligned but valid'.
Journal of Reading 32(4), 1989, 292-297.

A robust defence of readability formulas against criticisms that their application often leads to poor-quality written communication. In the process, Edward Fry offers an excellent review of current thinking on readability testing.

Fry (1990)

Edward B Fry. 'A readability formula for short passages'.
Journal of Reading 33(8), 1990, 594-597.

A persistent drawback of conventional readability formulas has been their lack of applicability to shorter passages of text. Most formulas require a passage of at least 300 words in order to attain any degree of consistency and reliability: with shorter passages, readability scores tend to fluctuate, often erratically. This presents a barrier to assessing the readability of short, but nonetheless important, texts such as the rules and procedures contained in driver's training booklets.

In this article, Fry presents a new *Short Passage Readability Formula*, designed for use with passages of 40 to 99 words—provided that they contain at least three sentences. The Formula requires two major inputs: a word difficulty level (established by reference to Dale and O'Rourke's *The Living Word Dictionary*) and a sentence-difficulty measure based on length.

Geisler and others (1985)

Cheryl Geisler, David Kaufer and Erwin Steinberg. 'The unattended anaphoric "this": When should writers use it?' Written Communication 2(2) 1985, 129-155.

The *unattended anaphoric* use of the word *this*, is the use of *this* alone to refer back to a preceding idea, proposition, procedure or quotation; for example, John believed that Mars is larger than Saturn. Even his brother knew that *this* wasn't right.

In this article the authors attempt to identify those circumstances that are appropriate for the use of *this* alone and those that are not.

A series of sentences were given to students attending the writing course at Carnegie-Mellon University and asked to indicate the antecedent to which the word *this* referred. They found that sentences were interpreted more easily if the *this* referred to the main or focal topic of the sentence; for example, John kicked the dog, which had bitten him. *This* angered the old man.

The authors propose a number of guidelines for the use of the unattended word *this* in such circumstances. First it should not be used where it refers back to an 'out of focus' topic. In such cases it should be accompanied by a noun or noun phrase; for example, The Disciplinary Committee read the case carefully, listened to the student, and questioned the teacher before coming to a decision. The entire campus community knew that *this (decision)* would set precedents for years to come.

There are, however, other occasions when either an attended or an unattended *this* can be used. In such cases using *this* alone would be less clumsy or more economical, but may lead to some loss of clarity. The authors suggest that the clarity of such sentences be assessed by writers asking themselves *this what?* If they cannot fill in the 'what' easily then either the referent needs to be added; for example, *this decision*, or the sentence needs redrafting.

Gibbs and others (1989)

Sharon Gibbs, WE Waters and CF George. 'The benefits of prescription information leaflets' (in two parts).
British Journal of Clinical Pharmacology part one: 27, 1989, 723-739; part two: 28, 1989, 345-351.

It is widely recognised that the information currently provided for patients about their prescribed medicines is inadequate. Drug actions and reactions are not usually discussed during general practice consultations; when they are, patients frequently misunderstand or forget details given to them orally.

For this study, generic information leaflets were developed for three commonly-prescribed groups of medicine. These were constructed according to general principles for the design of technical information and were 'style edited' by an educational psychologist to improve their readability.

These leaflets were then tested to determine their effects on patients' knowledge, behaviour and satisfaction with their medicines. Few systematic studies have been performed to examine the effects of leaflets. These two papers are therefore of particular interest because of their detailed account of survey methodology. The results illustrate the impact carefully-designed written material can have on the communication of medical information.

Goddard and Bowling (1987)

Anne Goddard and Ann Bowling. 'An international comparison of health education literature on breast disorders'.
Health Education Journal 46(3), 1987, 91-93.

A content analysis was undertaken of publicly available literature on breast disorders from six countries (France, Italy, Spain, Sweden, UK, USA). The information content of the literature was evaluated against a checklist of 20 criteria consisting of topics considered to be important in relation to self-care, risk factors, diagnosis, and treatment.

The content analysis revealed differences in both the amount and type of information provided in the various countries and showed that it is harder to obtain information on many topics in the UK than it is elsewhere. In particular, there seems to be a reluctance in the UK to give clear, specific, realistic information which might be regarded as 'bad news'. The assumptions underlying this appear to be that people do not want or cannot accept unpleasant information.

If preparatory information is to be accurate and realistic it must often include material on topics that are personally threatening (treatment side-effects, for example) or controversial (such as breast reconstruction). While this may heighten anxiety in the short term, the longer-term outcomes are likely to be more beneficial.

The research suggests that the success of mammography campaigns in Sweden and the USA in dramatically reducing mortality rates from breast cancer may be because the availability of frank, high-quality information materials has made women more receptive to screening programmes. There is a possibility that better literature might lead to better-informed choices and use of services by British women.

Goldsmith (1980)

Evelyn Goldsmith. 'Comprehensibility of illustration: an analytical model'.
Information Design Journal 1(3), 1980, 204-213.

This paper is based on the author's PhD thesis and presents a model for the evaluation of the comprehensibility of illustrations. This model comprises a number of elements, 3 *semiotic levels* and 4 *visual factors*, which Goldsmith argues are crucial to understanding pictures, particularly those which are intended to be in support of text. The 'semiotic' levels are:

- *Syntactic level* – a response to graphic signals as a an image or set of images.

- *Pragmatic level* – a response to the artist's meaning in terms of all the previous experience and present judgment of the viewer.

- *Semantic level* – a response to images in terms of the meanings the artist intended to set down.

Goldsmith exemplifies this by reference to a cartoon showing two unicorns stranded on a small mound surrounded by water, with an ark sailing away in the distance. The *syntactic level* requires an ability to distinguish the bounds of the separate images and to perceive pictorial depth. The *semantic level* requires recognition of the images as unicorns, water and an ark. But the point of the drawing is lost at the *pragmatic level* if the viewer is unaware of the story of the Flood and the current scarcity of unicorns. These levels are, in practice, often interdependent and consideration of the higher levels automatically presupposes the existence of those below.

Goldsmith exemplifies this by reference to a cartoon showing two unicorns stranded on a small mound surrounded by water, with an ark sailing away in the distance. The *syntactic level* requires an ability to distinguish the bounds of the separate images and to perceive pictorial depth. The *semantic level* requires recognition of the images as unicorns, water and an ark. But the point of the drawing is lost at the *pragmatic level* if the viewer is unaware of the story of the Flood and the current scarcity of unicorns.

In addition to these 3 semiotic levels Goldsmith identifies 4 visual factors:

- *Unity* which refers to any area in a picture which might be recognised as having a separate identity. The level of separateness will vary according to the intention of the picture or the interest of the viewer.

- *Location* – the spatial relationships between the separate images. It encompasses the various devices for depicting pictorial depth and the different gradients of tone, size, clarity, texture and so on.

- *Emphasis* – this also refers to the relationship between images, but is hierarchical rather than spatial. It is often not the simplicity or complexity in itself which is important but the amount of relevant detail.

- *Text parallels* – the relationship between the picture and its text.

The model Goldsmith has constructed is based on the interaction between the four factors identified and the three semiotic levels at which each factor can be considered.

	Levels		
Factors	syntactic	semantic	pragmatic
unity	1	2	3
location	4	5	6
emphasis	7	8	9
text parallels	10	11	12

This gives a total of 12 elements which it is proposed, contribute to the comprehensibility of supportive illustration. These elements are described in detail in the article and illustrated by examples of illustrations.

Goldsmith (1984)

Evelyn Goldsmith. *Research into illustration: an approach and a review.* Cambridge University Press, 1984.

This report presents a very detailed survey of research into illustration in the 15 years up to 1980. The research studies Goldsmith identifies fall into three broad categories: those relating to children; those relating to cross-cultural investigations; and a third group concerned mostly with understanding the perceptual and cognitive abilities of the viewer. The primary focus of the review is informative illustration, rather than the use of illustrations to enhance the attractiveness or the persuasiveness of a document. Goldsmith's book includes summaries of the major research studies, from which comparisons and general conclusions are drawn.

The most important consideration affecting the decision to use illustrations is whether or not the content of the text is visual. There is then a need to consider the relevance of the illustration, the level of visual literacy of the reader, and cultural factors. Goldsmith notes that:

> As far as can be judged from the literature, the ability to distinguish the bounds of images is universally very high, given an acceptable level of

visual acuity ... and any failure to understand a picture is unlikely to
occur at this level.

Detailed line drawings rather than stylised drawings or photographs
have been shown to be the most readily recognisable form of
depiction, and it is unlikely that anyone from about nine years
upwards is unlikely to experience any difficulty with this element,
unless the depiction is particularly obscure. A number of aspects were
identified as needing careful attention if the picture is for young
children or people unused to pictorial communication. These include
familiarity with the depicted object; a tendency to literal and specific
interpretation; insensitivity to the constraints imposed and support
offered by context; and implied motion by devices such as speed lines
has to be learned.

Goldsmith points out that there is a remarkable degree of concensus
among researchers as to the most effective devices for getting and
directing attention, including:

- Colour.

- Position.

- Size.

- Isolation.

- Complexity.

- Tonal contrast.

- Directionality.

- Implied motion.

These eight factors seem to be of prime importance when the
communication potential of a picture or series of pictures is being
considered, whoever the intended viewers may be. It seems however,
that while each of these factors has an attraction value, each may also
distract. At the time of the review, very little work had been done to
establish the relative weighting of these factors. Goldsmith notes that:
'in the absence of such information, all that can be said is that attention
can be focused by combining factors, or dissipated by allowing them
tocancel each other out'. There is evidence that, in a display containing
both text and pictures, the pictures will be the first to attract attention.

Beyond the adoption of a consistent method of presentation when relating text and illustration, natural scanning habits can be exploited to facilitate eye movements. In a horizontal display the eye moves to the right, in a vertical one it moves downwards.

Text clearly varies in the extent to which it lends itself to a pictorial form of expression.

Probably the first thing that needs to be taken into account when considering the relationship between text and picture is whether it is intended that one should replicate the other: and if not, then the proportion of the totalcommunication that each is expected tocontribute.

Finally, Goldsmith proposes that—with some modification—her model could be used in practice to determine the reasons why some illustrations fail to communicate as intended when subjected tofield tests.

Gordon and Sager (1985)

Daniel B Gordon and Naomi Sager. 'A method of measuring information in language, applied to medical texts'.
Information Processing and Management 21(4), 1985, 269-289.

This study set out to develop a series of quantitative measures of the information content of texts, based on the linguistic structure of sentences. Two contrasting types of text were used to develop the measures: narrative patient records (factual reports) and articles from the medical research literature (theoretical reports). Sentences from the patient records were analysed by computer (using the LSP natural-language processing system). Those from the medical research articles were analysed manually using the same methods of analysis.

The analysis employed the following counts and calculations based on courts of *words*, *operators* (that is articles, particles, prepositions or conjunctions) and *adjuncts* (a group of words that are of second rank in importance in a sentence):

1. the number of words in each sentence (an intuitive indicator of the amount and complexity of the information in a sentence)

2. the number of operators in each sentence (one measure of the amount of information in a sentence)

3. the number of words per operator (a rough inverse measure of the density of information in a sentence)

4. the number of operators in adjuncts (a measure of how complicated the local modifiers are in a sentence)

5. the number of operators not in adjuncts (a measure of how complicated the logical structure of the sentence is as a whole)

6. the maximum depth of nesting (including adjuncts)

7. the maximum depth of resting not including adjuncts

8. finally, the product of (2) and (6) above as a measure of overall complexity

The study demonstrated that a linguistically-based analysis of text sentences can lead to quantitative measures of the amount and complexity of the information they contain. Furthermore, within an individual piece of text the measure of overall complexity seems to reflect perceived differences in the complexity of the information.

Guthrie (1988)

John T Guthrie. 'Locating information in documents: examination of a cognitive model'.
Reading Research Quarterly 23(2), 1988, 178-199.

Being literate in today's society requires competence in complicated reading tasks. The purpose of reading documents, especially in work settings, is often to locate specific facts rather than to acquire or recall knowledge as is usually demanded in the classroom. Yet this is a skill many readers do not have. According to the 1986 National Assessment of Educational Progress (NAEP), about 50 per cent of American high school graduates fail reading tasks that require them to match three elements in a questionnaire with three elements in a corresponding source document (such as a railway timetable). When the number of elements was increased to six, only 11 per cent of the graduates were able to cope.

Guthrie suggests that performance in document search tasks depends heavily on analytical reasoning and proposes a five-stage cognitive processing model to account for performance:

- Forming a clear goal.

- Selecting an informational category.

- Extracting the relevant information.

- Integrating new information.

- Recycling until the goal is met.

Guthrie then presents experimental evidence from work with a group of 26 college students, to support this model. The results suggest that category selection is particularly important for good performance on document searching tasks. This reinforces the need for mutually exclusive categories, clearly described and presented. Many of the college students who took part in the experiments did not make use of the most efficient or effective strategies for obtaining the information they needed, possibly because they did not encounter well-formed documents in which using optimal strategies would really pay off.

Finally, the author questions the use of prose recall tests as a useful (and most used) measure of text comprehension, since there is a low level of correlation between the ability to recall and the ability to locate information.

Guthrie and Kirsch (1987)

John T Guthrie and Irwin S Kirsch. 'Distinctions between reading comprehension and locating information in text'.
Journal of Educational Psychology 79(3), 1987, 220-227.

Laboratory measures of reading comprehension are usually based on text recall. However, locating information such as facts, names or numbers is a very different task from being able to recall it later, and it seems reasonable to suppose that the cognitive processes underlying information location and recall are different in any case.

Guthrie and Kisch investigated this expectation by working with a group of 45 electrical engineers and technicians. The authors estimate that electronics technicians spend around 398 minutes a month comprehending information in manuals and another 217 minutes locating information.

The group was set a series of reading tasks tested their reading skills in four areas:

- Reading comprehension.

- Locating information in technical articles.

- Locating information in technical manuals.

- Locating information in schematic diagrams.

Factor analysis revealed two factors: one relating to comprehension and the other to locating information. The relationship between these two factors is complex. In the case of technical articles, locating information was shown to be independent of comprehension. However, in the more highly formalised document types (manuals and schematic diagrams) the two factors were indistinguishable.

Haberlandt And Graesser (1989)

Karl Haberlandt and Arthur C Graesser. 'Buffering new information during reading'.
Discourse Processes 12(4), 1989, 479-494.

A report of an experiment, conducted on undergraduates, into the possible relationship between reading speed, working memory and word type.

The key findings of this are that *word type* plays a significant role in cognitive load and that reading times:

- Increase more steeply for nouns than for function words.

- Increase more steeply for nouns than verbs.

- Increase more steeply for new nouns than for repeated nouns.

- Increase with the cumulative number of new arguments per sentence.

These findings are discussed in terms of a model of reading in which the availability of adequate buffer memory is a key factor.

Hans and Levine (1985)

George J Hans and Martin G Levine. 'The effect of background knowledge on the reading comprehension of second language learnings.'
Foreign Language Annals 18(5), 1985, 391-398.

This study involved research with 90 high school students who were studying Spanish as a foreign language. They were tested for their knowledge of baseball and 52 were classified as having limited knowledge while 38 had a high level of knowledge.

The students were given an authentic newspaper account in Spanish of a baseball game and were tested for comprehension using a 12-item multiple choice test consisting of explicit and implicit questions.

The results of the test showed that background knowledge was a significant factor that affected reading comprehension across two types of question. Moreover, background knowledge was found to be more important to comprehension than language skills.

Harris Research Centre (1985)

Home Improvements Booklets Survey.
Harris Research Centre, 1985.

Interviews, comprising open-ended questions, were held with 62 householders to guage their reaction to a booklet produced by the Department of the Environment on home improvements.

Most of the findings are specific to the booklet being tested. Those of general interest relate to the use of illustrations in public documents. Eight out of ten people made unprompted comments of approval of the illustrations, but two out of ten were critical of the use of cartoons. When prompted, six out of ten people found the illustrations amusing and suitable and thought they helped to explain the text. About one in 20 thought that they were unnecessary and did nothing to explain the text.

Hartley (1981)

James Hartley. 'Eighty ways of improving instructional texts'.
IEEE Transactions on Professional Communication 24(1), 1981, 17-27.

This paper presents suggestions for improving educational documents under three main headings: prose materials; graphic materials; and typographic considerations. Each suggestion is based on research findings and references are given to this research wherever possible.

The suggestions are directed specifically to educational texts and may not be directly transferable to the design of public documents.

Hartley (1982)

James Hartley. 'Information mapping: a critique'.
Information Design Journal 3(1), 1982, 51-58.

The Information Mapping concept for structured writing is described and reviewed. It is a set of procedures, developed by Robert Horn in the mid-1960s, to help writers to organise and to display their text. Information maps for self-instructional books are conspicuous for their physical features, the format in which they present information. An equally important aspect of such information maps, however, is that the content itself is selected and organised according to a set of underlying principles. The method of presentation and the organisation of content, may be thought of as the visible and invisible features of a mapped page.

Various difficulties in accepting the system are listed and solutions are suggested. It also notes the problems of evaluating the system and comments on some of the research which purports to do so.

Hartley (1984)

James Hartley. 'The role of colleagues and text editing programmes in improving text'.
IEEE Transactions on Professional Communication 27(1), 1984, 42-44.

The author compares the comments made on his article 'Eighty ways of improving instructional text' (see Hartley 1981) by nine of his colleagues with the suggestions for improving the article provided by a series of computer-based text editing procedures (developed by

Lawrence Frase at Bell Laboratories). The software applied in the study included checks for the following common problems:

- Spelling errors.
- Punctuation errors.
- Word repetition.
- Split infinitives.
- Passives.
- Abstract words.
- Sexist phrases.
- Awkward words or phrases.
- Readability scores.
- Sentence length (average and ranges).
- Sentence types (percentage of simple, complex, compound and compound complex sentences).

Hartley concludes that text-editing programmes are more thorough and systematic than humans, but cover a much narrower range of activities. Humans are more variable but offer a wider range of comments including textual comments as well as suggestions for improvement. He argues that both forms of editing have their usefulness, with computers able to take over much of the routine.

Hartley and others (1980a)
James Hartley, S Bartlett and A Branthwaite. 'Underlining can make a difference'.
Journal of Educational Research 73(4), 1980, 218-224.

Most people believe intuitively that underlining words or phrases in a text should help in learning and absorbing information. For the same reason printers use italic or bold type to indicate emphasis. Yet much of research prior to this study had failed to demonstrate that the use of underlining, either by teacher or student, has any effect on how students learn.

In this study sixth grade school children were given underlined or normal text and their recall tested using a cloze procedure.

The study found that both immediate and in the long-term (a week later) recall was significantly better in children who had studied underlined text and that this result was not obtained at the expense of other items of information in the text.

Hartley and others (1980b)

James Hartley, Mark Trueman and Peter Burnhill. 'Some observations on producing and measuring readable writing'.
Programmed Learning and Educational Technology 17(3), 1980, 164-174.

A piece of technical text was rewritten to a set of brief guidelines covering various textual, typographical and procedural aspects. The resulting text was then evaluated using a number of commonly used techniques.

Readability formulae – seven were used (Forecast; Lensear Write; Farr-Jenkins Patterson; Flesch; Powers revision of Flesch; Kincaid's revision of Flesch; and McElroy's FOG). The results from the application of formulae also predicted different levels of difficulty, and each of them gave inconsistent measures of difficulty for different samples of text.

Cloze tests The results indicated that two of the revised versions were easier to comprehend but not the third.

Personal judgments of readers on which of the texts was easier to read in terms of its layout, its paragraphs and its sentences.

Location of difficulties by readers pointing out where they thought *others* might have difficulties. The results from this were sparse but very informative.

The authors conclude that readability formulae can be applied quickly but that the results need to be used 'with a pinch of salt'. They found it more helpful to ask users of the text to make comparisons between the original and revised texts. The technique they recommend, though, was to ask users where they thought *others* might find points of difficulty in the text. This they found was a 'quick, easy and helpful method of assessing readability'.

Hartley and others (1984)

James Hartley, Mark Trueman and A Rodgers. 'The effects of verbal and numerical quantifiers on questionnaire responses'.
Applied Ergonomics 15(2), 1984, 149-155.

A number of researchers have tried to assign numerical equivalents to expressions of frequency such as 'always', 'often', 'occasionally', 'seldom' and 'never' (these expressions are generally referred to as *verbal quantifiers*). This paper summarises the results to date and describes three experiments designed to investigate whether or not such frequency scales achieve equal interval measurement when they are used in questionnaires.

In the first experiment, subjects were asked to give percentage equivalents to three sets of supposedly equivalent verbal quantifiers. The responses differed significantly.

In the second experiment, the subjects were asked to complete different versions of the same questionnaire to see whether the three sets of verbal quantifiers produced equivalent responses in a more concrete situation. They did not.

In the third experiment, the subjects completed one version of the questionnaire with a set of verbal quantifiers and two versions with different numerical quantifiers ('half of the time' or '50 per cent of the time'). The verbal quantifiers gave the same results as in the previous experiments. The numerical quantifiers gave different but consistent results.

The authors conclude that numerical quantifiers are probably more useful and less open to subjective interpretation than verbal ones and should be used whenever possible.

Hartley and others (1985)

James Hartley and others. 'Readability and prestige in scientific journals'.
Journal of Information Science 14(2), 1988, 69-75.

A review of ten studies looking at possible relationships between the degree of difficulty of journal articles and the prestige accorded to the articles and their authors. Readability measures were used to measure difficulty. The limitations of these measures are acknowledged, but not seen as totally invalidating the studies. Opinion polls and citation analyses were used to measure prestige.

The authors found that the results were not very conclusive, as most of the findings were not significant statistically. As a consequence they conclude that this sort of research cannot be pursued much further without the development of better measuring instruments.

Hartley and Trueman (1983)

James Hartley and Mark Trueman. 'The effects of headings in text on recall, search and retrieval'.
British Journal of Educational Psychology 53(2), 1983, 205-214.

Previous research into the role of headings had focused primarily on their value in assisting the recall of information after reading a text. The series of nine experiments reported in this article attempts partly to replicate earlier studies, and partly to build on them. These experiments focused on three separate variables:

- The use of headings in two different types of reading – reading for recall and reading for the retrieval of information.

- The effectiveness of headings in two different positions – marginal or embedded in the text.

- The effectiveness of two different types of headings – statements or questions.

The subjects were 14-15 year-old comprehensive school pupils of a range of ability levels and the text used was an adapted *Sunday Observer Magazine* article. Overall, the results showed that headings did improve both the recall and retrieval of information. However, neither the position nor the nature of the headings seemed to have any effect. By contrast earlier studies by the author had shown that it was easier to retrieve from texts with marginal headings (as opposed to embedded ones), and that headings in the form of questions help less able readers.

Hartley and Trueman (1985)

James Hartley and Mark Trueman. 'A research strategy for text designers: the role of headings'.
Instructional Science 14(2), 1985, 99-157.

This article presents results from a series of experiments with 14/15 year-olds into the role of headings in the comprehension of written material. The first series investigated the effects of three main variables:

- The position of headings (marginal or embedded).

- The form of headings (statements or questions).

- The nature of the task which the heading seeks to assist (free recall; searching unfamiliar text; or retrieval from familiar text).

The results indicate that the position of the headings, whether marginal or embedded, had little effect. Headings were, however, shown to facilitate recall, information search and retrieval performance.

The experiments were then replicated using a different text in a further four experiments with 11/12 year-olds. This time, the headings aided the 11/12 year-olds' search and retrieval, but not their recall. A further experiment with 14/15 year-olds, using the second text, showed that headings once again aided recall. Hartley and Trueman suggest that the variation may be the result of a developmental trend in children's capacity to use headings as recall devices.

The final set of three experiments tested whether headings presented as questions were more helpful to lower-ability readers than headings in the form of statements. No significant differences were found.

Hartley and Trueman (1986)

James Hartley and Mark Trueman. 'The effects of typographic layout of cloze-type tests on reading comprehension scores'.
Journal of Research in Reading 9(2), 1986, 116-124.

Experiments were conducted with 10-15 year old schoolchildren to test two different ways of presenting cloze-type tests

- Missing words represented by dashes, with one dash for each missing letter. Answers were to be written in the text.

- Missing words represented by lines whose length indicated the length of the missing word. Answers were to be written in boxes to the right of the text.

In the first experiment, with 334 10-14 year olds, the only significant difference was that girls performed better than boys on both versions of the test. This was confirmed by the second test, with 287 14-15 year olds, which also found that pupils performed significantly better in tests where dashes were used to indicate the missing words.

Although the details in the article do not give enough information to draw definite conclusions about the layout of other documents, such as forms, the results do show that different designs of similar documents produce very different effects.

Hayes and Flower (1980)

John R Hayes and Linda S Flower. 'Writing as problem solving'.
Visible Language 14(4), 1980, 388-399.

Over a period of several years, Hayes and Flower analysed protocols of writers who were asked to think aloud as they completed their writing task and were tape recorded as they did so. The resulting tapes were then analysed). From their research, the authors drew the following conclusions about the writing process:

- Writing is goal directed.

- Writing processes are hierarchically organised.

- Editing appears to take precedence over all other writing processes in the sense that it may interrupt the other processes at any time.

- Writing processes may be organised 'recursively'; for example, when the editing process identifies a major fault in the text, it may invoke the writing process in an effort to correct the fault.

• Writing goals may be modified as writing proceeds.

Hedges (1988)

Alan Hedges. *Social Security Literature.*
Department of Health and Social Security. 1988

In April 1988, the Department of Health and Social Security introduced new style, 16 page, A4 claim forms. These were designed to fulfil the function of leaflets (conveying information) as well as forms (collecting information). This research was commissioned to assess public reaction to this new format and to see whether it influenced people's perception of the Department. Depth interviews were held with 80 members of the public and eight advice workers who advise the public on social security benefits.

The report contains a large number of detailed comments on the specific leaflets being tested. More general findings were that:

• The approach of targeting leaflets at specific client groups (pensioners, unemployed people, people bringing up children) worked well.

• Well-spaced out text was liked and easy to read.

• Users liked the combined leaflet and form format.

• The length of the forms was off-putting.

Hedges and Ritchie (1986)

Alan Hedges and Jane Ritchie. *Designing documents for people.*
Social and Community Planning Research for the Department of Health and Social Security, 1986.

The main aim of this research was to identify what people need and want from printed communications issued by government departments. More particularly it was designed to answer three specific questions:

• How do people respond to and use benefit documents?

- What kind of information do people need about benefits and how can these needs best be met?

- How effective are existing DHSS benefit documents in meeting people's requirements?

Hedges and Ritchie focused on two quite different client groups: people who were approaching retirement and people receiving, or eligible for, supplementary benefit. The research was conducted in six discrete waves carried out between 1984 and 1986. During the first five waves of the research, information from clients was collected through a total of 24 group discussions and 44 unstructured exploratory interviews (involving a total of 183 people). At the sixth wave of research, five matched samples, each of 50 people, were given a structured questionnaire to test reactions to five different versions of a document. These were supplemented by in-depth interviews with a further 27 people.

Attitudes, expectations and motivations
In general, it was found that people have very low expectations of official documents. They expect them to be difficult to understand, uninteresting and therefore unlikely to supply answers to specific problems. Not surprisingly, therefore, they are more likely to talk to another person (most usually a friend, relative or colleague) than they are to consult a printed document.

General information needs
In addition to probing people's expectations and motivations, the group discussions and interviews also focused on a number of aspects of the need for information. This showed that users of DHSS documents generally preferred personalised information: that is, information specific to their own circumstances. The fact that people sought information from other people rather than from documents was found to be exacerbated by the 'invisibility' of much written information. The study revealed a very low level of awareness of benefit literature, and often the display and distribution systems are inadequate.

Claimants were asked how they retained their benefit documents. By far the most common behaviour was to keep papers for so long and then to have a 'clear out'. Decisions on whether to retain documents were made on two different bases: if they were likely to be relevant or of interest at a later stage; or if the documents indicated that they ought to be kept.

On the basis of these findings on general information needs, Hedges and Ritchie offer some practical recommendations:

- Documents that are a natural focus of interest to claimants (eg order books, entitlement notices) should be used as the main information carriers.

- Folders or wallets may help people to locate their benefit documents more easily and lead to greater use of written communications.

- The relevance of a document and/or the need to retain it should be immediately clear.

Specific benefit information needs
In the main, people do not need general explanations about a bureaucratic system—they simply want to know how the system applies to them and their specific needs change during the course of the claim process. Before claiming, people need to know whether they are eligible and how to go about making a claim. They also need reassurance that claiming is an acceptable and legitimate thing to do and that it will not be a humiliating or an undignified process. At the time of the claim, the most important piece of information is 'how much will I get' or 'am I getting the right amount'. After becoming claimants people need to know whether there is anything else they could claim, how changes of circumstances affect benefit entitlement and what to do if the level of benefit received changes suddenly.

The research also showed that if people can see the logic or sense of a written requirement or instruction, they are much more likely to register it and, more importantly, to internalise it.

Broad principles of document design
On the basis of the research a number of broad principles were identified for document design. People want access to material relating

as directly as possible to their own situation,without first ploughing through a mass of irrelevant information. This requires good signposting within documents, case-based information and selective mailing of documents. Hedges and Ritchie propose two general principles. First, explanations must be put in places where people are likely to look—entitlement notices, order books or giros—not just in bulky leaflets which they may either not see or not read. Secondly, trouble should be taken to relate the explanations as closely as possible to the circumstances of likely claimants.

Literature intended for the general public should be designed to reinforce the grapevines through which information is gathered—this may mean separate documents aimed at claimants and at professionals. There is also a need to help people overcome any emotional barriers—public documents should give the impression that the recipient is a valued person and has a right to his or her entitlement.

Hill and Mayon-White (1987)

Alison Hill and Richard T Mayon-White. 'A telephone survey to evaluate an Aids leaflet campaign'.
Health Education Journal 46(3), 1987, 127-129.

Leaflets on AIDS and how the HIV virus is spread were sent by direct mail to homes in Oxford in April 1986. A telephone survey to evaluate the effectiveness of the campaign was conducted by two skilled female interviewers before and after the leaflet drop. Telephone numbers were selected by determining a random position on a randomly chosen page in the local telephone directory. All the calls were made after 5 pm.

Of a sample of 134 people in the city who were questioned in a series of follow-up telephone interviews, only 51 (38 per cent) recalled receiving the leaflet at all. These people were more likely to be in social classes I and II and to read a quality daily or Sunday newspaper. The telephone survey further revealed a number of problems with a distribution of the leaflets which may have contributed to the low success of the initiative. As a research tool, however, the telephone survey proved to be quick to plan and relatively cheap to implement.

It was concluded that unsupported leafleting has only marginal impact and is not an effective medium for health education.

Holland (1981)

V Melissa Holland. *Psycholinguistic alternatives to readability formulas* (Document Design Project Technical Report 12).
American Institutes for Research, 1981.

Even if the statistical and validation problems of readability formulas are overcome, readability can never be a precise yardstick of how comprehensible, usable or effective a public document is. Nor can the formulae provide a prescription for writing and revising documents.

In this report the author reviews some psycholinguistic research that challenges the assumptions underlying readability formulae. This research indicates that there are sources of comprehension difficulty in words and sentences which are unrelated to their length and frequency. These sources include organisation within and between paragraphs; text content and function; graphical layout; and reader characteristics.

Holland concludes that 'accumulated' evidence suggests to us that readability level can appropriately serve only as a filter, to decide which texts are not acceptable. It is not appropriate as a ruler of effectiveness or as a design goal.

Holland and Redish (1981)

V Melissa Holland and Janice C Redish. *Strategies for understanding forms and other public documents* (Document Design Project Technical Report 13).
American Institutes for Research, 1981.

This report addresses itself to public forms as a particular type of discourse, and shows how they are similar to other types of text, where they differ, and how we can begin to understand forms as a type of text. Holland and Redish propose that forms have unique characteristics and that they require processes and strategies that differ in systematic ways from those needed to understand recreational reading or educational texts.

In an attempt to understand these strategies the authors carried out an experiment where subjects were asked to speak aloud all their thoughts and reasoning as they filled in an application form for a job in a government department. These protocols were tape recorded and the tapes analysed. The protocols were then compared for the subjects who completed the form in such a way that it would be well received with those who failed to do so.

As a result of the protocol analysis a number of strategies were identified and assigned to three levels:

- *Decoding strategies*, where the user devotes attention to the meaning of words or ambiguous sentences.

- *Form-using strategies*, in which the user goes beyond words and sentences and attempts to relate items across the form or to draw on personal knowledge to clarify the meaning of items (see also Flower and others 1980 for a description of the 'scenario principle').

- *Global strategies*, that arise as the reader locates the document in a societal and institutional context. Here the reader is looking for the intention behind the questions, predicting how answers will be interpreted, and displaying an awareness of the rhetorical situation and the text type.

When the protocols of the 'successful' form-fillers were compared with the 'unsuccessful' ones, a number of points emerged. The 'unsuccessful' form-fillers were far more likely to be concerned primarily with decoding strategies. In fact, they were very likely to make no global strategy comments at all and to ignore the intent of the form. This was reflected in other behaviour. The 'successful' form-fillers were likely to find a place to put down any piece of information they thought would be useful. By contrast the 'unsuccessful' ones were more constrained by the form, and failed to give potentially useful information if it was not specifically asked for.

The authors suggest that forms should be designed and written so that they encourage users to employ form-using and global strategies.

Holland and Rose (1980)

V Melissa Holland and Andrew M Rose. *Understanding instructions with complex conditions* (Document Design Project Technical Report 5). American Institutes for Research, 1980.

Prior research had looked at the ease with which subjects were able to understand a range of conditional sentences, from the simple, 'If A and B then do X' to the more difficult, 'If not either not A or B do X'. Many guidelines on writing public documents suggest that the more complex conditional sentences should not be presented as prose. The aim of this study was to identify the factors making these expressions difficult to understand and to determine the level of complexity at which alternatives to prose should be considered.

Holland and Rose begin by reviewing both the theoretical background and relevant prior research and conclude that little is known about what the factors are, and at what levels, and in which combinations, they contribute to the difficulty of complex conditional sentences.

In their own research, the authors looked at how subjects comprehended multi-category sentences of the form 'If you are X or Y', where X is a coordinate compound such as 'If you are male, or both married and not employed'. In all, 96 different instructions were tested on 40 adult subjects. The instructions were presented one at a time on a computer screen and the speed and accuracy of responses were recorded by the system. The results of the study are complex and almost impossible to summarise. However, in bare essentials, they show that:

- Each of the major sentence dimensions, number of categories, sentence type, and-or and negatives, seemed to contribute to the overall difficulty of the sentences.

- The dimensions seemed to be interactive in their effects

- when connections between categories were implicit and not explicitly stated (eg. if A, B, C or D) subjects interpreted them as 'and' rather than as 'or'.

- The use of semicolons exacerbated processing difficulties.

- The speed and accuracy of response were related, that is subjects both took longer to respond and were more likely to respond incorrectly to certain constructions.

An important finding was that, where incorrect responses were given, they were overwhelmingly more likely to be negative replies where they should have been positive than they were likely to be the other way round. The authors suggest this indicates that where subjects have difficulty understanding a complex series of categories they assume that it does not apply to them.

In drawing out the practical implication of their results, Holland and Rose identify a number of specific sentence constructions that are suitable for general use. However, in view of the complexity of their findings, the authors conclude that:

- The safest recommendation to make is that all complex instructions should be experimentally evaluated before being included in any document designed for public use.

Holland and Rose (1981)

V Melissa Holland and Andrew Rose. *A comparison of prose algorithms for presenting complex instructions* (Document Design Project Technical Report 17).
American Institutes for Research, 1981.

Results of earlier studies (including Rose and Cox 1980) have shown that conditional instructions (if 'X' then do 'Y') become increasingly difficult to process as the structure becomes more complex. This study was designed to investigate whether this difficulty can be alleviated by presenting conditional instructions in formats other than prose. The hypothesis was that the major sources of difficulty—disjunction (or), negation, hierarchical structure, and ambiguous punctuation would be eliminated by the use of algorithms.

Holland and Rose addressed four specific questions in this study:

- What kinds of logical or syntactic difficulties in prose processing might an algorithm alleviate?
- How does performance compare between two forms of algorithms a) flowcharts and b) lists of steps ('jump' questions)?

- How does a reader's performance on first exposure to algorithms compare with performance on prose instructions?

- Which format does the average reader prefer for complex conditional instructions?

The results of the study show that people generally processed lists and flowcharts faster and more accurately than prose. Indeed algorithms were almost error-free on occasion. Prose seemed to be more sensitive both to logic and structure changes in the stimulus instructions than algorithms. So that responses to prose become slower and more error-prone as the complexity of the instruction increases. Algorithms, on the other hand, seemed to have a relatively constant speed and accuracy, regardless of complexity. Lists were slower to process than were flowcharts, but they were equally accurate.

When the results of the initial trial were compared it was clear that response times for prose remained relatively uniform from the first to the fourth exposure. In comparison, the lists and flowcharts had very high response times on the first exposure—often three or four times the norms for the main experiment. These response times decreased rapidly with successive exposures. In addition, flowcharts were often misinterpreted when they were first presented, whilst lists seemed to be easier to follow and were highly accurate from the beginning.

Subjects overwhelmingly preferred algorithms. Flowcharts were ranked first two and a half times as often as lists; and lists three times as often as prose. However, it must be noted that these preference ratings were obtained at the end of the experiment. Had they been obtained at the outset the results would almost certainly have been different. Thus, in general algorithms were easier and more accurate to process than prose, except where the reader had no prior experience of them. Where the readers were inexperienced, algorithms of both types (lists and flowcharts) were processed more slowly and, in addition, flowcharts were likely to be misinterpreted.

Of the two types of algorithm, flowcharts seemed to be processed more quickly than lists. There was, however, no difference in the accuracy. As already noted, lists were far less likely than flowcharts to be misinterpreted when a reader encountered them for the first time.

The authors conclude, therefore, that where flowcharts are used they should be accompanied by brief explanatory notes.

Holmes (1987)

A Holmes. 'Understanding legislation drafted in plain English'. Quoted in:
Plain English and the Law.
Law Reform Commission of Victoria Report No 9, 1987.

Lawyers and law students were given one of two versions of pieces of written legislation: the original draft and a 'translated' plain English version. They were then asked to apply the legislation to a number of hypothetical legal cases.

There was no significant difference in the level of accuracy of answers between those using the original draft and those using the plain English version. There was, however, a difference in the length of time taken to complete the task. The plain English version took between a third and a half the time that the original version took to complete.

Horowitz (1985)

Rosalind Horowitz. 'Text patterns' (in two parts).
Journal of Reading 28(5/6), 1985, 448-455 and 534-541.

Horowitz reviews the literature on readers' use of text patterns to process writing and concludes that experienced readers are aware of the overall structure of texts, and use this to comprehend and organise their recall. Poor readers, on the other hand, are unaware of the structure and therefore unable to use it.

Horowitz identifies five text structures which are commonly present in school texts:

- *Temporal* (eg 'George eats garlic at 5 pm. Suddenly Georgette threatens to leave George. Shortly thereafter George promises he won't eat garlic. By 6 pm Georgette reconfirms her love for George').

- *Attributional* (eg 'George checked the counters for his favourite foods: onions, ribs, lima beans, and garlic').

- *Adversative* (eg 'Although George eats garlic, Georgette does not').

- *Compare-contrast* (eg 'The cause of the break-up is that George eats garlic').

- *Problem-solution* (eg 'The problem is that Georgette dislikes garlic. The solution is that George gives it up').

Horowitz goes on to point out the implications of this research for teaching reading. She also makes the point that anything which helps to make the text structure more obvious can aid comprehension.

Hukin and others (1986)

TN Hukin and others. 'Prescriptive linguistics and plain English: the case of 'whiz-deletions''.
Visible Language 20(2), 1986, 174-187.

At one stage, readability formulas were offered as a way of improving written texts. As their limitations became apparent, writing guidelines and design principles have been offered in their place. The authors of this article note that these guidelines and design principles are themselves now subject to criticism.

Guidelines for document designers, published by the American Institutes for Research, is a highly acclaimed plain English handbook. In producing the guidelines, the authors drew on relevant research and took great care to point out that there will be exceptions to almost every guideline. Even so, the authors of this article show that at least one of the guidelines is regularly broken even in good writing. The guideline studies was 'Avoid whiz-deletions'. This is described as follows:

> In English, many subordinate clauses are introduced by the words 'which is', 'who were', 'that are' etc. These 'little words' help make the structure of the sentence clear to the reader – they make it easier for the reader to understand how the subordinate clause relates to the rest of the sentence. Removing these 'little words' is called 'whiz-deletion'. 'whiz-deletion' can often make a sentence unclear or ambiguous; it can place a greater than necessary burden on the reader. Wherever possible, replace the missing 'which is', 'who was' etc.

The authors reviewed the psycholinguistic research that had been cited to support this guideline. Generally they found that it was not directly relevant. Therefore they looked at samples of both plain English and unsimplified writing to see how extensively reduced relative clauses, or 'whiz deletions', were used.

The samples of plain English were taken from *How plain English works for business: twelve case studies*, published by the U.S. Department of Commerce. This collection was chosen because it contains writing samples that are considered models of plain English, and because it was edited by the same people who wrote *Guidelines for document designers*.

For every sample of plain English in this book, they counted:

• The total number of words.

• The number of reduced relative clauses.

• The number of full relative clauses.

In all cases full relative clauses were very rare, and reduced relative clauses were eight times as likely to be used.

Broadening their survey, they also looked at randomly chosen samples of good, but unsimplified writing from a variety of published sources. They found that full relative clauses were four times less common than reduced ones.

A detailed analysis of the sample documents showed that reduced relative clauses almost never made a sentence unclear or ambiguous. In fact, on the contrary, they more often reduced ambiguity. Other identified advantages of using reduced relative clauses were that they:

• Promote better sentence rhythm.

• Make complex sentences easier to parse and thus easier to understand.

• Can reduce the emphasis on one part of a sentence, so that another part can be emphasised.

The authors point out that, although they focused their attention on just one of the 25 guidelines in *Guidelines for document designers*, they could have selected a number of others instead, with similar findings.

The guideline to 'Use the active voice', for example was violated frequently in the documents surveyed—including the ten plain English ones.

Other guidelines that were often ignored were:

- Write short sentences.

- Avoid nouns created from verbs.

- Unstring noun strings.

International Standards Organisation (1984)

Development and principles for application of public information symbols (Technical Report 7239).
International Standards Organisation, 1984.

This report outlines design criteria which should be applied to the development of public information symbols. These criteria include the following:

- *Proportions of a symbol* – long, narrow forms are not as easily perceived as forms in which height and width are similar. A height to width ratio of 1:4 is the maximum recommended for use in public information symbols.

- *Symmetry* – symbols that are designed with left-right symmetry are more easily perceived.

- *Directional characteristics* – where symbols have either explicit or implicit directional characteristics, the direction should be shown by an arrow, with the symbol designed so that it allows reversal.

- *Solid or outline forms* – silhouette is more effective than outline. Solid forms should therefore be used in preference. If however, symbols in outline form must be used, the interior of the symbol should differ in colour or in pattern from that of the background.

- *Number of details* – the ratio of perimeter to area of the symbol should be minimised. Only details that contribute to better comprehension should be included.

- *Minimum dimension of significant details* – there should be 1mm of significant detail for every metre of viewing distance. Such details should also be drawn in lines of 0.5mm of line thickness for every metre of viewing distance.

- *Reproduction / reduction* – care should be taken at the design stage to produce originals that are suitable for significant reduction in size.

- *Negation* – if a concept can be conveyed either by a positive or a negative symbol, the positive image should be used.

- *Combination of symbols* – composite symbols should be formed from as few component elements as possible. Such composite symbols should be subject to the same testing as any other new symbol.

- *Interaction between symbols* – When symbols are designed it should be borne in mind that they are frequently displayed as a group and interaction can occur between adjacent symbols.

- *Apparent size* – where symbols are to be grouped the dimensions may have to be modified to compensate for any apparent perceptual inconsistency.

- *Symbol size* – to ensure that a symbol is conspicuous it needs to be at least 25mm for every metre of viewing distance. When conspicuity is of less importance, the size of the symbol can be smaller and still maintain good legibility. In such cases the symbol should be at least 12mm for every metre of viewing distance.

Jansen and Steehouder (1984)

Carel Jansen and Michael Steehouder. 'Improving the text of a public leaflet'. *Information Design Journal* 4(1), 1984, 10-18.

From this detailed case study of a Dutch government leaflet dealing with rent rebates the authors evolved a provisional set of eight criteria for evaluating the design of written public information:

- The text should reflect the reader's course of actions, and not merely describe any official rules and definitions.

- Instructions should always be simple and economical.

- Instructions should be easy to carry out.

- It should be obvious for the reader when certain rules apply.

- The text should guide the reader to passages which are relevant to his / her situation.

- The text should be written in a direct style.

- The language of the text should be simple.

- The text should accurately reflect the content of the official regulation.

Jansen and Steehouder maintain that leaflets are read for two reasons. Some people read them for general information while others will have specific questions to which they want answers. They believe that, in most instances, it will not be possible to write one leaflet to meet both these needs. Their eight criteria relate to leaflets written for the reader wanting specific information.

The experiment involved the testing of four different versions of the same text, which differed in the degree to which they met the eight criteria, and an interactive computer program. In total 761 subjects were given an imaginary case study and asked to find out how much rent subsidy the person would be entitled to. Those testing the computer program were all employees of the Twente University of Technology.

Overall only the 6.2 per cent of the subjects using the texts got the right answer. There was no significant difference in the performance of those using the three different prose texts, but the text composed of flowcharts proved to be significantly better than the other three with 15.1 per cent of subjects getting the right answer. Those using the computer program performed markedly better—34.3 per cent getting the right answer.

In an attempt to understand why a flowchart should increase comprehension as compared with prose, three subjects were given one of the texts used in the earlier experiment and were asked to 'think aloud' as they carried out the calculation.

This showed that the three subjects tended to use the prose text in a global rather than a precise manner. The precise information in the text was either left unread or it was only read after one or more unsuccessful tries to solve the problem.

Secondly the subjects tended to postpone some actions until they came to a passage where they needed the results of those actions. They then reconstructed the instruction from memory.

Finally the subjects often read passages that were irrelevant to the case study. Although the text contained sufficient cues (such as headings, underlinings) which indicated they could skip these passages, they were afraid to do so.

The authors suggest that, in addition to indicating that algoriths are likely to be more efficient than text, the research has identified a number of additional criteria for writing prose leaflets:

- The instructional character of the text should be stressed in the introductory passage.

- The text should be fragmented so that users have to complete each instruction before they can proceed with the next step.

- The leaflets should provide users with a form on which the results of the calculations and decisions can be noted in a convenient way.

Jonz (1989)

Jon Jonz. 'Textual sequence and second-language comprehension'. *Language Learning* 39(2), 1989, 207-237.

This study contrasts reading comprehension processes between native and non-native (undergraduate) speakers of English.

The key finding of this research is that non-native speakers of English appear to be less sensitive to the higher-level rhetorical features of text than native speakers. When confronted with difficult texts, they tend to rely more heavily on lower-level 'surface features', such as lexical and syntactic factors to facilitate comprehension.

Keenan (1984)

Stacey A Keenan. 'Effects of chunking and line length on reading efficiently'.
Visible Language 18(1), 1984, 61-80.

It is well established that people segment texts into meaningful phrases and sentences ('chunks') as they read. Many researchers have investigated whether reading can be facilitated by printing text so that it reflects the way in which it is read. Three main methods are used to do this:

- Printing only one phrase, or chunk, on each line.

- Printing extra space between chunks, but putting as many words and chunks per line as will fit.

- Using two lines for each chunk and printing extra space between chunks horizontally.

It has been shown that unskilled readers comprehend more and read faster with texts that are printed with one chunk per line. There is, however, conflicting evidence about whether chunked text aids comprehension for adult readers.

Using 24 subjects who were clerical staff at AT&T Bell Laboratories, Keenan set out to investigate whether text with one phrase or chunk per line aided reading in comprehension and proof-reading tasks. Contrary to her expectations, the chunked format was read significantly more slowly in all tasks. Keenan concludes that while both chunking and shorter line-lengths have positive effects on reading efficiency, the highly variable line-lengths that result from chunking have a stronger negative effect. It is suggested that this may also account for some of the conflicting findings from previous research.

Keller-Cohen (1987)

Deborah Keller-Cohen. 'Organisational contexts and texts: the redesign of the Midwest Bell telephone bill'.
Discourse Processes 10(4), 1987, 417-428.

In this paper, Keller-Cohen reviews some of the organisational factors which affected the redesign of a regional telephone bill at Midwest Bell. Financial considerations, organisational time frames, and employee training and experience were all shown to have a significant impact on the processes by which a new telephone bill was developed.

Midwest Bell set up a small committee consisting of Bell employees, customers and community figures to develop a new telephone bill as part of a commitment to improve customer services. Keller-Cohen observed the redesign process and interviewed many of the key players. It became apparent that several characteristics of the organisation played a role in shaping the final outcome. For example, th einitial poposals for the new design were based on the experience and intuition of Bell employees. There was little attempt to collate the views of customers at this preliminary stage. Many of the staff involved in the project had worked for many years at Bell and were therefore not easily able to bring fresh insights and perspectives to the problem. Keller-Cohen identified a further problem in that each version of the revised bill was tested using techniques from social psychology, rather than from psycholinquistics which might have been expected to reveal more immediately useful data. These factors, the overall budget for the project, and the very tight time frames involved did not allow for the possibility of any laboratory tests.

The author concludes that

> Often, one attempts to explain the shape, structure, or content of a text by looking inward, by relating elements later in the text with those found earlier. The process reported here argues against the validity of such an approach because it ignores the history of the text ... the 'biography' of a text. The organisational context is, in other words, an important source of variation in the construction of texts in institutional settings.

Kemper (1986)

S Kemper. 'Imitation of complex syntactic constructions by elderly adults'.
Applied Psycholinguistics 7, 1986, 277-288.

Few researchers have looked at how linguistic abilities change and develop with age, and this article begins with a brief review of the limited research findings that were available. Earlier work by the author[*] had demonstrated an age-related decline in the variability and accuracy of adults' use of grammatical and syntactic structures. This paper follows up this finding by looking specifically at embedded clauses.

---

[*]   D Kynette and S Kemper. Aging and the loss of grammatical forms a cross-sectional study of language performance. *Language and Communication* 6, 1986, 65-72.

A total of 32 subjects were used: 16 aged between 70 and 89 years and 16 between the ages of 30 and 49. All lived independently or with a spouse or relative in the same middle- class neighbourhood. All were in good health, had no significant sight or hearing defects, and spoke English as their native language. The two groups were also matched for the mean number of years of schooling they had completed.

Each subject was interviewed at home, and was read a total of 32 sentences in turn, and asked to repeat each sentence 'as exactly as possible', but correcting any ungrammatical or unacceptable ones. The sentences included four different types of embedded clause:

- *Gerunds* (eg 'Baking tires me out').
- *Wh- clauses* (eg 'What I did interested my grandchildren').
- *That- clauses* (eg 'That the cookies were brown surprised me').
- *Relative clauses* (eg 'The cookies that I baked were delicious').

For each type of clause a total of eight sentences were compiled. These varied in grammatical correctness, length of the sentence and position of the embedded clause.

The replies to each sentence were coded into four categories:

- *Exact imitations*, including those where the grammar was corrected.
- *Paraphrases*, preserving the semantic content, but altering the syntax.
- *Abridgements*, by omitting a clause or one or more phrases.
- *Others*, where both the semantic content and the syntax was altered.

The younger adults produced grammatically correct imitations of all 32 sentences. Their responses were not affected by the correctness, length or position of the embedded clauses.

On the other hand, elderly adults produced many more paraphrases, abridgements, and 'other' types of response. The sentences that caused greatest problems were those that had long embedded clauses at the beginning. The most common response to these was to give an abridgement and, in particular, to delete the embedded clause. Compared with their younger counterparts, the elderly had more difficulty with ungrammatical sentences; long embedded clauses; and embedded clauses at the beginning of the sentence.

Kemper concludes that, when taken together with the results of her earlier research, this study shows a pattern of linguistic deterioration in healthy adults over 70 years of age. She postulates that this may be due to memory limitations.

Kempson (1984)

Elaine Kempson. *The language of forms.*
Elaine Kempson for the Department of Health and Social Security, 1984.

This empirical study focused on user preferences relating to the language and presentation of selected public documents. The research involved 12 group discussions (involving a total of 96 people), backed up by 160 postal questionnaires. Participants were given a series of letters where the basic text was the same but the following changes were made:

Salutations – two thirds of participants did not notice whether there was a salutation or not. When they did, they liked the letter with a personalised salutation most, the one with no salutation least.

Pronouns – twice as many people preferred the use of 'he/she' as preferred 'they' to refer to a single child whose sex was unknown.

Contracted verbs – a third of participants could not see any difference between the letter which used contractions and the one which did not. On the whole, however, 50 per cent more people preferred the use of non-contracted verbs (do not) as preferred the contractions (don't).

Typeset compared with typewritten text – roughly equal numbers preferred each of the letters.

Kempson also investigated preferences regarding the wording of declarations and warnings on forms. Again participants were given a range of options to consider.

Declarations The majority of participants thought that a declaration should begin with 'I declare', should include the phrase 'to the best of my knowledge' and should say that the information is 'true' rather than 'true and complete'. The option which met these criteria was:

> I declare that the information I have given is true to the best of my knowledge.

189

A quarter of group discussion participants said that declarations made them frightened or anxious, nearly a half said they made them more careful. They had no effect at all on nearly a third of participants.

Warnings Nine out of ten participants thought that there should be a warning on forms. The most common reason (given by half of them) was that they thought that they ought to be warned if there was a possibility of prosecution for giving false information. However almost a half of participants said that printed warnings had no effect on them at all. Elderly people were more likely to find them frightening. As to the wording of warnings, participants thought that they should include either 'deliberately' or 'knowingly' and should use the phrase 'may be prosecuted' rather than 'may be committing a criminal offence' or 'we may take you to court'. The option which met these criteria was:

> If you deliberately give false information you may be prosecuted.

Kern (1980)

Richard P Kern. *Usefulness of readability formulas for achieving army readability objectives: research and state-of-the-art applied to the army's problems.*
US Army Research Institute for the Behavioural and Social Sciences, 1980.

This report was prepared to help the United States army evaluate the usefulness of readability formulae for identifying material that is suitable for readers at a given reading level.

It concludes, after reviewing the research literature, that

- Readability formulae do not predict comprehension and cannot be used to match material to reader.
- Rewriting to lower the formula reading score does not increase comprehension.
- Requiring that text be written to a particular readability level focuses attention on meeting the score requirement rather than organising the material to meet the readers' information needs.

Kerr (1983)

Scott Kerr. *Making ends meet: an investigation into the non-claiming of supplementary pensions.*
Bedford Square Press, 1983.

A book reporting the findings of a series of related studies conducted over the period 1976-1982 to find out why some pensioners do not claim supplementary pensions. In particular, it focused on the factors differentiating those who do and those who do not claim. This is in contrast to earlier published research which looked solely at why pensioners do not claim. One of the factors investigated was lack of knowledge, either of entitlement or the application process. Earlier research indicated that this was one of the most frequently cited reasons for not claiming means-tested benefits.

A series of 92 depth interviews of eligible non-claimants in receipt of rebates showed that attitude was a far more important barrier to claiming means-tested benefits than lack of knowledge. At a very basic level, the benefit was not seen as a 'right'. Pensioners expectations of the level of income they needed were often very low, and the connotations of applying—that is asking for help—were unacceptable, and the expected outcomes of applying—the potential insult to the family—were unacceptable.

These attitudinal factors combined with the multiple handicaps associated with old age. These handicaps included reduced mobility, poor health, low levels of confidence or ability to articulate, poor vision and hearing, and possibly mental confusion and disorientation.

Kirby and Gordon (1988)

John R Kirby and Christopher J Gordon. 'Text segmenting and comprehension: effects of reading and information processing abilities'.
British Journal of Educational Psychology 58(3), 1988, 287-300.

The complex process of reading can be disentangled into a number of distinct text-processing activities. At the most fundamental level, reading involves visual and phonological analysis followed by word identification. Beyond this basic level of word recognition, other levels of analysis come into play, decoding the syntax and extracting meaning.

Syntactic analysis allows the reader to break up a stream of text into chunks—a smaller number of higher-order units, corresponding roughly to phrases or clauses. This process is a prerequisite for skilled reading because it allows the reader to transform a sentence into more manageable units which lie within the limits of working memory.

This study tests the hypothesis that segmenting text into appropriate syntactic units improves comprehension, especially in the case of readers with poor comprehension but adequate vocabulary. The authors conducted a series of tests on a group of 352 primary school children (Grades 6-8) to explore this hypothesis. The experimental design involved manipulating texts into appropriate and inappropriate segments, and then testing for readability.

Inappropriate segments
> Michael was born in an industrial
> > city in Northern
> > > England where he spent the
> > > > early years of his life.

Appropriate segments
> Michael was born
> > in an industrial city
> > > in Northern England
> > > > where he spent the early years
> > > > > of his life.

The results indicated that poor comprehenders, regardless of their vocabulary skills, benefited from appropriate segmenting. Kirby and Gordon suggest that syntax analysis may be a 'bottleneck' for these readers.

Kirsch and Jungeblut (1986)

Irwin S Kirsch and Ann Jungeblut. *Literacy: profiles of America's young adults* (final report).
National Assessment of Educational Progress, Princeton, New Jersey, 1986.

In the spring of 1985, the National Assessment of Educational Progress

(NAEP) conducted a survey to develop new perspectives on the literacy skills of young Americans aged between 21 and 25 years. The survey stressed the complexity and diversity of literary tasks in American society rather than using a simplistic single standard for literacy. NAEP convened panels of experts whose deliberations led to the following definition of literacy: 'using printed and written information to function in society, to achieve one's goals, and to develop one's knowledge and potential'.

An initial screening of 40,000 households was used to identify a nationally representative sample of between 3,600 and 5,000 young adults (aged 21 to 25) and several hundred 17 year-old school leavers. Black and Hispanic groups were oversampled so that reliable reports could be generated.

Approximately 3,600 young adults were interviewed and were assessed in performing such document tasks as:

- Reading and interpreting prose.

- Identifying and using information located in documents.

- Applying numerical operations to information contained in printed material.

The study provides considerable insights into the literary skills and proficiencies of America's young adults. Major findings were that, while the overwhelming majority of young adults adequately perform tasks at the lower levels on three literacy scales (prose, document and quantitative literacy), sizable numbers appear unable to do well on tasks of moderate complexity.

Chapter I provides the rationale for conducting the study and the purpose and conceptual framework of the research are set against a brief discussion of previous attempts at assessment. Chapter II reviews the methodology (focusing on the assessment design), the data collection activities, the scoring and entry of data, and the scaling of the simulation tasks. Major sections of Chapter III deal with the dimensionality of literacy skills, scaling the adult literacy tasks, and describing and anchoring the literacy scales. Chapter IV profiles proficiencies for the total group of young adults assessed on each of three literacy scales. Chapter V compares young adults with in-school populations and describes performance at five levels of reading proficiency. Young adults are characterized in Chapter VI using three variables as a framework—race and ethnicity, parental education, and respondent's education. Chapter VII presents analyses investigating the relationship among demographic characteristics, educational variables, literacy practices and the four literacy outcome measures. The oral-language assessment is described in Chapter VIII.

Kirsch and Mosenthal (1990)

Irwin S Kirsch and Peter B Mosenthal. 'Exploring document literacy: variables underlying the performance of young adults'. *Reading Research Quarterly* 25(1), 1990, 5-27.

The purpose of this study was to identify some of the critical variables that underpin young adults' performance across a range of document tasks. In the absence of a method for systematically comparing and contrasting the structure and content of different documents, the researchers adopted an exploratory approach by analysing secondary data from a literacy study conducted by the National Assessment of Educational Progress in 1985 (this dataset comprised the responses by 3,618 young adults, aged 21 to 25, to a total of 61 individual document tasks).

Kirsch and Mosenthal were able to identify three groups of variables by developing their own relational grammar and by analysing the original documents used in the assessment. These groups consisted of document, task and process variables. The results of a multiple regression analysis revealed that five variables are likely to be good predictors of document difficulty for general populations of young adults. Between them, these five variables were shown to account for 89 per cent of variance in the distribution of percentage correct scores.

- *Number of organising categories* – the number of explicit organising categories a respondent needs to recognise in a document to be able to perform a simple task.

- *Number of task specifics* – the number of separate pieces of information a respondent needs to process to complete a simple task.

- *Degrees of correspondence* – the extent to which a respondent is required to make use of higher-level inference or interpretation in order to follow an instruction and complete a document-based task.

- *Type of information* – the degree of effort needed to locate or provide requested information from a document.

- *Number of document specifics* – the number of separate, explicit pieces of information in a document.

Klare (1979)

George Klare. 'Writing to inform: making it readable'.
Information Design Journal 1(2), 1979, 98-105.

In this article, Klare offers some practical guidance for those who have to write for and communicate with the public.

The first series of guidelines relates to words. It is suggested that writers should ask themselves three questions. Is the word longer than necessary? Will intended readers know the word? Is that particular word necessary? Will intended readers know the word? Is that particular word necessary? Research has suggested six qualities of words that can be helpful when changes are needed:

- Frequency or familiarity.

- Brevity.

- Association value – words which call up other words quickly and easily also add to readability, especially when the other words (or their meanings) appear later in the text.

When it comes to sentences, three questions are suggested. Is the sentence longer and more complex than necessary? Will intended readers understand the sentence? Is the variety needed, or should I simplify the sentence? Six research-based suggestions can be helpful. These are to:

- Be brief.

- Use the active voice.

- Use affirmative constructions.

- Use statement rather than question form.

- Use less embedding of words, or phrases, in sentences.

- Use lower word depth (i.e. the number of sub-clauses a reader must store while reading)

Koh (1985)

Koy Moy Yon. 'The role of prior knowledge in reading comprehension'. *Reading in a Foreign Language* 3(1), 1985, 375-380.

The author postulates that a reader's ability to understand a text is related to prior knowledge and culture, as well as to purely linguistic abilities. This paper describes a research study which set out to test two null hypotheses. The first was that there is no significant difference in the level of comprehension between groups of readers that cannot be explained in terms of linguistic proficiency. Secondly, that there is no significant difference in the level of comprehension of subjects with regard to familiar and unfamiliar texts.

The subjects, 60 students at the National University of Singapore, were divided into three groups:

- Business students, educated in Chinese medium schools.

- Science students, educated in Chinese medium schools.

- Science students, educated in English medium schools.

The groups differed, therefore, both in their language ability and in their prior knowledge of business and scientific information. Four English language texts of 400 words were used, covering business studies, science, history, and politics. Two of the texts were therefore familiar to some of the students but not to others. The other two (history and politics) were assumed to be unfamiliar to all the students. Cloze tests, where every seventh word was deleted, were used to assess the students' comprehension of the material.

The results showed that the students with the higher proficiency in English gained significantly higher comprehension scores for the texts which covered subjects that were unfamiliar to all groups. There was, however, a fairly clear and significant indication that prior knowledge also played a role in comprehension. The business students with a low proficiency in English gained comprehension scores for the business text that were equal to the science students who were proficient in English. Similarly, the two groups of science students gained higher comprehension scores for the science text than did the business students. The highest score of the test was for the science students who were proficient in English for the English-language science text.

These results confirm earlier research that the comprehension of a text involves a combination of linguistic proficiency and prior knowledge, with the absence of one factor sometimes being compensated for by the presence of the other.

Larkin and Simon (1987)

Jill H Larkin and Herbert A Simon. 'Why a diagram is (sometimes) worth a thousand words'.
Cognitive Science 11(1), 1987, 65-99.

The authors develop the idea that while diagrams and verbal descriptions may be equivalent in terms of information, the operations which humans need perform on them to extract information are quite distinct. The specific advantages of diagrams over verbal descriptions are explicable in terms of computational efficiency. Larkin and Simon postulate that:

- Diagrams can bring together all information that is intended to be used together, thus avoiding large amounts of searching for relevant information elements.

- Diagrams typically use location to group information about a single element, and avoid the need to match symbolic labels.

- Diagrams automatically support a large number perceptual inferences, which are very easy for humans.

The advantages of diagrams, in the view of the authors, are therefore largely computational. Diagrams are not better representations because they contain more information but because the indexing of the information they contain can support extremely useful and efficient computational processes. The ideas presented in this paper go some way to providing an explanation of why diagrams can be so useful.

Lasisi and others (1988)

MJ Lasisi, Sola Falodun and AS Onyehalu. 'The comprehension of first-
and second-language prose'.
Journal of Research in Reading 11(1), 1988, 26-35.

This article reports on research designed to illuminate how national
culture interacts with second-language reading comprehension,
specifically within a Nigerian context.

Law Reform Commission of Victoria (1987)

Report: Plain English and the Law.
Law Reform Commission of Victoria. Report No 9.

An Australian commission, led by Professor Robert Eagleson, was set
up to review the techniques, principles and practices of drafting
legislation, legal agreements and government forms. From this they
have recommended steps that should be taken to adopt a plan English
drafting style.

Although the report focuses on legal documents and their use by
lawyers, many of its recommendations are just as relevant to other
types of document.

It highlights a number of factors which reduced the intelligibility of
the documents. They included:

• Linguistic defects.

• Excessive sentence length.

• The creation and use of unnecessary concepts.

• Poor organisation of material.

• Unattractive layout.

At the same time it recommends the use of:

• Good modern typography.

• Cross-referencing.

• Indexes.

• Use of formulae, charts and maps.

Appendix 1 includes a useful set of design guidelines which, though written for legal documents can just as usefully be applied to other sets of documents. As well as including much of the advice frequently found in other guidelines, these stress:

- The importance of considering the purpose of a document before you start writing.

- The need for an awareness of the audiences of a document, including their interests and needs.

- The importance of the organisation of the document, and of making this visible through clear layout.

Ledwith (1984)

Frank Ledwith. 'Immediate and delayed effects of postal advice on stopping smoking'.
Health Bulletin 42(6), 1984, 332-339.

A study designed to test the effectiveness of leaflets in helping people to kick smoking. Subjects were recruited covertly through newspaper advertisements and were divided into three groups:

- A control group of 459 people who were sent no information.

- A 'leaflet' group of 481 people who were sent the leaflet only.

- An 'advice' group of 899 people who were sent the leaflet, plus an offer of individual advice (this offer was taken up by a third of the group).

It emerged from the research that the provision of a leaflet seemed to have a latent effect. When, some months later, there was a large increase in the price of cigarettes, the group who had received the leaflet were far more likely to have given up smoking. Ledwith concluded that the higher rate of cessation by the advice group was due, in part, to the series of follow-up letters they received. The effect could not be attributed simply to the impact of the personalised advice, since only one third had taken up this offer. Thus leaflets alone were not a sufficient stimulus for people to give up smoking, but they may have a latent effect which can be activated through further stimuli such as follow-up letters or powerful externalities like a steep price rise.

Naturally, care needs to be taken in generalising from the results of this study to other public information campaigns.

Lee (1986)

JF Lee. 'Background knowledge and L2 reading'.
Modern Language Journal 70(4), 1986, 350-354.

This study investigated the effects of three types of background knowledge on the comprehension of texts in a reader's second language. The factors investigated were:

- The presence of a title page and picture page to provide a context for the text.

- The use of concrete terms within the text to give clues to its content area.

- The reader's prior knowledge or experience of the content of the text.

The subjects were 32 GCE Advanced level Spanish language students, divided for purposes of the study into four groups:

- Group 1, who received texts with title page, picture page and concrete terms

- Group 2, who received texts with title page and picture page

- Group 3, who received texts with concrete terms

- Group 4, who received texts with no background prompts

Each group was given two texts in Spanish, one covering a topic familiar to them and the other an unfamiliar topic. They were asked to read the text once, at their normal reading speed, and then to write down in English (their native language) all that they could recall.

The results showed that all three components of background knowledge (title / picture; concrete terms; and prior knowledge) play some role in the way learners of a second language read, comprehend, and recall passages. The interaction between these and the reader is extremely complex.

Recall of the familiar text was enhanced when the readers were provided with a title and picture page and particularly when the text also contained concrete terms. In contrast, the non-familiar text was recalled best when no title and picture page was provided. This was attributed to the fact that the picture, like the text, depicted a situation that was unfamiliar to the reader.

Lefever and Dixon (1986)

A Lefever and P Dixon. 'Do written instructions need examples?' *Cognition and Instruction* 3(1), 1-30, 1986.

A report of an experiment, with 76 students on an introductory psychology course, that looked at the extent to which exampes and instructions were used in carrying out simple series-completion and classification tests. The results suggest that caution may be needed when using examples.

The authors found that most students consistently used the examples, rather than the instructions. When the examples and instructions conflicted, 92 per cent followed the example. The results were not due to problems with the instructions, as these were followed correctly when they were presented without examples.

Lefrere and others (1983)

Paul Lefrere and others. *Effective forms: a case study of the development and testing of two postal claim forms for Supplementary Benefit.* Open University, 1983.

In 1982 the Department of Health and Social Security developed a prototype postal claim form for unemployed people claiming Supplementary Benefit, which an Open University team evaluated form and then redesigned. This report describes both the evaluation of the prototype form and the processes of drafting, design, testing and revision involved in producing the form that was finally introduced in April 1983.

Lefrere also indicates some of the general lessons that were learned and which could be applied to the development, design and testing of other administrative forms. These lessons include guidelines on language, on typography, on design and the use of colour, together with a methodology for testing forms.

A number of specific points identified by the testing are worth noting. The word 'savings' was taken by most people to exclude the cash in their pockets and money in current bank accounts. 'Income' was not understood to encompass social security benefits or retirement pensions. Users had particular difficulty with branching directions (for example, 'If you answered "no" go to section 7'). These problems can be overcome by clear instructions and better typographic signalling. It also helps if sections have a heading and are numbered rather than lettered. Where inconsistent column widths are used some sections will be missed. Users find leaflets with complicated concertina folding difficult to follow.

A full account of this research, which relates it to other studies, is contained in Waller (1984).

Levine and Haus (1985)

MG Levine and GJ Haus. 'The effect of background knowledge on the reading comprehension of second language learners'. *Foreign Language Annals* 18(5), 1985, 391-197.

This study investigated the effect of background subject knowledge on the reading comprehension of high school students in a second language. A group of 203 students of the Spanish language were given a report of a baseball game taken from a Spanish daily newspaper. The text had been tested to ensure that it was within the reading capabilities of the students. When the students had read the article they were given a twelve-item multiple choice comprehension test in Spanish. Of the items, four required direct recall of information in the text. The remaining eight required the reader to use both the text and prior knowledge to come up with an answer.

In addition, the students' knowledge of baseball was assessed by means of a multiple choice questionnaire and they were assigned into either a 'high knowledge' or a 'low knowledge' group. They were also assigned to two levels of language ability.

The results showed a significant effect of background knowledge, not only for the questions where readers would require such knowledge, but also for the four questions where the answer was actually contained in the text.

Levine and Haus also showed that background knowledge could sometimes be more important than language level. Background knowledge appeared to help students at the two language levels equally for the four questions specifically covered in the text.

Lewis (1988)

David Lewis. *Information design research: literature survey.* Information Design Unit for the British Library, 1988.

A review of the information design literature covering a two-year period (1986 to 1988), with particular emphasis on research findings of practical relevance to the construction of public documents.

The review complements and updates earlier literature reviews carried out by Elaine Kempson for the Department of Health and Social Security (covering the years 1979 to 1986), and which are incorporated into this publication, *Designing Public Documents*.

Lewis and Walker (1989)

Clive Lewis and Peter Walker. 'Typographic influences on reading'. *British Journal of Psychology* 80(2), 1989, 241-257.

It is intuitively plausible that the primary linguistic message conveyed by a written word or phase may be modified by the perceptual qualities of the typeface in which it is displayed. This article reports on an empirical investigation of the phenomenon of 'typographic illusion'.

In a preliminary study, 20 undergraduate volunteers were asked to rate commonly-used typefaces in terms of perceived qualities such as heavy-light, fast-slow, and hard-soft. The results indicated that typefaces do in fact possess perceptual qualities about which subjects generally agree, and that the adjectives selected for this study were reliably descriptive of at least some of these qualities. In the first experiment, test adjectives were presented to subjects in typefaces which were either consistent or inconsistent with their meaning. Subjects were asked to perform a speeded binary classification task. It was anticipated that subjects' response would be slowed on those occasions when typeface and word were incongruent—that is, if a semantic code is accessed from a word's visual or surface features.

In the second experiment, the scope of the basic paradigm was widened by requiring responses to a broader range of test items. This time, rather than assessing test adjectives (heavy-light) directly with typeface characteristics, eight pairs of animal names were selected. Additionally, evidence was sought that the interaction would generalise to a situation where subjects responded, not to the word's direct meaning, but on the basis of characteristics indirectly inferred from the test word.

In combination, these results clearly indicate that the typography of a word can be perceptually encoded and can activate representations in schematic memory. These findings stand in contrast to the view, prevalent in perception and memory research, that between initial pattern recognition and final perceptual recombination stages, the surface details of a written word are without significant influence. The authors recognise that their results are confined to situations in which words were presented in isolation. However, they point out that there are many times when responses to single word cues may be critical, such as when a motorist passes a traffic sign at speed.

LoMaglio and Robinson (1985)

Larry J LoMaglio and Victoria J Robinson. 'The impact of passive voice on reading comprehension'.
IEEE Transactions on Professional Communication 28(4), 1985, 26-27.

Twelve students entering the National Technical Institute for the Deaf, New York, were tested to assess their ability to comprehend sentences written in the passive voice. The students were presented with 36 sentences written in either the passive or the active voice and were required to choose a sentence having the same meaning but written in the opposite voice, from four possible answers. Six of the test items involved passive sentences, which lacked an agent (eg 'The child was loved').

The mean score overall was over 90 per cent, but 50 per cent of the students taking the test failed to comprehend the test items involving passive sentences with no agent. In fact 91 per cent of the total errors made on the test were made on these six items. The authors conclude that sentences which include an agentless passive should be avoided wherever possible.

Lundeberg (1987)

M Lundeberg. 'Metacognitive aspects of reading comprehension: studying understanding in legal case analysis'.
Reading Research Quarterly 22(4), Fall 1987, 407-442.

Reports the results of a study, using protocol analysis and interviewing, of the differences between the strategies used by 'experts' and 'novices' when reading reports of legal cases. The novices were, in fact, legal novices; they were educated to at least masters level in subjects such as Education and English.

The research identified a number of differences between the strategies of the two groups, and the author uses these to produce guidelines for effective reading, which she has tested and found useful.

One of the key differences between the strategies of the two groups was that the experts, but not the novices, did some preliminary surveying of the document before they read it right through. This included looking at headings, getting a clear idea of the context of the case by checking on the parties to the case, the type of court, the date and the judge, and overviewing the document to see—and mark—key parts such as the facts and actions sections.

She also found that the novices tried to assign names to the plaintiff and the defendant, and added incorrect information to supplement what as included in the document. This finding can be seen as supporting the 'scenario principle' approach to documents advocated by Flower and others (1980).

Lynton (1985)

Maggie Lynton. *Government forms testing: use of market research for the testing of government forms.*
Canberra Department of Sport, Recreation and Tourism, 1985.

This report offers practical guidelines on the testing of printed documents (forms, leaflets, and letters) with the general public. Written primarily for the staff of government departments, the report includes an aid for the evaluation of submissions from outside consultants for a forms-testing study as well as being a guide to those departments intending to conduct a forms-testing study using their own internal manpower resources.

The paper outlines the criteria against which documents should be evaluated, such as comprehensibility, user-friendliness, and legibility. Lynton then proposes three main techniques for testing documents:

- Structured interviews.

- Unstructured or semi-structured interviews (including protocol analysis and observation techniques).

- Group discussions.

Practical guidance, based on the author's experience as a market researcher, is offered on each of these methods. She particularly recommends one-to-one interviews for the testing of both forms, and group discussions plus interviews for evaluating leaflets. She strongly advises against using 'remote' methods such as telephone or postal interviews for either type of document. Sampling methods and sample sizes are also discussed, with the conclusion that useful qualitative research can be carried out with quite small samples. Two examples are quoted which each used a sample of 70 people.

Finally the paper offers practical advice specifically to government departments whose own staff are about to carry out testing of public documents for the first time.

McGarvie (1982)

Michael J McGarvie. *Information in advice centres: the use of Government leaflets in advice centres* (Master's dissertation). Centre for Information Science, The City University, 1982.

Interviews were conducted with one worker in each of 18 advice centres in the London Borough of Lambeth. These included both generalist as well as specialist centres. All but two had displays of leaflets. However, the leaflets were only consulted as a written information source by eight workers and never replaced advice giving. The workers did, however, feel that the leaflets were useful to give to clients after an advice interview. In particular, they said that benefits leaflets were the ones most likely to be taken away.

On the whole workers found the leaflets readable but they felt that their clients would probably find them difficult to understand. Three people specifically mentioned leaflets which contained calculations as being difficult. They also felt that their clients were not aware that leaflets existed, as very few people asked for specific ones. They were of the opinion that more publicity was needed for leaflets and that radio and TV (ten people) could be used as another means of conveying the information contained in the leaflets.

Six workers said that the DHSS was bad at supplying leaflets: they were often out of stock and there was usually a long delay before receiving the ordered leaflets. Four said the DHSS was particularly good and efficient. Ten workers had not noticed any recent improvements in the design of leaflets. Seven thought that some had improved and the DHSS leaflets—particularly Family Incomes Supplement, Supplementary Benefit and Child Benefit—were singled out as being good examples. The improvements noticed for these leaflets were that they included more pictures and visual displays which were easier to understand. Also the language and format had been simplified.

Only five workers said that clients often came in with leaflets or came in asking for them. Twelve workers said that people do not seem to be aware that there are leaflets available and they thought that DHSS offices and post offices should have better stocks of leaflets on display.

McGuire (1989)

Christine McGuire. 'Towards an acceptable text'.
Health Education Journal 48(4), 1989, 203.

A short communication outlining the interim findings of research into the problems of developing appropriate health education materials for ethnic minority groups funded by the Health Education Authority.

Mali and Sykes (1985)

Mali and Sykes. *Writing and Wordprocessing for Engineers and Scientists.*
McGraw-Hill Book Company, 1985.

Includes a readability formula—The Technical Clarity Index—that pays more attention than most formulae to the meaning of the words in the passage being assessed.

The formula is based on counts of:

- *Average sentence length* – that is the number of the words divided by the number of sentences.

- *Average number of general, non-technical, complex words* – the number of non-technical words with three or more syllables per 100 words.

- *Average number of technical, complex words per* – the number of technical words with three or more syllables per 100 words. 'Technical words' includes acronyms and abbreviations; jargon and specialised scientific/engineering terms; numerical descriptions and quantitative expressions.

Malicky and Norman (1989)

Grace Malicky and Charles A Norman. 'The reading concepts and strategies of adult nonreaders'.
Journal of Reading 33(3), 1989, 198-202.

Relatively little attention has been paid to understanding the literacy development of adults who are virtual non-readers. The purpose of this study was to explore the nature of illiteracy in adults who have made little or minimal progress in learning to read or write.

The experimental design for this project consisted of a series of literacy tasks to determine how these adults actually interact with print. The first was a task in which familiar print (such as a brand name) was presented in each of three ways:

- Picture context.

- Logo or trademark in isolation.

- Typed words in isolation.

All the adults were able to read at least some of the (24) environmental print items correctly when provided with a picture context (mean = 12.2). The adults did almost as well on the logo format (mean = 11.8) but performed more poorly on the typed print format (mean = 7.4).

The second task involved interaction with passages containing familiar language of both predictable and unpredictable nature. Responses to these two sets of tasks were rated in terms of the relative use of print-based and knowledge-based information.

The results of this study support the hypothesis that adult non-readers place greater reliance on knowledge-based rather than print-based cues. While use of unfamiliar, unpredictable passages did result in somewhat greater use of print cues, only about a fifth of the adults made adequate use of these cues and half were unable to use either knowledge or print cues on that type of material.

Mapes (1982)

REA Mapes. *D1 application form: home address difficulties.* Swansea University, 1982.

This research was commissioned because the staff at Drivers and Vehicle Licensing Centre were facing difficulties coding the address section of completed driving licence application forms.

Professor Mapes proposes two hypotheses to explain the causes of these difficulties:

- That completing the address part of a form is an unconscious mechanical act—the 'motor effect'.

- That there is public disinterest in and lack of familiarity with the recent changes of postal addressing.

422 people were selected in random street surveys and asked to complete one of four different address formats.

Form A was similar to that used on the application form up to 1982.

Address	
Post Town	
Postcode	

50.9% correct

Form B was similar to the layout on the revised application form.

Address	
Post Town	
Post Code	

73.6% correct

Form C was intended as an easier alternative to B.

Address	
Town	
Post Code	

80.2% correct

Form D was designed to test the 'motor effect' and to provide an easier format for post code details than B.

No & Road	
Area or Village	
Town	
Post Code	

84.1% correct

The three forms B, C and D were significantly better than A. Of these three, D was marginally better than C which, in turn, was marginally better than B. However the use of the abbreviation 'No.' gave rise to difficulties and it was recommended that 'number' be written in full.

It is particularly interesting that form B, with just two lines for the address, was a good deal better than A, which had three lines. The use of two lines did not, as had been expected, lead to address over-crowding. This happened only three times—all of them being people living in rural areas.

Market and Opinion Research International (1985)

Attitudes among VAT registered traders towards VAT publications.
Market and Opinion Research International for HM Customs and Excise, 1985.

This study was carried out in two parts: a quantitative stage, which consisted of 214 structured telephone interviews, and a semi-qualitative stage comprising 21 personal interviews. The respondents in both stages were staff in companies and firms whose job it was to handle the VAT returns.

The results showed that, in general, VAT registered traders prefer to have their queries answered in person (most usually by telephone) rather than having to refer to VAT leaflets.

The most favoured suggestion for improving communications was to have more leaflets distributed with the VAT return forms—when prompted, 9 of 21 interviewees agreed with this suggestion.

People were not opposed to the use of leaflets as a means of communication, but they did have views on the way they should be advertised and distributed. Advertising in the local or national press was preferred to either radio or television. Distributing leaflets with VAT returns, by VAT visiting officers, and by making them available in a wider variety of places were all preferred to suggestions that leaflet reference libraries be created at VAT offices, that there should be more enquiry counters at the VAT office or that audio or video cassettes could be produced instead of leaflets.

Matthews and others (1982)

Christopher Matthews and others. 'Commonsense, skill and research in forms design.'
Information Design Journal 3(2), 1982, 87-95.

The authors, who were employed by the Central Office of Information, describe a 'commonsense redraft' of the application form for the Criminal Injuries Compensation Scheme.

The redesigned form, the leaflet and the full explanatory document were subjected to a 'diagnostic test' by a commercial market research company. This test consisted of 18 extended interviews with ex-applicants to the Criminal Injuries Compensation Scheme, who were recruited through the Islington Victim Support Scheme, and one with the organiser of that scheme. Two of the more genral findings are that:

- The notes at the beginning of the form which were printed on tinted paper (as compared with white boxes for the replies) were not always read.

- There was little spontaneous enthusiasm for the numbering of the question subsections on the form.

Mayer (1989)

Richard E Mayer. 'Systematic thinking fostered by illustrations in scientific text'.
Journal of Educational Psychology 81(2), 1989, 240-246.

In the first of two experiments, 34 female college students who had rated their existing knowledge of car mechanics as 'very little' were asked to read an explanatory text about vehicle braking systems that either contained labelled illustrations or unlabelled illustrations. After reading the documentation, those students who had been given labelled illustrations were shown to have greater understanding and to be able to recall more information about braking systems. To clarify the effects of labelled illustrations, two new control groups were introduced in a second experiment and given texts which contained illustrations only (without labels) or just the labels.

The findings of the study are consistent with the notion that illustrations can affect the cognitive processing of the reader. In particular, the labelled illustrations used in these studies seem to have helped students guide selective attention and build internal connections. Not surprisingly, providing labels that repeated explanatory information from the text helped students recall that information better than if no labels were presented.

Mayer suggests that the results of this study support a model of learning in which illustrations can help readers to focus their attention on information in a text and reorganise that information into a coherent mental model.

MIL Research Ltd (1982)

Cash help: a report on a research project to test the communication effectiveness of the new 'Cash Help' leaflet.
MIL Research Ltd for the Department of Health and Social Security, 1982.

The main purpose of the research reported here was to test the communication effectiveness of a revised version of the DHSS leaflet *Cash Help*. Fifty depth interviews were held during April 1982 in Newcastle and Havant, Hampshire. All interviewees were either already receiving supplementary benefit or appeared to qualify for it. Their ages ranged from 16 to 88 years.

The main points of interest to emerge from the study included:

- The use of colour and its bright attractive appearance was felt to make the leaflet more approachable and less threatening.

- The list of eligible categories of people on the cover helped people identify immediately whether the leaflet applied to them.

- The format, a four sheet fold-out, caused considerable problems.

Elderly and disabled people found it physically difficult to open the leaflet out further than the first fold, especially if they were arthritic. The result was that most of them tried to read it whilst the leaflet was folded and this often led to confusion about which page followed on from which. Others experienced difficulty in working out the order of the pages. Many respondents said they preferred the book format of the earlier form. The report concludes that 'the folding of the pages and the format of the leaflet was a source of continuous confusion'.

There was a concern that, instead of the address and telephone number of the local DHSS office being stamped on the claim form, there was an instruction telling people where to find the telephone number in the telephone book. This seemed to deter some people without a telephone from filling in the form.

Some of the wording used also caused problems: for example, 'I claim supplementary benefit' was sometimes misconstrued as meaning 'I am already claiming supplementary benefit'. The use of the heading 'you and your family' led some of the pensioners who lived alone to assume it did not apply to them. A minority were unhappy with the term 'income' which suggested salary or investment income, whereas they were in fact on a pension or other state benefits.

The step-by-step instructions on how to claim were found to be simple and straightforward. People were not usually offended because the steps were oversimplified because they believed this would be useful to other users of the leaflet.

The use of illustrations was liked where it clarified the text. However, some people considered a picture of posting the completed form in a postbox to be insulting.

MIL Research Ltd (1984a)

MIL Research Ltd. *Report on a qualitative study of the revised BOTB services leaflet.*
Prepared for the Central Office of Information. MIL, 1984

The testing of this booklet involved 20 qualitative depth interviews with potential users and identified a small number of points which are of general interest:

- The black cover was considered too sombre by some respondents.

- The reversed out bright yellow lettering on the cover was difficult to read.

- The red print used in the booklet was liked by most respondents, but some found it difficult to read.

- The question and statement headings were particularly liked.

MIL Research Ltd (1984b)

Report on a three stage qualitative study of the NP15 leaflet.
MIL Research Ltd for the Department of Social Security, 1984.

A detailed study of a revised version of DHSS Employers' guide to National Insurance contributions.

This involved 200 telephone interviews designed to find out how the original guide was used and what problems it raised. More detailed personal interviews were then held with 55 of the people who had been identified as making more frequent use of the guide. These people were shown the revised version and asked to comment on it.

The results showed that people are more likely to telephone the local DHSS or Tax Office with queries than they are to use the booklet. More specific criticisms of the original guide included:

- The use of unfamiliar code numbers to refer to other documents; a need for better cross-referencing; and a need for better indexing.

Specific comments on the revised booklet included:

- A preference for the A4 format, because it looked less official, made the document look shorter, and was easier to file with other A4 documents.

- The brown print was not generally liked – because it is more difficult to read in poor lighting. Some people, however, thought that brown was a more 'modern' colour than blue.

- The flow-chart was welcomed enthusiastically in principle, but because it did not cover its subject comprehensibly it was found to be difficult to use in practice.

MIL Research Ltd (1986a)

Inland Revenue 'Employers' guide to PAYE': a report on a qualitative study into employers' response to a new style and format for the Guide.
MIL Research Ltd for the Inland Revenue and the Central Office of Information, 1986.

The Inland Revenue redesigned the PAYE Guidance Booklet (P7). This research compared the existing and redesigned booklet by in-depth interviews with 50 small businessmen and women followed by a problem-solving exercise. The results showed that a large majority of people preferred the A4 size of the new guide to the existing A5 format. There were two main reasons for this preference. First, it was the same size as other associated documents and a more convenient shape for storing in a filing cabinet. Secondly, it allowed the size of the print to be larger, making it less daunting and easier to read. The inclusion of more white space in the new layout made it look more modern and friendly and easier to use. The space was also found useful for making notes.

The use of colour and illustration in the revised guide reinforced the good impression already created by the size and layout. The coloured highlighting for paragraph headings and coloured print for sub-headings made it easier to scan a page for relevant information. The introduction of coloured margins and illustrated chapter-headings added to the visual appeal of the guide. The majority of respondents were not, however, conscious of the illustrations.

In general, users preferred the less formal tone of the revised guide, which used layman's language. The step by step way of presenting information was also liked and was not considered condescending. The more detailed contents page of the existing guide made it easier to use, even though the initial impression it gave was off-putting. Because the key word in a paragraph heading would not always be the first word, it was suggested that it should be highlighted on the contents page. For the same reason it was suggested that redundant words should be omitted.

The existing guide gave both page and paragraph numbers on the contents page. Respondents found this confusing and preferred the revised contents page, which gave paragraph numbers only.

The use of flowcharts in the revised guide was liked by most respondents. A few, however, found the idea of having to use the charts quite off-putting.

The problem-solving exercise brought to light further minor faults with the revised guide. More importantly it showed that some difficulties arose because the text assumed too much prior knowledge on the part of the user. The problem-solving exercise also showed that if the guide is to be used by and useful to people a comprehensive and easy to use index and reference system is essential.

MIL Research Ltd (1986b)

Reform of social security client group targeting: report on a qualitative and quantitative research study.
MIL Research Ltd for the Central Office of Information and the Department of Health and Social Security, 1986.

Traditionally, the DHSS has advertised each benefit separately. Recently, however, attempts have been made to change this targeting by producing booklets which concentrate on groups of individuals who may qualify for more than one benefit, for example one parent families, letting them know which of the many benefits available are relevant to their needs. The DHSS was interested in extending this approach to all benefits and commissioned a market research study to help with this.

The specific aims of this research were to determine the client groups that cover the entire benefit population most thoroughly, to reduce these to the smallest number that would still maintain the maximum representation of target groups and to identify the group names with which people most readily identify. The project was carried out in three distinct stages involving nine group discussions and 16 depth interviews.

These were designed to provide basic background information on people's approach to their benefit entitlement and to establish how they group their own needs and those of others.

The first, qualitative, stage it confirmed earlier research about people's level of knowledge about benefits. While some people knew exactly which benefits they were eligible for, many others did not. The official sources of information, most particularly DHSS office itself, were regarded as inaccessible, complicated and generally unsatisfactory. The most common source of information was friends or acquaintances, particularly those who had already claimed the benefit themselves. Official leaflets were not always available, and where they were they were thought to be daunting or unintelligible. There was, however, a good deal of support for leaflets aimed at groups of people, rather than covering individual benefits. People felt that this would help them identify for themselves the benefits for which they were eligible and would avoid the need to wade through many irrelevant leaflets before finding the right one. It was also thought that it would lead to a reduced number of leaflets, improving their availability and helping people to understand and apply for their entitlements.

The qualitative research identified 14 main client groupings. These were: expecting a baby, single parents, families with children, low-income households, the employed in need, unemployed, school-leavers, students, pensioners, people coping with death or bereavement, armed services staff and their dependents, disabled and handicapped people unable to work due to sickness or industrial injury and caring for a sick, disabled or elderly person. Respondents also felt that a summary leaflet would be useful in addition to these client-group titles. The summary leaflet would act as a kind of index and give a complete list of all benefits available as well as a brief guide to the separate leaflets.

The second, quantitative stage involved interviewing 307 people from each of the major categories of actual or potential client groups. These interviews were designed to produce a shortlist of possible titles and contents for leaflets. The results confirmed those of the qualitative research. Some clients identified very easily with distinct groups, such as 'the unemployed' and 'the retired', while others identified with a number of groups. Where people identified with more than one group it seemed that the marital and, in particular, the parental status was of greater importance than the other factors such as unemployment, low income or disability. The researchers recommend that a grouping system based on various types of need involved would be preferable to a system based solely on types of people.

The final stage was a small-scale qualitative study comprising 20 interviews with small to medium sized employers and self-employed people, to examine the implications of proposals to make benefit payments to employees through their pay packet. Few of them thought that they would use leaflets, preferring instead to telephone their local DHSS office if they needed specific information.

Moriarty and Scheiner (1984)

Sandra E Moriarty and Edward C Scheiner. 'A study of close set text type'.
Journal of Applied Psychology 69(4), 1984, 700-702.

This experimental investigation set out to measure the effect on reading of varying the spaces between individual letters. The primary measure used was the number of words read within a given time period (105 seconds). The testing was carried out on a group of 260 undergraduate students. Both serif and sans-serif typefaces were used, and the spacing—or kerning—varied.

It was found that the students read the close-spaced type more quickly (370 words in the allotted time) than they read the regularly-spaced typeface (332 words). Contrary to expectations, there was no significant difference in the speed of reading serif or sans-serif type.

Mosenthal and Kirsch (1989)

Peter Mosenthal and Irwin S Kirsch. 'Understanding documents'
(a regular monthly column in the *Journal of Reading*).

A very clear series of short articles aimed primarily at those who teach document design skills which covers the following topics:

- Lists [33(1), 1989, 58-60].
- Combining simple lists [33(2), 1989, 132-135].
- Intersecting lists [33(3), 1989, 210-213].
- Nested lists [33(4), 1990, 294-297].
- Graphs and charts, 1 [33(5), 1990, 371-373].
- Graphs and charts, 2 [33(6), 1990, 454-457].
- Forms, 1 [33(7), 1990, 542-545].
- Forms, 2 [33(8), 1990, 636-641].
- General reference maps [34(1), 1990, 60-63].

National Consumer Council (1984)

National Consumer Council. *Plain English for Lawyers: some guidelines on writing and designing legal documents.*
NCC, 1984.

The report concentrates on the language of legal documents and includes some useful glossaries of legal phrases with their plain English equivalents.

National Opinion Poll (1981)

National Opinion Poll. 'Mrs, Miss or Ms'.
NOP Review, February 1981.

A national opinion poll was commissioned by the *Daily Mail* on the female form of address. Only 12 per cent of the 1909 adults interviewed in a random sample in November 1980 said they liked the term 'Ms', while 40 per cent expressed clear dislike. Although equally popular with men and women, those who favoured the term were much more likely to be under 35.

Nine out of ten respondents said they never used the title Ms, while only 1 per cent said they always used it.

Nehiley and others (1982)

JM Nehiley, J Stephens and J Sutherland. 'Cartoons: when are they effective?'
Journal of Extension 20, 1982, 14-20.

This article begins with a review of previous research into the use of illustrations in publications written for the general public. The authors conclude that illustrated publications can have a positive effect on comprehension by people with limited reading abilities and low incomes. At the same time illustrated publications can also lead to increased comprehension among audiences with higher reading abilities.

The specific objectives of the study reported here were to determine whether adults with limited reading abilities given a cartoon-styled publication would have significantly higher levels of comprehension than similar adults given the original publication. A second objective was to test whether the levels of comprehension of a cartoon-styled publication would be significantly lower for adults with limited reading abilities than for those with higher reading abilities. Finally, the authors looked at whether individuals with limited reading abilities reported a significantly higher opinion of cartoon-styled publications than did individuals who had no reading difficulties.

The publication tested was a guide to growing vegetables, both in its original publication format, and as a revised version developed for gardeners with limited reading abilities. The revised version used illustrations to demonstrate gardening techniques such as soil preparation, planting and plant maintenance. In addition, hand lettering was used instead of set type in order to create 'a more personal communication'.

The subjects participating in the study were 80 gardeners with limited reading abilities; 119 journalism students participating in a communications course; and 100 audience members attending an extension home landscaping and design meeting. Both the original and the revised publications were tested using both the Fry and Flesch readability tests. According to these measures, the original publication was written at the 11th grade level while the revised one was written at around 4th or 5th grade level. Comprehension levels were assessed using a 15-question test, and opinions on the relative merits of the two formats were assessed by questionnaire. The t-test was used to evaluate differences in means on the comprehension test scores for the two groups of participants. Data were also analysed using the chi-squared test, with the 0.5 level of significance as the criterion for rejecting the null hypothesis.

The results showed that the illustrated publication resulted in higher levels of comprehension among people with limited reading abilities than the original publication. There was no significant difference between the comprehension levels of the illustrated publication by people with limited reading abilities compared with those with higher abilities. Overall, between 80 and 90 per cent of subjects preferred the illustrated publication, with no significant difference between the different ability groups.

Newman and others (1983)

Ian M Newman and others. 'Usage patterns of educational pamphlets and options to improve their effectiveness'.
Journal of Drug Education 13(4), 1983, 337-346.

The authors conducted a telephone survey of all the people who had requested free or inexpensive educational materials from the Alcohol and Drug Information Clearinghouse over a period of one calendar year.

The findings of the survey revealed that:

- 30 per cent of those questioned had distributed to other all the information materials they had requested.

- 33 per cent had distributed a half or more.

- 25 per cent had distributed less than a half.

- 12 per cent had lost the materials.

In all, of the 62,450 items requested almost a third (19,641) had not been distributed. This finding led to a review of policy regarding the distribution of educational materials and the factors affecting the policy reformulation are described.

Newstead and others (1987)

SE Newstead, P Pollard and D Riezebos. 'The effect of set size on the interpretation of quantifiers used in rating scales'.
Applied Ergonomics 18(3), 1987, 178-182.

The results of two short empirical studies are presented in this paper, which looks at how people interpret quantifiers that are commonly used in questionnaires and in rating scales. The results indicate that the interpretation of certain quantifiers varied according to the context in which they were employed. Low magnitude qualifiers (such as 'few', 'several') appeared to signify a much greater proportion of the whole when they described small sets rather than large ones. In other words, their meaning varied as a function of set size. The significance of this finding is that it is virtually impossible to find quantifiers for use in rating scales that achieve the desirable property of interval scaling (the commonly employed term 'several' is particularly ambiguous in this respect).

The studies demonstrated that the main problem in selecting unambiguous quantifiers occurred in the middle range of 0.35 to 0.65. Despite this, some quantifiers were clearly more consistent in their interpretation and more appropriate to use than others (like 'half').

The paper concludes with some recommendations for choosing an appropriate quantifier:

- The quantifiers selected should have a clear and distinct meaning, which can be easily defined.

- Split quantifiers (eg 'some ... not') should be avoided, especially as people may miss the negative.

- Those quantifiers which exhibit the least variation as a function of set size (eg all / many / half / some / none) are to be preferred.

Nova Research Ltd (1986)

Revised P35 tax form diagnostic research.
Nova Research Ltd for the Central Office of Information and the Inland Revenue, 1986.

A complete redesign of the employers' P35 tax form was undertaken following an O&M analysis of the pattern of mistakes made on the existing form. The form was produced in two variants, one in black and white, and the other in blue-black and white, to assess the effect of introducing colour. A research study was then commissioned by the Inland Revenue to evaluate the effectiveness of the redesigned form and its accompanying notes.

Depth qualitative interviews were held with 32 people from small firms who were usually responsible for the completing the P35 form. Of the two new versions of the form, the blue one was reported to be more 'friendly' and less 'bureaucratic'. Some people thought that this would encourage users to complete the form, while others felt the 'unofficial' appearance might lead some people to be less conscientious when completing it. The blue colour did not appear to contribute significantly to the ease of completion of the form, although the strong contrast between the blue-black type and white background was thought to improve the clarity of the form. Several respondents spontaneously commented that red would be an undesirable colour for this type of form (other unacceptable colours were orange, bright yellow, and pink). The use of bolder, larger print and the use of a layout with more white space were both thought to make the form very much easier to follow.

Some of the results from this study may be transferable to the design of other public documents. For example, it was found that explanatory notes were rarely referred to (unless specific problems were encountered with the form), suggesting that greater design emphasis should be given to the notes as an important integral part of completing a form. Subjects also liked having response boxes in the sections of the form dealing with general questions and declarations.

Owen and others (1984)

T Owen, BM Hibbard and JO Robinson. 'An evaluation of two antenatal information booklets'.
Health Education Journal 43(2/3), 1984, 60-62.

Two antenatal information booklets were compared using the Flesch Index of readability and reader interest, and the FOG readability formula. In addition, knowledge tests were carried out using three groups of women, two receiving one or other of the leaflets, and a control group receiving no information at all.

The two leaflets tested were:

- Leaflet A – *You and your baby,* produced by the British Medical Association. The text of this was felt 'may not be a very effective source of information, being written in an impersonal style, using small print, long sentences and difficult language'. It also contained 'brief and visually appealing' advertising.

- Leaflet B – *The book of the child,* produced by the Scottish Health Education Group. This was considered to be 'a "glossy" publication containing no advertising material and designed to be visually attractive, easily understood and informative'.

As expected, leaflet B achieved significantly better scores on both Flesch indices and FOG readability scores. When it came to knowledge scores, however, while there was little difference between the two groups receiving the booklets. Both groups were significantly more knowledgeable than the control group (which had received no information). The results were also analysed by social class, since it had been expected that the easier to read and more attractive leaflet B would be more suitable for women in social categories III to V. In fact this was not the case. The simpler booklet conveyed more information to women in social categories I and II but not to those in III to V. A tentative eplanation put forward was that:

> the same factors which may have influenced the results in the upper social classes may actually have operated in reverse for the lower classes. The lack of explicit diagrams, the free advertising and free offers may well be the factors that make it more appealing to these women, who stereotypically watch ITV and use euphemistic language when discussing matters such as menstruation and conception.

Whether one agrees with this explanation or not, the results of the study underline, once again, the importance of testing public leaflets and forms on their intended audience.

Pakin (1984)

Sandra Pakin. *Documentation development methodology: techniques for improved communications.*
Prentice Hall, 1984.

This book describes a document design methodology (DDM) which was evolved by Sandra Pakin in the early 1980s. In the words of the author, the DDM is 'a methodology for people committed to producing good documentation. Those looking for a quick-and-dirty way to meet a documentation obligation will find that DDM is not for them'. The book consists of six main sections.

Part 1 *The DDM* summarises the overall methodology and explains its use.

Part 2 *Planning* discusses how to structure a project, how to plan a document and how to prepare for production.

Part 3 *Review* describes how to review and test the document.

Part 4 *Writing* explains how to translate the plan of a document into readable text.

Part 5 *Graphics* covers page format and layout, text and graphic standards and development of figures and illustrations.

Part 6 *Production* discusses production control, support services such as word processing, and production methods for page preparation and reproduction.

The main intended audience for the book is people working in professional data processing or with management information systems who need to produce documents of some substance. Much of the book's content, however, is generalisable to other public documents.

Palmer (1990)

Alison Palmer. *Severe Disability Allowance – report on a small-scale market research study into a revised claim form and wrap-around leaflet.*
MIL Research Ltd for the Department of Social Security, 1990.

A small-scale qualitative research study was carried out by personal depth interviews with 28 potential claimants of the Severe Disability Allowance (SDA). The main objectives of the study were to:

- Assess the SDA Claim Pack's strengths and weaknesses in terms of communicating information about SDA.

- Compare two alternative cover designs.

- Gauge target group reaction to and comprehension of 'disability' stipulations.

Overall, the SDA Claim Pack was found to be very acceptable to the target market in terms of its format (a wrap-around leaflet), its overall presentation and its ease of handling. Of the two cover designs, the use of blue text on a white background was strongly preferred to black on brown. In terms of communication effectiveness, however, the leaflet fared badly in two respects. The formal definition of 'disability' emerged as the question presenting claimants with the most difficulty. This was possibly inevitable since the officially-agreed eligibility criterion of '80 per cent disabled' is difficult for people to grasp. The survey interviews showed that the leaflet failed here because it was too wordy, over-complex, and potentially distressing to disabled readers and their carers.

It was noticeable that few interviewees read the final sections of the Claim Form. As presented, the information appeared low key and lacked impact. Palmer recommended that reference to a telephone helpline should be made at key points in the form that are recognised to cause difficulties for claimants.

Palmer and MacLeod (1989)

Alison Palmer and Alison MacLeod. *Form AG1 development research: report on the findings of a small-scale qualitative study.*
MIL Research Ltd for the Department of Social Security, 1989.

The report is of a small-scale qualitative study carried out by depth interview with 16 potential claimants of Department of Social Security help towards certain NHS charges.

The key findings and recommendations which emerged from Palmer and MacLeod's research on claim form AG1 were that the front page of the form should give a clearer indication of what the benefit covers and who it applies to. Non-essential detailed information should be relegated to other parts of the form. The integration of explanatory notes with the questions can also be helpful, as long as a clear distinction is made between background information and information specific to a particular question. Based on the authors' observation of user behaviour, it was clear that the way people filled in form AG1 did not always follow the same structured logic as employed by the form designer. Finally, it was noted that the main routing currently used in form AG1 would benefit from rationalisation and simplification.

Palmer and MacLeod (1990a)

Alison Palmer and Alison MacLeod. *Report on a two-stage qualitative research study into DS2: the new claim pack for Attendance Allowance.*
MIL Research Ltd for the Department of Social Security, 1990.

This study tested and evaluated a new Social Security claim pack

(DS2) for the progressively ill and for their carers who may be eligible to receive Attendance Allowance. The researchers explored reaction to a number of information design aspects of claim pack DS2 through a series of personal depth interviews with 42 individuals.

The overall reaction to the claim pack by professionals, patients and carers was positive, especially with regard to the use of the wrap-around format. It was felt that this resulted in a 'slow release' of information which seemed to encourage claimants to read the supporting leaflet information before they completed the form. In conclusion, the researchers suggested that a significant improvement to the claim pack could be made by making it clearer which was the form and which the leaflet.

Palmer and MacLeod (1990b)

Alison Palmer and Alison MacLeod. *Report on a qualitative research study on the revised SF3000 form amongst potential applicants for community care grant and budgeting loans from the Social Fund.* MIL Research Ltd for the Department of Social Security, 1990.

Form SF300 is used by people seeking help from the Social Fund. The Department of Social Security prepared two draft versions of form SF300 with wrap-around supporting leaflets, in both portrait and landscape mode. These were then tested extensively among the key target groups. The two versions were found to differ in respects other than their orientation, and the following general conclusions may not be valid outside the context of this particular study.

Potential claimants perceived the vertical (pink) wrap-around leaflet more as a cover for the enclosed form than an integral part of the claim pack. This encouraged claimants to discard it as though it were merely a wrapper. The landscape format was better received. It seemed to encourage claimants to open the claim pack more slowly, which seemed to help them absorb the information bit-by-bit. The landscape format was also reported to offer a more spacious feel, with fewer questions per page. On the other hand, the portrait leaflet's colour (pink) was perceived as a more sympathetic colour for the form than the more official-looking green of the landscape leaflet. It was also felt that the use of photographs on the (pink) cover tended to soften the

rather 'official' image of the claim pack and so foster a sense of
identification among target groups.

Parkinson (1990a)

Chris Parkinson. *A study of words, concepts and terms used on
Department of Social Security forms.*
Document Design Unit, Department of Social Security, 1990
(unpublished).

A study carried out by the DSS Document Design Unit to investigate a
number of features associated with the use of DSS documents by the
general public. The aim of the research was to identify any problems
that people completing the DSS forms might have with the specialised
meaning of the words and phrases used.

The research was conducted by means of a short questionnaire
administered to a random sample of 251 members of the public in the
streets of London and Nottingham. The survey addressed three
general questions.

How do people interpret certain words and phrases used on DSS documents?
The aim here was to discover how members of the public interpreted
the terms 'qualify', 'entitled', and 'can get' by means of a multiple-
choice question. It was found that 'entitled' and 'can get' were often
interpreted differently from the sense actually intended in DSS
documents, thus leading to the possibility of confusion.

*Do people actually understand the meaning of some of the words and
concepts used in DSS forms?*
Parkinson found that certain concepts like 'backdate' and 'arrears'
were widely misunderstood. The study demonstrated that significant
improvements in understanding could be achieved by using simplified
versions of the concepts, such as 'before' (an 18 per cent improvement
over 'backdate') or 'at the end of' (a 26 per cent improvement on
'arrears').

Do people use the same terms as those used in DSS documents?
Terms commonly used in DSS documents, such as 'doctor's note',

'government pension' and 'employer's pension' were not necessarily
the same as the terms naturally used by members of the public. The
results showed that those surveyed preferred to use 'sick note' (77 per
cent), 'old age pension' (70 per cent) and 'company pension' (69 per
cent).

Parkinson (1990b)

Chris Parkinson. *Summary of research into illustrations.*
Document Design Unit, Department of Social Security, 1990,
(unpublished).

A summary of some of the published information design research into
the use of illustrations on forms and documents, Parkinson's review is
broken down into six broad areas:

- The effect of illustrations on the comprehension of text.

- Readers' preference for illustrated texts.

- Cultural differences in the perception of illustrations.

- The effects of illustrations on those who are learning a second
  language.

- Research problems.

- Other relevant research.

The author cautions that most of the previous research had been
limited to studies on educational texts for children or had been carried
out in particular situations which means that the findings are not
directly applicable with any certainty to DSS leaflets.

Parkinson (1990c)

Chris Parkinson. *A quantitative and qualitative study into different ways
of presenting complex information.*
Document Design Unit, Department of Social Security, 1990,
(unpublished).

The aim of this study was to compare and evaluate three different
ways of conveying complex written information, in this case
information about eligibility for a range of welfare benefits.

One of the main findings of the study was an indication that people seem to prefer complex information to be presented as a series of questions as these were perceived to be simpler and easier to understand. Information presented as structured text was judged by most of the study's respondents to be the most difficult to understand.

Pettersson (1982)

Rune Pettersson. 'Cultural differences in the perception of image and colour in pictures'.
Educational Communication and Technology Journal 30(1), 1982, 43-53.

Cross-cultural studies form one of two major areas of information design research into illustrations. The other is the perception of illustrations by children. This article reviews the research into cultural differences in the perception of images and colour, and proposes some ecological and technological reasons for these differences.

On the whole, research suggests that people from less developed and more rural communities dislike straight lines or rectangles in pictures. Angular, abstract art is found only in industrialised communities where 'modern cities are dominated visually by the squares and rectangles of building modules'. In other words, physical geography seems to exert an influence on people's visual perception. Drawings made by 'primitive peoples' are never framed by parallel lines and right angles. These seem to be the result of 'various technical dictates and are not a reflection of man's true, natural preference'.

Colour perception also varies with environmental factors. Equatorial people are ecologically adapted to life in a climate characterised by bright sunlight and dark nights. In both these conditions colour and contrast decrease in intensity. As a result, such people seem to have enhanced black and white vision. Conversely, as latitude increases so, too, does the importance of colour vision. Colour preferences seem to mirror the findings on colour perception. People with less well-developed colour vision prefer bright colours, those with enhanced colour vision prefer more subtle and subdued colours.

Finally, Pettersson identifies culturally-related differences in colour naming. Research has identified eleven colours that are readily perceived by all ethnic groups: red; yellow; green; brown; blue;

orange; pink; purple; black; white; and grey. Some languages have as
few as two expressions for colours, roughly equivalent to 'dark' and
'light'.

PPCR Market Research Ltd (1989)

*Comprehension of Social Security benefits appertaining to sickness: a
qualitative investigation into consumers' understanding and
comprehension of **the system** for claiming Social Security when sick and
the forms involved in this system.*
PPCR Market Research Ltd for the Central Office of Information, 1989.

A key aspect of the Department of Social Security's policy of helping
frail and vulnerable people to remain in the community is to ensure
that the carers of these people receive as much practical help and
support as possible. As a result, a DSS leaflet *Caring for Someone* was
produced to inform non-professional carers about some of the benefits
and services to which they might be entitled. The primary intended
audience for the leaflet was full-time carers, but it also aimed to reach
people who may play a lesser role, restricted perhaps to doing the
shopping or collecting benefits.

The research was commissioned in order to evaluate the first draft of
the leaflet to see how effectively and how clearly it communicated in
plain, friendly, jargon-free language two key points. First, that readers
should be made to realise that they might actually be 'carers', even if
in only a casual or part-time capacity. Secondly, that they should
understand the broad criteria for entitlement to benefits and services,
and be given pointers to the most appropriate support services and
what to do next. Given the importance of these points, it was felt to be
essential to make sure that the cover design and text conveyed the
sense that the leaflet was useful and that it should be used.

The research methodology consisted of 40 one-hour depth interviews
with carers recruited from a panel. Respondents were given the leaflet
at least one day before the interview. Four client groups were
involved: elderly people; people with physical disabilities; children
with special needs; and the mentally ill. Most were not claiming any
benefit.

The majority of the sample did view themselves as 'caring'—the term used on the leaflet cover—although acknowledgement of themselves as 'carers' was more restricted. People were less likely to be seen as 'carers' where they were close members of the family, where they did not live with the charge, and if the charge was seen to be relatively independent. The problem here was that the leaflet was not felt to be relevant by those with a low level of self-identification. Only half the sample said that they would have picked up the leaflet in real life if they had noticed it.

Overall impressions of the first draft of the leaflet were positive. In particular, it was felt to offer an intelligible overview or 'starting point'. The leaflet's appeal was increased by its coverage of both benefits and services. On the negative side, there was some confusion over whether the benefits referred to the carer or the charge. There were also a few overall comprehension problems, but these were thought more than likely to be related to the complexities of the benefits system per se.

Few of the people interviewed had read the leaflet thoroughly before the interview, and the mechanics of their reading tended to reflect an initial identification of the main areas of interest (by scanning the contents and headings) followed by quick—and selective—reading. In this regard, there was often over-strict self-editing: often the reader misjudged the potential of a particular section for being relevant to their needs.

PPCR Market Research Ltd (1990)

Community Charge Benefit: a qualitative evaluation of leaflet cover design, layout and text.
PPCR Market Research Ltd for the Department of Social Security, 1990.

This empirical study, intended to assess the proposed text and design of CCB1, a new information leaflet about Community Charge Benefit, was conducted by means of depth interviews with 30 potential claimants. These revealed that the use of illustrations in the leaflet was generally welcomed. They were felt to break up the monotony of the text and were additionally useful in reinforcing signposting. Where drawings of people were used, faceless illustrations were perceived as avoiding certain dangers of stereotyping, and of suggesting that the benefit might only be relevant to certain types of people.

The research revealed a number of important problems with the language used in the poster that accompanied the leaflet.

The term 'benefit' tended to suggest cash in hand to many people, rather than the intended meaning of rebate or reduction.

A number of users felt that the more vernacular 'poll tax' should feature somewhere in the poster, even if only in parenthesis.

The leaflet's information about a telephone 'Freeline' was received as a good idea and with evident enthusiasm.

Pruyn and Jonkers (1984)

JFA Pruyn and R Jonkers. 'Reach to recovery: evaluation of an educational booklet for women with mastectomy'.
Journal of the Institute of Health Education 22(3), 1984, 92-9.

This paper describes the testing of a booklet written for women who had undergone mastectomy. The research involved administering a written questionnaire to 53 former patients and 33 health care workers. The study revealed some important differences between the assessments of the booklet made by patients and those made by health care staff. First, the health staff seemed to form an overall assessment on the practical and non-specific grounds of its efficiency and general interest. Patients, on the other hand, based their assessment on the patient-oriented benefit, readability, and exhaustiveness of the text, as well as its general interest. In terms of the content of the booklet, the statistically most significant difference was that patients were more likely to consider that aspects of after-care had not been covered in sufficient detail.

The survey also looked at how best to distribute the booklet. Here, the respondents were asked three questions to find out who should distribute the booklet to its readers, when would be the most suitable time to do so, and whether it should be distributed to the friends or relatives of the patient as well as the patient herself.

On the basis of this study the authors propose a three-stage process in the production of health information booklets for the general public:

- Producing a draft booklet in close consultation with care workers, ex-patients and volunteers from after-care groups.

- Testing the booklet with other patients and care workers.

- Revising the booklet in the light of findings from the tests.

Rasinski (1990)

Timothy V Rasinski. 'Adult readers' sensitivity to phrase boundaries in texts'.
Journal of Experimental Education 58(1), 1990, 29-40.

Previous research has shown that phrasing or segmenting texts is an important factor in reading fluency and comprehension. This paper sheds new light on the interaction between reading ability and text difficulty.

Sixty undergraduates were selected at random from students at Kent State University, of which half had passed a reading proficiency test and were identified as good readers. The other half had failed the test and were experiencing some difficulty in reading college-level materials. The subjects were instructed to identify and mark locations in a series of texts where they thought they could identify significant phrase boundaries. The research revealed a significant difference in readers' ability accurately to identify phrase boundaries, although this was manifest only for relatively difficult texts. It was concluded that poor readers are less sensitive to phrase boundaries in text, and this lack of sensitivity is a key determinant of their ability to process more difficult texts.

The key findings of this exploratory study suggest that phrasing ability is a salient variable in skilled and proficient reading for adult as well as younger readers.

Raskin (1986)

R Raskin. 'The quest for style'.
IEEE Transactions on Professional Communications PC29(3), 1986, 10-18.

This article reviews five computer programs for analysing and editing the style of wordprocessed documents. The five were:

- Grammatik II
- Right Writer
- Electric Webster
- Punctuation and Style
- PC Style

Each was tested on three documents: a business memo, a press release in letter form and a newsletter covering neighbourhood news. All three contained a number of commonly made errors. The strength and weakness of each program are discussed.

The author condludes that:

> Overall these programs are interesting nit pickers, but they really function only at the microscopic level. But when it comes to evaluating style in relation to context, they all fail. To judge content, flow, organisation and sentence structure, I recommend that you find a sympathetic and grammatically knowledgeable friend who likes to read and is willing to help.

The same conclusion was reached two and a half years earlier by James Hartley writing in the same journal (see Hartley, 1984).

Readability formulas (1981)

'Readability formulas: used or abused.'
Forum, *IEEE Transactions on Professional Communication* Vol PC 24(1), 1981.

A series of essays on the usefulness of readability formulae.

Kenneth Powell – *Readability guides are helpful if...*
Most formulae are based on 50-75 per cent comprehension only (Flesch 50, Dale Chall 50, Fog 50, Fry 50-75, Smog 90-100 per cent). The

formulae are far from exact. For those correlated to reading grades, the standard error is plus or minus one and a half grades. Moreover, readabilitly formulae do not tell writers how to improve their writing.

Janice Redish – *Understanding the limitations of readability formulas*
Readability formulae are popular because they are easy and inexpensive to use. Handy as they are, they are very limited tools. Eight limitations are discussed:

- They can only be used on prose passages of more than 100 words.

- They assume the text is composed of well-formed grammatical sentences. They are not sensitive to either word order or grammar.

- All except those with a vocabulary list are insensitive to gibberish, made up words and acronyms.

- Many people generate their own lists of acceptable vocabulary without testing these words first.

- They reward the writer for reducing the number of words in a sentence but this might make the text unreadable by eliminating connecting words.

- They do not measure how relevant the content is for the intended audience.

- They do not give any indication of how well organised the entire document is.

- They do not measure typographic features that affect how readers react to, understand and use documents.

Lawrence Frase – *Ethics of imperfect measures*
This essay describes the 'Writers Workbench' which calculates several readability measures; comments on misspelled words; comments on awkward phrases in sentences; measures text abstractness; and compares these properties to other texts.

It also describes the underlying thinking behind this system which is based on concerns about the misuse of readability formulae.

Bertram Bruce and others – *Why readability formulas fail*
Readability formulae fail because of factors not covered by the

formulae. They also lack solid statistical grounding. Klare for example showed that, of 65 students, less than half indicated positive correlations between comprehensibility and scores.

Furthermore, readability formulae were frequently used inappropriately.

Redish (1979)

Janice C Redish. *How to draft more understandable legal documents.* American Institutes for Research, 1979.

The author begins by making a series of seven assertions about legal documents and how they are drafted.

- Many legal documents cannot be read and understood by a lay person.
- People without legal training have to read and understand many legal documents.
- Much legal writing is unintelligible even to lawyers.
- Tradition (not necessity)—and a lack of understanding of the audience—are the major reasons that legal language is so obscure.
- Legal language can be made clear without losing its necessary precision.
- It is not the technical vocabulary but complex sentence structure that makes legal writing so difficult to understand.
- Clarity is not the same as simplicity, brevity or 'plain English'.

Redish goes on briefly to discuss document design as a process rather than a series of operations. She then offers a series of ten guidelines, illustrating each with examples, that are intended to promote better legal drafting.

Redish (1981a)

Janice C Redish. 'How to write regulations (and other legal documents) in clear English'. *In*: Richard A Givens (ed.), *Drafting documents in plain language.*
Practising Law Institute, 1981, 207-265.

Using copious examples, Janice Redish describes an overall design methodology for creating public documents and offers specific guidelines for each stage of the process. Briefly summarised these are as follows:

STEP 1 - PLAN BEFORE YOU WRITE

- Get agreement on scope and policy before you write.
- Understand the agency's purposes in writing the rule.
- Think about all the different people who might have to read (and apply) your rule.
- Understand the way readers will use your regulation.
- Understand the constraints you must deal with.
- Involve your reviewers in the decisions about policy, audience, purpose and style before you write and keep them informed as you draft.

STEP 2 - SELECT APPROPRIATE CONTENT

- Include only information your audience needs.

STEP 3 - ORGANISE THE CONTENT AND MAKE IT CLEAR TO READERS

- Remember that most people use public documents as reference documents.
- If the document is a series of procedures, lay them out in chronological order.
- If different rules or parts of the document apply to different audiences, consider organising the document into a separate section for each audience.
- Show your organisation to your readers.

STEP 4 - WRITE A CLEAR FIRST DRAFT

- Use pronouns and simple names for the reader and the agency.
- Write in the active voice.
- Use action verbs instead of nouns made out of verbs.
- Write short sentences.
- Rewrite double negatives as positive sentences.
- Adjust your vocabulary for your audience.
- Avoid archaic legalisms.
- Don't try to cover all possibilities.
- Use 'may', 'must' or 'will' instead of 'shall'.

STEP 5 - REVIEW AND REVISE.

STEP 6 - EVALUATE THE DOCUMENT.

Redish (1981b)

Janice C Redish. *The language of the bureaucracy*
(Technical Report 15).
Document Design Project, American Institutes for Research, 1981.

The author identifies the characteristics of traditional bureaucratic language. In bureaucratic style of writing nouns tend to be over-used to replace pronouns, verbs, and adjectives. Bureaucratic writing tends to be full of jargon and slightly legalistic. Bureaucratic documents are often poorly organised, with uninformative headings and opaque tables of contents. They show a lack of concern for what the audience needs to know and there is a general lack of coordination in their production and distribution.

Redish then looks at some of the reasons that explain the feasures of bureaucratic language. In the case of legal documents the professionals feel that if lay readers could understand legal language, it would lose some of its mystique. In the case of official publications, the government tends to present itself as an impersonal guardian of the public welfare. The traditional bureaucratic language used is passive and is meant to indicate a strong, impersonal and therefore impartial institution.

Other factors relate to institutional inertia and the traditional models that writers feel obliged to follow. This may be exacerbated by time pressures which prohibit changes in procedures, by the institutional review process which can be cumbersome and hierarchical, and by a lack of training in producing good public documents.

Redish (1985)

Janice C Redish. *Beyond readability: how to write and design understandable life insurance policies.*
Committee on Consumer Affairs, American Council of Life Insurance, 1985.

A small booklet setting out some valuable guidelines for compiling public documents. Redish concludes with a 23-item checklist which can be used to assess an insurance policy (or, indeed, any public document). This checklist is derived from the guidelines and covers factors relating to layout, language, typography, and graphic design.

Redish and others (1981)

Janice C Redish, Daniel B Felker and Andrew M Rose. 'Evaluating the effects of document design principles.'
Information Design Journal 2(3/4), 1981, 236-243.

This paper develops a model of the process of designing documents based on research carried out at the US Document Design Centre (see overleaf).

The authors argue a detailed case against using readability measures in the evaluation of leaflets for the general public. They argue that an audience-centred evaluation, where a sample of potential users reads and answers questions about the document, is a far more appropriate tool for evaluation.

Work at the Document Design Centre has shown that changing a single feature (or just a few features) of a document, such as the insertion of informative headings will not yield startling improvements. Where substantial revision is undertaken, it is possible to

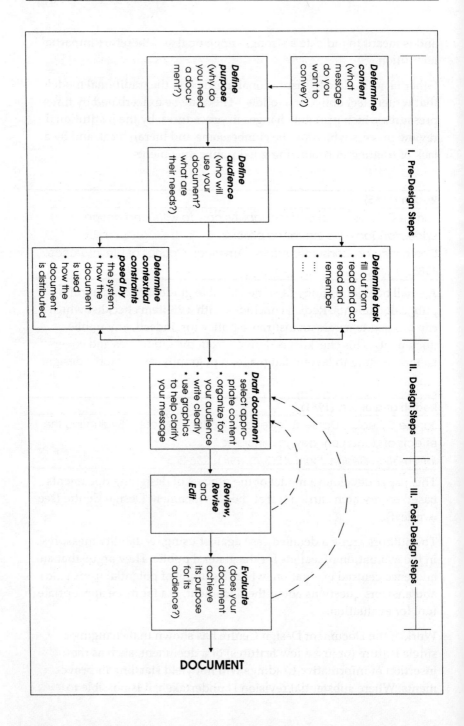

Determine content
(what message do you want to convey?)

Define purpose
(why do you need a document?)

Define audience
(who will use your document? what are their needs?)

Determine task
* fill out form
* read and act
* read and remember
* ...
* ...

Determine contextual constraints posed by
* the system
* how the document is used
* how the document is distributed

Draft document
* select appropriate content
* organize for your audience
* write clearly
* use graphics to help clarify your message

Review, Revise and Edit

Evaluate
(does your document achieve its purpose for its audience?)

DOCUMENT

I. Pre-Design Steps

II. Design Steps

III. Post-Design Steps

observe significant differences in user performance. The authors illustrate this by reference to a specific study based on reactions to a US government federal regulation governing the use of two-way radios on recreational boats.

The regulation was tested on 105 subjects who were given a 13-question comprehension test. 53 were experienced and 52 inexperienced in boating. One half of each group were given the original regulation, the other half the revised document. The rules were evaluated in terms of:

• The number of correct answers given by respondents.

• The average amount of time taken to answer the test questions.

• A subjective assessment made by each of the subjects of how difficult the rules were to follow.

This study was carried out by government writers with the help of researchers and it is concluded that 'non-research trained document designers can plan and conduct a useful empirical evaluation of a public document'.

Reid and Beveridge (1990)

DJ Reid and Michael Beveridge. 'Reading illustrated science texts: a micro-computer based investigation of children's strategies'. *British Journal of Educational Psychology* 60(1), 1990, 76-87.

Research has shown that the effect of illustrations on children's learning of science is related to ability. In this study, 180 children aged 14 were asked to learn about three illustrated science topics which were graded in increasing order of difficulty.

The topics were presented to them on a BBC microcomputer, and the software was programmed to record the time each child spent on both the segments of text and the illustrations. The software program also recorded the precise locations in the text where illustrations were accessed. It was found that significantly longer times were spent looking at the illustrations as the topics became more difficult. For every second that the least able (the bottom 17 per cent) children spent accessing pictures, they spent about four seconds reading the text. In contrast, for the higher ability children, this ratio was reduced to about one-to-six. Lower ability children tended to access illustrations much more often.

The most important conclusion to emerge from this research is the evidence that it provides to support the view that children of different abilities employ different strategies when decoding illustrated texts.

Research Business (1986)

The Research Business. *Action Special 1985: qualitative research – new cover design.*
The Research Business, 1986.

The *Action special booklet* was designed to complement a BBC Radio One programme and contains information about job opportunities, career options and training courses for young people leaving school. This research focused on five different cover designs and six sample layouts and was conducted using six group discussions.

The original booklet was criticised for using pictures that were superfluous, though *relevant* pictures were felt to improve it. The question and answer format was felt to be more interesting and to make the information easier to handle than a series of statements presented in a block of text.

Overall, the views of covers indicated that the young people thought they should convey information that is relevant to the contents, and be printed in attractive colours.

Some pictures were found to alienate the readers if they were seen as irrelevant to the text or depicting people who did not reflect the readership. The use of diagrams was appreciated, enabling the quick assimilation of information as well as being easier to use and more attractive. But graphics used for purely 'cosmetic' reasons were particularly criticised. Diagrams and flowcharts needed to be used carefully to avoid making the pages seem cluttered.

Research Surveys of Great Britain (1985)

The right to buy your home: evaluation of a publicity campaign directed at Council tenants.
Research Surveys of Great Britain, 1985.

This evaluation of all aspects of a publicity campaign to encourage council tenants to buy their homes, found that the leaflets were by far the most frequently mentioned aspect of the campaign (32 per cent), followed by TV advertising (20 per cent). They also led to much higher levels of knowledge than either press or TV advertising. However, the decay in prompted awareness after a 6 week period was greatest for the leaflet (33 per cent to 23 per cent) and smallest for the press advertisement (31 per cent to 30 per cent).

Reynolds (1988)

Linda Reynolds. 'Legibility of type'.
Baseline 10(1), 1988, 26-29.

The guidance that emerges from this review of some of the factors affecting the legibility of type is aimed particularly at readers who may not have a formal information design background, but who nonetheless are involved in the production of documents for the general public using in-house desktop publishing facilities.

Rice and others (1989)

G Elizabeth Rice, Bonnie J F Meyer and David C Miller. 'Using text structure to improve older adults' recall of important medical information'.
Educational Gerontology 15(5), 1989, 527-542.

Research has clearly established the existence of a 'levels effect' that results in a tendency for readers to remember key information more clearly the higher the level of its location in the structure of text, at the level of a heading, for instance. This experimental study made use of the 'levels effect' to investigate older adults' recall of important medical information.

Seventy older adults (over 65) read and recalled two passages containing information about arthritis and high blood pressure. Half the group read passages in which the text structures had been revised so that target ideas (those identified as the most important by medical specialists) were located at the highest levels of the content structure. The experiment was designed to investigate the degree to which recall is affected by four variables: revised text structure, education, medical condition, and age.

The results showed that the text revisions were moderately successful at increasing recall of target ideas. Education had the strongest effect of any variable on the recall of target information and detail, followed by age. Medical condition had little perceptible effect. An overall conclusion of the study is that the continuing sensitivity of older adults to prose structure (manifested in the levels effect) can be put to use to increase recall for important information. These findings have clear implications for the design of instructional materials for older adults.

Rimer and Glassman (1984)

Barbara Rimer and Bernard Glassman. 'How do persuasive health messages work? A health education field study.'
Health Education Quarterly 11(3), 1984, 313-321.

The authors set out to test empirically the validity of a definition of comprehension, and also to assess the significance of comprehension in determining whether or not a health education measure was acted upon.

They suggested that comprehension has three elements:

- *Psychological meaning* – the extent to which the reader can relate the message to their own life. This could be tested by asking a question like 'what would be the benefits for you of taking more exercise?'

- *Operational meaning* – the extent to which the reader can make use of the information: 'could you design an exercise schedule?'

- *Lexical meaning* – the extent to which the reader has understood, and can define, key words and phrases: 'tell me what "aerobic" means'.

The experiment involved a group of 65 randomly selected adults and a similar control group. The experimental group were given a booklet about heart disease and exercises and were tested when they had completed reading the booklet and re-tested four weeks later. Similar tests were carried out with the control group.

The experimental group scored higher on comprehension and on retention (comprehension four weeks later). Participants were also asked if they had changed their exercise pattern. Those who scored high on the measures of *psychological* and *operational* comprehension were more likely to have increased the amount of exercise they took. There was no significant correlation between measures of recall and recognition and increased exercise.

They conclude that comprehension is a complete phenomenon, and that attempts to measure comprehension which focus on recall and recognition can miss important factors. It is more important to measure the *psychological* and *operational* aspects of comprehension as these are more likely to lead to changes in behaviour.

They also note that significant information was forgotten in the four week period between the test, and recommended that health educators should find ways of making their messages more memorable.

Ritchie and Wilson (1979)

J Ritchie and P Wilson. *Social Security Claimants: a survey amongst the customers of a local social security office carried out on behalf of the DHSS.*
Office of Population Censuses and Surveys, 1979.

The aim of the study was to explore the opinions and experiences of the customers of a local social security office to examine how they view the service they receive.

Interviews were held with 348 people using unstructured questionnaires, which consisted mainly of open questions. About 50 per cent were supplementary and 50 per cent contributory benefit customers and the sample was stratified by the benefit claimed.

The study looked at:

- Contacts with the local office.

- Attitudes towards claiming social security benefits.

- Publicity, knowledge and information.

- Knowledge of assessment, appeals and payment.

- Views on the social security system.

- Causes of dissatisfaction among customers.

Over three quarters of the customers thought the public should be made more aware of the benefits. One third of them wanted to know which benefits people in their circumstances might be able to claim. The kind of information wanted reflected the general level of confusion and ignorance about the benefits.

A half of the customers had seen some general publicity about benefits and the same proportion had seen a DHSS leaflet. Noticeably fewer pensioners had done so.

In most cases the leaflets had been obtained from the local office or a post office. The other main sources of publicity were newspapers, television and notices in post offices.

All the customers who thought the public should be made aware of the benefits available were asked to suggest ways in which this could be achieved. The results are given in the table below.

Customers' suggestions for improving the publicity about benefits

Suggestions	Relative frequency
General	
Television advertisements	∎∎∎∎∎∎∎
Advertisements in newspapers/magazeines	∎∎∎∎∎∎∎
Posters in streets, railway stations, buses, bus shelters, shop windows	∎∎∎∎
Publicity on the radio	∎∎∎
More information at places of work	∎
Put circulars through people's doors	∎∎∎∎∎∎
Send out a car with a loudspeakesr (as on polling day)	∎
Produce a weekly paper (like a shopping guide)	∎

/ *continued*

Provide information for members of the public who are likely to be eligible for benefits

Send letters to people who might be eligible	■■■■
Visits to people's homes by social workers and health visitors	■■
Visits to people's homes by DHSS officials	■■■■
Give talks to special groups or at public meetings (eg women's institutes, pensioner clubs)	■■■■
Neighbours should be encouraged to inform people	■■■

Extent the information available for customers

Leaflets and posters in social security offices	■■■■■
Send leaflets/information with giros and order books	■■■■■■
Make the pamphlets clearer	■
Give more information during interviews at the office	■

Extend the publicity available in public places

Leaflets and posters in post offices	■■■■■
Leaflets and posters at libraries	■
Leaflets and posters in doctors' surgeries/health clinics	■■
Leaflets and posters in hospitals	■
Leaflets and posters in employment exchanges	■

Base: informants who felt that the public should be made more aware of the benefits available

---

Rose (1981)

Andrew M Rose. 'Problems in public documents'.
Information Design Journal 2(3/4), 1981, 179-196.

A useful account of a study carried out by the US Document Design Project to identify the extent and nature of the difficulties the general public faces when using public documents. It is useful mainly for the range of techniques it describes for identifying such difficulties. These included the following:

A critical incident survey
In this study, the interviewer asked the respondent to recall a specific instance when he or she filled out a form or helped someone else with a form and then to provide details about any problems that arose. Researchers then, independently, sorted the problems into categories.

From these categories a classification of user problems was evolved, which would be a useful checklist for designing a questionnaire-based evaluation of a document.

A critical documents project
The aim of this project was to identify a reasonably large but manageable number of critical and frequently-used public documents. It then determined how difficult each one was to use and understand, using a panel of judges. This proved a useful technique as there was a large degree of agreement among the judges.

Other document assessment techniques
Finally, three different techniques were used to identify the problems associated with each of the documents:

- A search for violations of document design guidelines.

- An analysis by an expert.

- An assessment of the information processing requirements of each document.

The main conclusions that were drawn from this study are that 'document design guidelines, if bolstered by some assertions regarding the document's purpose, make a good list to use to check a document for potential problems'. The work presented here confirms that people can agree in advance on the documents likely to cause problems. It is suggested that all public documents should also be field-tested by having an audience of potential users actually attempt to use them prior to final production.

Rose and Cox (1980)

Andrew M Rose and Louis A Cox. *Following instructions* (Technical Report 4), American Institutes for Research, 1980.

This study looked at the relative difficulty of conditional sentences (that is sentences of the form 'If Y then do X'). A total of 128 sentences was shown to each of 24 subjects. These represented 16 different conditional structures using 'and', 'or', and 'not' (for example, 'If you are B and not A then do X' or 'If you are not either A or B'). Each of these 16 structures was repeated eight times by substituting for A and

B single-male, single-female, married-male, married-female and the reverse of each pair (for example 'If you are single and not male then do X' or 'If you are not either female or married then do X').

Subjects were presented with these sentences in random order on a computer screen. Specially developed interactive software then recorded the accuracy and the speed of the reply. The results revealed that:

- 'Ors' take longer to process than 'ands' so that strings of 'ors' should be avoided.

- Wherever possible negated or embedded clauses should be avoided in the design of instructions (for example 'Not male and not married' should be changed to 'Female and single').

- Pseudoambiguous conditional instructions of the form, such as, 'If you are not A, and B, then do X' should be rewritten 'If you are B and not A then do X'. For example, in 'If you are not male and single, then go to question 5' it is not clear whether, single females should go to question 5 or not—to clear up any ambiguity it should be rewritten 'If you are single and not male, then go to Question 5'.

- Instructions which included 'not both' and 'not either' were especially difficult for the subjects. Instructions of the form 'If you are not (both/either) A or B then do X' should be rewritten as 'If you are not (both/either) B or not A then do X'.

Rowe (1982)

Camille L Rowe. 'The connotative dimensions of selected display typefaces'.
Information Design Journal 3(1), 1982, 30-37.

Like David Bartram (see Bartram 1982), Rowe used semantic differential scales to evaluate the typefaces. The 24 subjects were all lay people. The typefaces they evaluated were Helvetica, Garamond, Bodoni, Palatino and Times Roman (all general typefaces) as well as Cloister Black, Excelsior Script, Broadway, Libra and Legent (novelty typefaces chosen because they differed greatly from one another and because most of them had not been studied before).

From this study Rowe identified five main factors associated with particular typefaces:

- *Potency* – 7 scales – hard/soft; constrained/free; strong/weak; dark/light; masculine/feminine; rugged/delicate and tight/loose.

- *Elegance* – 4 scales – rich/poor; beautiful/ugly; expensive/cheap, and meaningful/meaningless.

- *Novelty* – 3 scales – simple/complex; legible/illegible, and usual/unusual.

- *Antiquity* – 2 scales – old/new and old-fashioned/modern.

- *Evaluation*– 2 scales – bad/good and dirty/clean.

Each of the typefaces is then discussed giving the results of this factor analysis. There is correlation between 'potency' and Bartram's 'potency' and 'elegance' and Bartram's 'evaluation' but no correlation in any of the other factors.

Ryder and Hughes (1985)

Randall James Ryder and Melody Hughes. 'The effect on text comprehension of word frequency'.
Journal of Educational Research 78(5), 1985, 286-291.

Various studies have identified word knowledge as the single most important factor in text comprehension. This study set out to test whether word frequency, which might be assumed to be related to word knowledge, had any effect on comprehension. Here frequency is defined, not as the number of times that a word appears in a document, but how frequently it appears in the language.

Using school students they tested two passages, one in which low frequency words were used, the other using high frequency words. Following reading students were tested for comprehension. 'Results indicated no significant differences between the two passages on either of the comprehension tests.'

Sanderson and others (1989)

Penelope M Sanderson, Jeffrey M James and Karen S Seidler. 'SHAPA: an interactive software environment for protocol analysis'. *Ergonomics* 32(11), 1989, 1271-1302.

This paper describes *SHAPA*, a software package for performing verbal (and non-verbal) protocol analysis. *SHAPA* has been specifically developed with the aim of engendering a feeling of direct engagement with the protocol data and so making the manipulation of data as direct as possible. The researcher can configure *SHAPA* to encode protocols using a wide variety of theoretical frameworks or vocabularies. The software allows protocol analysis to be performed at any level of analysis, and it supplies tools for data aggregation, manipulation and analysis.

The outputs generated by *SHAPA* can be used alone or in combination with other performance variables to build a rich picture of the influences on sequences of verbal or non-verbal behaviour. *SHAPA* should make protocol analysis more reliable by facilitating more appropriate encoding and by providing clearer access to the 'story' a protocol tells. However, the authors emphasise the point that using software does not guarantee that the results are more valid.

Schumacher (1981)

Gary M Schumacher. 'Schemata in text processing and design'. *Information Design Journal* 2(1), 1981, 17-27.

Schema theory suggests that the comprehension of text is an interactive process involving not only the text but the knowledge and experience that the reader brings to it. To illustrate this point Schumacher quotes the following passage:

> The procedure is actually quite simple. First, you arrange things into different groups. Of course, one pile may be sufficient depending on how much there is to do. If you have to go somewhere else due to lack of facilities that is the next step, otherwise you're pretty well set. It is important not to overdo things. That is, it is better to do too few things at once than too many. In the short run this may not seem important but complications can easily arise. A mistake can be expensive as well. At first the whole procedure will seem complicated. Soon, however, it

will become just another facet of life. It is difficult to foresee any end to the necessity for this task in the immediate future, but then one can never tell. After the procedure is completed one arranges the materials into different groups again. Then they can be put into their appropriate places. Eventually they will be used once more and the whole cycle will have to be repeated. However, this is part of life.[*]

For many people it is far from clear exactly what this simple event is. However, the brief comment about washing clothes makes the passage immediately interpretable. With this interpretation of comprehension it is possible to identify three reasons why readers fail to comprehend a passage. First, the reader simply may not have the appropriate schemata available to interpret a passage. For example, someone who has no knowledge of what is involved in washing clothes would not be able to comprehend the above passage. Secondly, a reader may have the correct schema but the passage cues are not sufficient to activate the knowledge on the part of the reader. This would be the case for anyone who initially had trouble comprehending the passage, but found it trivial on being given a context. Thirdly, readers may find an interpretation of the passage which handles the information but which is different from that intended by the author. For instance, the above passage could be interpreted as photocopying journal articles or even bricklaying.

Although the concept of schema has had a long history (going back as far a Kant's 1781 *Critique of Pure Reason*) it is only recently that the concept has attracted extensive research and theorising, and consequently there is little evidence from which specific applications to text design can be drawn. Most of the research has been undertaken with brief passages of text in well-controlled experimental settings.

It does seem from observational evidence that it is imperative that producers of text determine as accurately as possible the type of

---

[*] Taken from an experiment conducted by the psycholinguists J D Bransford and M K Jonson 'Contextual prerequisites for understanding: some investigations of comprehension and recall'. *Journal of Verbal Learning and Verbal Behaviour* 11, 1972, 717-726. [In the experiment, those subjects who were told the topic before hearing the passage remembered more than twice as many ideas as those who had not been told. They also rated the passage twice as understandable as those who had not been told the topic.]

knowledge readers are likely to have when they read a passage of text. This will be important in determining both the context and what concepts, relationships or inferences will need to be emphasised through typographical cuing. It is also necessary to bear in mind that the purposes for which a document is being read will influence the schemata the reader is likely to use in processing the text.

Schumacher and Waller (1985)

Gary M Schumacher and Robert Waller. 'Testing design alternatives: a comparison of procedures'. In: Thomas Duffy and Robert Waller (eds), *Designing usable texts.*
Academic Press, 1985.

The authors describe a range of procedures for evaluating document design, and assess these against six characteristics they consider to be desirable. These characteristics are:

- Time – how quickly the procedure can provide useful information.

- Usable form – whether the procedure produces data in a form that is easily analysed.

- Goodness-of-fit – whether it provides the right level of information.

- Reliability.

- Validity.

- Ease of use and cost.

Readability formulae
These are relatively easy to use, low in cost, quite reliable and timely. However, they do not provide a valid index of many of the factors that influence a document's usefulness. Similarly the goodness-of-fit is restricted. Finally, the information is provided in a form that is too general to help in document design. They are, therefore, most useful in giving a global assessment of documents for general audience use.

Performance tests
These usually focus on one design feature and study its impact on the ability of readers to remember, understand and use the text. Such tests can be carried out quickly, easily and inexpensively.

The data provided are not, however, easy to use and provide little guidance on how to modify a text. There are also doubts about validity. They are, therefore, most useful in establishing general principles of design. They can help designers to see the final impact of a particular design feature, but not to indicate how to redesign a document to make it more effective.

Structural analyses
These are detailed analyses of text content. They fail on all six desirable characteristics and appear to be of limited usefulness in document design evaluations.

User ratings
These are relatively easy to obtain, relatively inexpensive and have a reasonable goodness-of-fit. They are, however, time-consuming, suffer from reliability and validity problems and the results may not be easy to use. They are most useful for obtaining a global impression of a document.

User edits
Inexperienced individuals are assessed as they use a document, in order to determine potential design problems. A user edit is an inexpensive and easy-to-use method of evaluating a document. The procedure is, however, quite time-consuming and the data are difficult to summarise.

Protocol analyses
Individuals are asked to 'think aloud' as they attempt to understand a document or complete a form. Such analyses are relatively easy and inexpensive ways to collect data relevant to the design of a document and how that document is processed. There are some doubts about reliability and validity, but if used cautiously and carefully they can be a very useful method of evaluation.

Micro-eye-movement procedures
These are useful in helping to determine theoretical principles of document design that influence reading behaviour. They are, however, expensive and require specialised skills to operate the

equipment, and there are serious doubts about the generalisability of the results.

Macro-eye-movement procedures

Three methods of analysing a reader's eye movements are described and the authors conclude that 'this system holds promise for investigating some general design issues that have not been addressed by other methods. It remains to be seen how generalisable information obtained from this procedure is to real-world settings.'

Macro-processing procedures

A procedure like the Study-Protocol Recorder is the first system to allow systematic measurement of long-term reading behaviour on large text segments. The data collected, however, will probably be of little use for the design of a specific document.

Shilling (1981)

Dana Shilling. Plain English document design.
Information Design Journal 2(3/4), 1981, 244-240.

Shilling describes a number of techniques for plain English document design. In terms of overall design, documents should be divided into discrete, not too long, units with adequate white space between them. Wide margins are useful, not only to provide visual relief, but also to allow users to insert notes or make additions to the document. Standard size papers should be used so that documents fit into standard envelopes and filing cabinets. Black ink on white paper provides an efficient and easy-to-read document at minimal cost. Coloured paper can be a useful aid to processing when multiple copies of a form are involved.

Typography is also an important consideration. The most useful typefaces for public documents are those that have a relatively large body height, are moderately expanded, and have a fairly uniform type colour. Very delicate typefaces, or those with unusually long ascenders and descenders are too light in colour and may lead to eyestrain. For the same reasons dark, heavy faces are unsuitable for the main body of the text. Very formal and very informal or highly-decorated typefaces are inappropriate. The most suitable typefaces are possibly those in the

Century series; Times Roman; Gill Sans; News Gothic; and Helvetica.
Headings and subheadings should always be clearly identified.

An overall consideration is that a balance needs to be struck between
the needs of those who read and use a document and those who
process it at the office end.

Siegel (1979)

Alan Siegel. 'Drafting simplified legal documents: basic principles and
their application'. *In*: Duncan A MacDonald (ed.), *Drafting documents
in plain language*. Practising Law Institute, 1979, 175-252.

The author outlines six basic considerations that should be borne in
mind when legal documents are being drafted. These are content;
organisation of content; the need for legal compliance; language of the
document; its length; and finally its design. Siegel offers further
guidance on each of these considerations.

He also identifies four different approaches that are often made to
simplifying documents, using, as an example, a loan note. These are:

- Revising the content.

- Simplifying the organisation of the document.

- Simplifying its language.

- Reducing its length.

None of these, the author argues, is likely to be sufficient on its own.

Siegel and Glascoff (1981)

Alan Siegel and Donald G Glascoff. 'Case history: simplifying an
apartment lease'. In: Richard A Givens (ed.), *Drafting documents in
plain language*.
Practising Law Institute, 1981, 169-205.

This case study draws on a property leasehold agreement to illustrate
two methods by which a legal document can be revised.

In the first method, the existing document is used as a base, and its
contents translated into plain English, with a supplementary look at
the legal requirements. The other method involves creating an entirely

new document from scratch. That is, starting from the legal and administrative requirements of the transaction and then drafting an agreement which expresses the rights and responsibilities of, in this case, the landlord and tenants.

Siegel and Glascoff conclude that the more comprehensive second method is to be preferred when simplifying documents whose contents can be strongly influenced by complex external factors such as legislation.

Simply Stated (1982)

Simply Stated. 'Six graphic guidelines'.
Simply Stated 30, 1982.

A set of six guidelines based on the experience and expertise of the United States Document Design Centre.

- Use highlighting techniques (such as bold type, italics and white spaces) but do not overdo them.

- Use 8 to 10 point type for text.

- Avoid making lines of type too long or too short. The best line length is 50-70 characters.

- Use white space in margins and between sections.

- Use ragged right-hand margin.

- Avoid using all capital letters—use other highlighting techniques, such as bold type, italics or colour instead.

Sless (1985)

David Sless. *Form evaluation: some simple methods.*
Canberra Department of Sport Recreation and Tourism, 1985.

Sless offers practical guidance on the testing and evaluation of government forms. He maintains that, in general, the balance of opinion among information designers favours qualitative rather than quantitative methods. While no single method is superior to all others, there are some that are more useful to designers with limited resources or experience in evaluation.

These methods can be grouped under two headings: analytic methods and user studies. Analytic methods include the use of checklists, consistency studies, and analysis of errors. User studies include techniques such as interviews and observation studies.

Sless underlines a number of other important points. First, no form should be revised until it has been evaluated in its existing format. Secondly, any redesign should be preceded by the preparation of an 'image of user' document for each type of person who will be required to use the form. Thirdly, consideration needs to be given to the 'grammar of forms' or the rules for form design. Finally, the author looks at the question of who should carry out the evaluation, and concludes that designers should evaluate each other's work. Practical guidance is offered on each of these points and, in conclusion, he outlines a six-stage design process for developing a new form.

Stage one – planning the relationship between the form and the administrative system.

Stage two – constructing 'images of the form users'.

Stage three – developing a protocol of the questions that will go into the form. These should then be evaluated with user studies and modified three times before the optimum wording and order of questions is reached.

Stage four – designing the form and evaluating the artwork through analysis and user studies.

Stage five – after introducing the form, its performance should be assessed by user studies and error analysis.

Stage six – revising the form in the light of findings from its use.

Sless (1987)

David Sless. *Name and address please: a guide for forms designers* Communications Research Institute of Australia, 1987.

The author examined the name and address sections of 2,239 completed forms and, based on this analysis, presents a set of conventions for forms designers. These covered both the height and the width of response boxes.

- *Height of boxes* – 8 mm was the optimum for general use, but 7 mm was considered adequate if the form is not likely to be completed by elderly or disabled people.

- *Width of boxes* – 40 mm should be allowed for each given name; 50 mm for the family name. 140 mm should be allowed for the address and postcode.

He proposes that captions are best placed outside the response box.

Smagorinsky (1989)

Peter Smagorinsky. 'The reliability and validity of protocol analysis'. *Written Communication* 6(4), 1989, 463-479.

Smagorinsky reviews the development of protocol analysis techniques and their use as tools for analysing the process of composition. He examines recent claims and criticisms of the techniques and concludes that they are valuable, but only if conducted according to rigorous principles and procedures.

Smagorinsky makes a series of recommendations for using protocol analysis techniques.

The method of protocol analysis should emerge from a theoretical framework underlying the problem the researcher is trying to study.

The results of a protocol analysis should be substantiated by several forms of evidence—the protocol transcript should be compared with the written product, and independent judges should agree on the segmenting and coding transcripts.

The researcher should identify variables that affect the subjects, and thus influence the content of the protocol transcripts.

Finally, Smagorinsky argues for the need for more research into the technique itself, not least with regard to its possible applications in other areas of the social sciences.

Smith and Goodman (1984)

Edward E Smith and Lorraine Goodman. 'Understanding written instructions: the role of an explanatory schema'.
Cognition and Instruction 1(4), 1984, 359-396.

This paper deals with how people use and understand written instructions, such as those for assembling a simple electrical or mechanical kit. Typically, written instructions consist entirely of a linear sequence of steps which need to be executed to arrive at a final outcome. Theoretical considerations suggest that performance might be improved if explanatory information which offered a rationale for each step were included in written instructions. To test this hypothesis, the authors prepared three sets of instructions, for assembling an electrical circuit, and organised them in different ways:

- Typical linear organisation *(linear instructions)*.

- Steps to be executed plus explanatory information emphasising the structure of the circuit *(structural instructions)*.

- Steps to be executed plus explanatory information emphasising the function of the circuit *(functional instructions)*.

In the first of three experiments subjects, college engineering students were asked to read and then carry out the instructions by assembling the circuit. When they were later asked to recall the instructions orally, those who had followed the structural or functional instructions performed better than those who had followed the linear set.

The results of the second experiment confirmed an observation noted in the first, and showed that there was a demonstrable advantage in terms of reading speed associated with structural and functional instructions.

In the final experiment, subjects were given the task of assembling a second electrical circuit without any written guidance. Those who had previously used structural or functional instructions were better at this task than those who had previously followed the linear steps. It was concluded that this indicated that they had gained a more complete understanding of the principles of elementary circuit building.

Smith and Smith (1984)

Ron F Smith and Kay L Smith. 'A comparison of readability formulae as applied to newspaper stories'.
Journal of Reading 28(1), 1984, 20-23.

A number of newspaper articles were tested using the Flesch Formula, the Dale-Chall Formula, the FOG Index and the SMOG Grading. This showed that the different tests did not rank stories consistently casting doubt on their usefulness.

Stahl and Jacobson (1986)

SA Stahl and MG Jacobson. 'Vocabulary difficulty, prior knowledge and text comprehension'.
Journal of Reading Behaviour 18(4), 1986, 309-323.

Earlier studies have demonstrated the individual effects of both vocabulary difficulty and prior knowledge on reading comprehension. The purpose of this investigation was to try to find out if the two interact and if prior knowledge can compensate for vocabulary difficulty.

It is known that most readers skip words they do not know, as long as they still manage to comprehend. Stahl and Jacobson hypothesised that if the vocabulary in a passage becomes too difficult, readers use their prior knowledge to understand the overall meaning, while disregarding many of the words.

Sixty-one sixth grade high school students were tested in four groups. Each student received a 500 word passage about a ritual feast of the Yanomamo Indians living in the Amazon, but the texts varied between the groups.

- Group 1 received a simple language version.

- Group 2 received a simple language version and pre-instruction about the Yanomamo tribe.

- Group 3 received a difficult language version.

- Group 4 received a difficult language version and pre-instruction about the Yanomamo tribe.

All four groups were given two comprehension tests. The first comprised 14 questions, five of which were designed to be textually explicit (where the answers are contained in the text); five textually implicit (where the answers need to be inferred from the text); and five scripturally implicit (where the answers needs to be inferred on the basis of prior knowledge).

The second test involved sentence verification, where 23 sentences were selected from the simple language text and were either reproduced as in the text or slightly modified to convey the opposite meaning. The students were asked to indicate which sentences 'were in the story or meant the same as a sentence in the story'.

The results show that both vocabulary difficulty and pre-instruction had significant effects on comprehension. There was, however, no significant indication that they interacted. It should be noted that these two studies were looking at pre-instruction rather than prior knowledge or schemata.

Stark (1988)

Heather A Stark. 'What do paragraph markings do?'
Discourse Processes 11(3), 1988, 275-303.

Stark investigated the role of paragraph markings in texts by means of two linked empirical studies.

In the first study, answers were sought to the question 'how informative is a paragraph marking?' Subjects were asked to identify and then reinstate paragraph boundaries into three texts where the original paragraph markers had been removed. If paragraph boundaries are arbitrary, subjects would not be expected to agree with one another, nor with the original author. The results showed that a paragraph division is not entirely specified by the content of a text: the subjects provided a range of responses, sometimes in agreement, sometimes not. But their justification of their decisions were surprisingly uniform. Overwhelmingly, they believed themselves to be responding to topic changes or the introduction of new topics. However, subjects agreed with each other and with the author more than they would as a result of chance.

The second study looked at the effectiveness of paragraph cues by examining how the presence and positioning of paragraph boundaries affects comprehension. The results showed that paragraph cues are indeed effective. When placed in a plausible position, they encouraged readers to believe that the beginning of the paragraph marked the beginning of an important new idea.

Steffensen (1986)

M Steffensen. 'Register, cohesion and cross-cultural reading comprehension'.
Applied Linguistics 7(1), 1986, 71-85.

The term 'register' refers to the variety of language which is appropriate in a given situation. It is external to the text and therefore depends upon factors such as the topic covered, the purpose of a document, and the people involved in producing or receiving it. A technical paper written for discussion by experts would, therefore, differ in register from an article written on the same topic in a popular newsletter to stimulate discussion amongst lay people. 'Cohesion', on the other hand, refers to the linguistic relationships between different parts of a text. It is internal to the text and refers to the choice of grammar and words to create an organised piece of text.

In this paper, Steffensen looks at the relationships between register, cohesion, and background knowledge, drawing on the results of three cross-cultural studies. The first of these studies investigated the comprehension of adult subjects from the United States and India, who read letters about an Indian wedding and an American wedding. The results showed that subjects:

• Read their 'native' passages more quickly than the 'foreign' passage.

• Recalled significantly more of their 'native' passage correctly.

• Elaborated the 'native' passage by introducing into their recalls additional details that were consistent with the original text.

• Produced more errors in their recall of the 'foreign' passage.

While the first study used written texts, it was followed up by a similar experiment using oral ones. In the second study American and Australian Aboriginal women listened to two texts about an illness and its treatment. One of the texts was based on Aboriginal beliefs, the other on Western beliefs. After hearing one text read, each subject was asked to supply some personal information about herself to inhibit short-term memory and then to recall the story orally. The same procedure was repeated for the second text and both recalls were tape-recorded.

The results corroborated those of the first study:

- More of the 'native' text was recalled.

- There were more elaborations in the recalls of the 'native' text.

- There were more distortions in the recalls of the 'foreign' text.

Steffensen concluded that previous knowledge is an important factor in the comprehension of a text.

The third study involved the recall of a text which was biased towards a minority group of readers. This text was a story describing an incident involving 'sounding', a ritual of verbal insults that occurs primarily in black inner-city communities in the United States. The text was read by rural white and inner-city black students and their oral recalls tape-recorded. The results showed that readers who shared the author's cultural background were significantly more likely to understand the passage than those who did not.

While the link between register and background knowledge is fairly evident, the link between cohesion and background knowledge is, perhaps, less so. The wedding-letter texts used in the first experiment each contained six complex sentences with a causal or adversative conjunction. Four of these were considered to have particular cultural significance, that is, the cause-effect relationship was based on information specific to that culture. Analysis of the recall protocols of the American text showed that the American subjects recalled more cohesive elements in culturally-significant sentences than did the Indian subjects. In fact, the Indian subjects were more likely to recall only one part of the causal statement. There were also a number of cases in which the cohesive element was used incorrectly to join two propositions that did not have a cause and effect relationship in the original text.

In conclusion, Steffensen argues that

> the results of this preliminary study provide some support for the claim that when there is a breakdown in comprehension, certain aspects of textual cohesion will be lost in the process of reading and recalling.

A fourth experiment was conducted to test the proposition that register, cohesion and background knowledge all interact in the process of comprehension. To do this the first 302 words of the Indian wedding letter were specially prepared so that each clause was contained on a separate page in a booklet. Two subjects, an Indian woman and an American woman, read this text, a clause at a time, in an interview setting. They were asked to describe what they had already learnt from the text and what they expected to follow.

The results showed that the text was more easily understood when the reader possessed the appropriate background knowledge. In particular, such knowledge prevents ambiguous sections being inappropriately interpreted. They also demonstrated that background knowledge and register can together affect the processing of cohesive devices in the text.

Suen and Komoda (1986)

C Y Suen and M K Komoda. 'Legibility of digital type-fonts and comprehension in reading'. In: J C van Vliet (ed.), *Text processing and document manipulation.*
Cambridge University Press, 1986, 178-187.

Two experiments were carried out to investigate the effects of font styles on legibility and reading proficiency. Three commonly-encountered fonts were chosen: Letter Gothic, Courier and DEC-Writer. These were selected to exhibit a range of serif and non-serif, dot-matrix without ascenders and descenders and letter-quality properties. Both upper- and lower-case characters were tested.

The legibility test was conducted with seven subjects, all with normal vision. Each completed ten sessions of approximately two hours, over a period of two weeks. During these sessions they were asked to recall individual letters that were flashed very briefly onto a microcomputer screen and followed by a masking after varying periods of time. The more legible fonts should lead to better recall especially at the shorter intervals between seeing the letter and seeing the masking stimulus.

The results showed that the san serif Letter Gothic font was the most legible font, and the dot-matrix DEC font the least legible. More detailed analysis showed that, with both Letter Gothic and DEC-Writer, there was a tendency for some lower case letters to be mistaken for upper case. With Courier the reverse happened.

A second experiment was undertaken to see if the above results could be generalised to reading. A total of 36 subjects were given a number of texts to read, one word at a time, on a microcomputer screen at a rate of 600 words a minute. In all, there were nine experimental texts of about 160 words in length, each produced in each of the three fonts being studied. Each subject read each of the texts, but in one font only. The subjects were then given a series of multiple choice questions based on the texts.

Once again, the dot-matrix DEC-Writer font, which lacked ascenders and descenders, invoked the lowest performance. There was, however, little difference between Letter Gothic (san serif) and Courier (serif).

Swaney and others (1981)

Joyce H Swaney. *Editing for comprehension: improving the process through reading protocols*
(Technical Report 14).
American Institutes for Research, 1981.

Three experiments were designed to explore the process of skilled editing. The aim was to understand why editing often fails, and to determine what can be done to make it more effective.

In the first experiment, 24 adult volunteers read four documents which had been revised by skilled editors. After reading each document, the volunteers completed a comprehension test. The results showed that while three of the documents had been improved by the revision, the fourth appeared to have been made worse.

In the second experiment, protocols of subjects reading the fourth document were collected in order to pinpoint why there were comprehension difficulties. The document was then revised once more and tested on twelve new subjects.

Comprehension tests from this third experiment revealed that the error rate had dropped dramatically.

Swaney concluded that standard editing techniques sometimes fail to improve clarity, even when used by skilled editors. She argues that reading protocols can provide a powerful editing tool when standard editing techniques fail. Even so a number of queries are raised:

- How many protocols are needed to revise a document?

- How can questions best be asked with protocols? In this experiment they were asked after the protocols and were very valuable in bringing to light misunderstandings which the subjects were not aware of as they read.

- Will all editors benefit from collecting protocols? How do you move from an awareness of a problem to its solution?

- Can protocols be used in training editors?

Swarts and others (1980)

H Swarts, L S Flower and J R Hayes. *How headings in documents can mislead readers*
(Technical Report 9).
American Institutes for Research, 1980.

Previous research has shown that the use of headings in a document can help both the comprehension and recall of its contents. The purpose of this series of experiments was to investigate the effect of inaccurate, incomplete or vague headings.

In the first experiment, 55 subjects were read the headings from three documents which related to business administration, and were asked to write down what they expected those sections to cover. One of the documents contained vague headings, another misleading headings, while the third was a rewritten document whose headings focused on the readers' needs. The subjects' written predictions of content were then scored for each heading as 'correct', 'partially correct' or 'incorrect'.

The results showed that the rewritten document headings led to 74 per cent correct predictions of content, the original document with vague headings to 50 per cent correct predictions, and the original document with misleading headings led to no correct predictions at all.

In the second experiment, the subjects were given ten key sentences and asked to match them to the appropriate heading. In this case the rewritten document led to 60 per cent accurate matchings, the original with vague headings to 50 per cent accuracy, and the original document with misleading headings to only 10 per cent accuracy.

The authors conclude that where heading are ineffective they tend to be vague and focused on broad concepts. Effective headings, on the other hand, are accurate, specific and focus on the readers' needs and goals.

The third experiment addressed the importance of headings within the context of the document as a whole. Can clear prose outweigh misleading headings? Can misleading headings make a difference to usability even in generally clear documents? To find out, five versions of the same insurance policy were tested. Three used a plain English text. Of these one had clear headings, one had vague and misleading headings, and the third no headings at all. The other two versions used the original hard-to-read text, one with misleading headings and the other with helpful headings. Each version was tested on five people. The subjects were given a list of questions and were asked to search for the answers in the document, without having read it first. The subjects were also asked to look at the questions again and to predict under which heading they thought each answer should, logically, be found. The following factors were calculated for each version of the text:

- The time it took to answer the questions.

- The number of times answers were correctly matched to the headings they were found under.

- The number of questions answered correctly.

The only factor which was found to be significant was the last of these. In fact, subjects reading insurance policies with clear headings did not take significantly less time to answer questions than those whose policies had misleading headings. More surprisingly, they did not do significantly better at matching answers to their headings. This result, therefore contradicts the findings of the first two experiments. The clear prose versions, however, all performed better than the versions with the original text.

The conclusion drawn is that clear prose generally outweighs misleading headings. This seems to agree with the findings of Charrow and Redish's study of headings in warranties (see Charrow and Redish 1980). However, the authors point out that their findings may not apply to all documents. The plain English insurance policies were all designed so that they would be easy to use. It is suggested that the role headings play seems to be dependent on the length, style, purpose, and degree of familiarity of a document. Thus headings may assume a greater importance in densely printed documents, such as regulations.

The report concludes by outlining ways of writing headings that will help readers to locate information within a document. Heading should set the scene explicitly for the reader using phrases such as 'How this policy affects use and your family'. In some cases a keyword will be sufficient . Such cases depend on:

- The extent to which the reader can be expected to understand the document's assumptions, purpose, structure and scope. Tthe more unfamiliar a document is, the more the reader will need to use heading cues to understand the framework of the document as a whole.

- How clearly intended readers will understand the terms in the heading.

- The choice of keywords that are both accurate and specific.

Talkback Research (1985)

Talkback Research. PSA contact forms
Talkback Research, 1985.

A total of 45 interviews were held with both contractors and officials, to assess reactions to a revised Property Services Agency booklet setting out 'General conditions of Government contracts' for small businesses.

There was no indication that a clear and straightforward presentation was considered condescending. On the contrary, the easier the document was to use, the more favourably it was received by both contractors and officials.

Tomaselli and Tomaselli (1984)

Kayan G Tomaselli and Ruth Tomaselli. 'Media graphics as an interventionist strategy'.
Information Design Journal 4(2), 1984, 99-117.

This paper describes a project to design and evaluate health education graphics in order to communicate with semi-literate readers in a black township in South Africa.

The project demonstrated that the design of media graphics needs to be context-based. Design should be preceded by in-depth research, not only of the problem, but also of the target readership and their interpretive patterns. Reliance on research done elsewhere can never be entirely satisfactory, since social, political, and economic conditions differ.

Townsend and others (1990)

Michael AR Townsend and others. 'Headings within multiple-choice tests as facilitators of test performance'.
British Journal of Educational Psychology 60(2), 1990, 153-160.

There is a great deal of evidence to support the view that learning from prose can be enhanced if headings are inserted ahead of sections of text. As well as helping people to retain information, headers may contribute to more efficient reading by helping readers to switch between one knowledge schema and another.

Townsend reports on an empirical study to test the effect of introducing headings into a multiple-choice test. The experimental sample comprised 287 undergraduate students enrolled in an educational psychology degree. All students were asked to complete an identical multiple-choice test, except that some contained headings while others did not. The students were then asked to complete a questionnaire by which they self-rated their attitudes to headings.

The results showed that the presence of headings made little contribution to actual test performance. At the same time, the majority of students endorsed a belief that headings serve important cognitive functions. It appears that headings may facilitate performance more at the time when learning material is being encoded rather than at the time of retrieval during the test.

Trent (1982)

Curtis Trent. 'What should a title say?'
Journal of Extension 10, 1982, 18-22.

An interesting research project which looked at the influence of cover titles and illustrations on a potential user's selection of a publication.

A set of six pamphlets relating to health and nutrition were selected for testing. The covers of these were simply illustrated and each pamphlet was printed on a different coloured paper. The titles were straightforward and were written in the 'how to' format—'How to save money', 'How to control your weight'. For comparison an additional set of publications was produced. The new pamphlets were identical to the original ones in colour, shape, size and content, but the illustrations were removed from the cover and the titles were changed so that they were more informative—for example the pamphlet corresponding to 'How to save money' was entitled 'Convenience foods'.

Multiple copies of the two sets of pamphlets were placed randomly on a display board which was subsequently placed in six different locations. Selection of pamphlets made from the board by the general public were monitored. When a pamphlet was taken from the board, the monitor approached the person taking it and the reasons for its selection were recorded. A total of 195 people were interviewed in this way.

The results showed that there was a significant presference for the 'how to' illustrated pamphlets, over pamphlets that simply specified subject content. The selection ratio was about three to one. It was not, however, possible to determine the separate effects of the wording of the title and the cover illustration. Clearly the different versions of the pamphlets should have varied in one aspect only.

The results are, therefore, of limited value to designers of public documents. What is more useful is the technique used to monitor the selection of pamphlets by the general public.

Trice (1986)

Ashton D Trice. 'Elements of personalisation in covering letters may affect response rates in mail surveys: a further analysis of Worthen and Valcarce (1985)'.
Psychological Reports 58(1), 1986, 82.

Ashton Trice reanalysed 23 previous studies cited by Worthen and Valcarce (see Worthen and Valcarce 1985). Trice suggests that where questionnaires ask for personal information, a form letter tends to be preferred to a personalised letter. This may be because the use of personalised salutations leads respondents to question the confidentiality of the research.

Urquhart (1980)

Christine Urquhart. 'Reading, looking and learning'.
Journal of Information Science 1(6), 1980, 333-344.

This review of research relating to reading and comprehension is written from the standpoint of an information officer who needs to understand both how subject specialists read and understand material and what aids and hinders their comprehension.

The research areas covered by the article include the psychology of reading; text structure and content and its effect on comprehension and learning; reading strategies and the possibilities of altering reading behaviour by increasing reading speed or improving learning patterns; and the ways that the mind and eye interact in the visual processing of text.

Vanderplas and Vanderplas (1980)

J M Vanderplas and J H Vanderplas. 'Some factors affecting legibility of printed materials for older adults'.
Perceptual and Motor Skills 50(3), 1980, 923-932.

Reading speed and acceptance ratings were obtained as a function of type size, type style, line width, and line spacing in two experiments with samples of older adults. Significant differences were found for different styles as well as different sizes of type. Roman styles of type were read more quickly than Gothic styles. Reading speed also increased as type size was increased—participants were happier with type sizes of 12 point upwards, although there was not much significant increase in reading speed beyond 14 point. Significant interactions were also found between different line widths and spacing for different sizes of type of the same style. The implications of these findings for the design of printed materials for use by older adults are discussed briefly.

Verhoeven (1990)

Ludo T Verhoeven. 'Acquisition of reading in a second language'.
Reading Research Quarterly 25(2), 1990, 107-112.

The purpose of this longitudinal study was to investigate differences in reading acquisition between children learning to read in their native language and those learning to read in a second language.

Verhoeven studied Dutch and Turkish children in the first two grades of primary school in the Netherlands as they learned to read in Dutch. The children were given a number of tasks to assess their word recognition and comprehension skills.

The Turkish children were found to be less efficient in various reading processes in Dutch than their monolingual Dutch peers. However, evidence emerged from the study that both Dutch and Turkish children rely on highly comparable strategies. During the first two grades, both word recognition and comprehension skills appear to be most strongly influenced by children's oral proficiency in the second language. This finding suggests that children learning to read in a second language should be helped to build their oral skills, and that reading instruction should be matched to those skills.

Wagenaar and others (1987)

Willem A Wagenaar, Rob Schreuder and Gert Jan Wijlhuizen.
'Readability of instructional text, written for the general public'.
Applied Cognitive Psychology 1(3), 1987, 155-167.

This paper addresses a question that is central to information design practice: 'Is there an easy way to predict the readability of a written text simply by analysing its formal properties?'.

The readability of nine texts written for a general audience was assessed using twelve different scores. Five were obtained from the structural analysis proposed by Kintsch and colleagues at the macro level of text comprehension. Four of the other measures were related to reading speed, and the three remaining were a subjective measure of readability; the Flesch index; and a cloze percentage test. The most effective measures of readability were provided by the Flesch score at the micro level and Kintsch's number of re-instatements at the macro level.

The pattern of correlation between the twelve metrics revealed a close relationship between subjective assessments, cloze scores, Flesch indices, the number of propositions per 1,000 words, and all four measures of reading speed. The remaining readability measures—those proposed by Kintsch—did not correlate with this group, nor was it possible to demonstrate any significant association amongst the measures in the group. A principal components analysis identified two important factors which were identified as text difficulty at the micro and at the macro levels. Wagenaar and colleagues conclude that a full description of readability requires analysis at both these levels. The problem is that the available methodologies for analysing readability at the macro level rely extensively on manual techniques and are very time-consuming to apply. It is suggested that, in many cases, the most efficient way of identifying examples of poor readability is probably to test draft materials with the help of a small sample drawn from the population for which the text is intended.

Walker and others (1986)

Peter Walker, Sylvia Smith and Alan Livingston. 'Predicting the appropriateness of a typeface on the basis of its multi-modal features'. *Information Design Journal* 5(1), 1986, 29-42.

There exists a range of adjectives which can be used to describe perception through more than one of the senses: sound, vision or touch. These same adjectives are also used to describe the personalities of people. Examples of such 'multi-modal' adjectives include words like 'smooth', 'hard' and 'warm'.

The three aims of this study were:

- To demonstrate that non-specialists apply such adjectives, in a consistent fashion, both to typefaces and professions.

- To discover whether the adjectives were being taken to represent the same qualities when applied to typefaces and to professions.

- To demonstrate that the judged appropriateness of a typeface to represent a particular profession can be predicted partially by the degree to which they share the same multi-modal features.

Thirteen professions were selected that could be represented by a single word and for which there was a well-established stereotype. These were Baker, Blacksmith, Builder, Butcher, Chemist, Dentist, Doctor, Florist, Hairdresser, Optician, Photographer, Solicitor, and Watchmaker. A selection of 14 display typefaces was also chosen.

Subjects responded to each typeface on a series of 13 seven-point scales. Nine of the scales were pairs of antonyms of multi-modal adjectives: soft-hard, weak-strong, bright-dull, light-heavy, quiet-loud, relaxed-tense, warm-cool, smooth-rough, slow-fast. The other four scales were sad-happy, unfriendly-friendly, feminine-masculine and modern-traditional. The subjects were drawn from the general public, with one group of 33 responding to the typefaces and a second group to the professions.

The results showed that non-specialists can respond both to typefaces and to professions using adjectives that refer to perceptual qualities in different sensory modalities. In doing this there was a significant degree of agreement amongst the subjects. There was some evidence that, when an adjective was applied both to a typeface and to a profession, it was used to refer to the same quality. This was assessed by determining which other adjectives it correlated with in each context. It was noted, however, that this evidence was indirect only, and that further research was in progress.

To test whether it is possible to predict the appropriateness of a typeface to represent a profession the mean ratings for each typeface were compared with the mean ratings for each profession. There was some correlation (both positive and negative) between particular typefaces and professions, but not for all.

The hypothesis was, therefore, tested further by showing 20 new subjects each professional title in six different typefaces. They were asked to rank the typefaces for their appropriateness to represent each of the professions. The results indicated that the appropriateness of the typeface to a particular profession is partially determined by the extent to which they share the same multi-modal features. This was true, however, for only seven of the adjective pairs: strong-weak, bright-dull, heavy-light, loud-quiet, happy-sad, tense-relaxed, cool-warm.

The researchers conclude that the results, if confirmed by further research, could have a number of implications for graphic design practice. The most significant of these is that it would be possible to compare the profile of ratings for the corporate body producing the printed literature with the profile for each of a number of alternative designs. It would also be possible for graphic designers to use the technique to learn from clients the corporate personality they wish to have created.

Waller (1979)

Robert Waller. 'Functional information design: research and practice'. *Information Design Journal* 1(1), 1979, 43-50.

Waller argues that only rarely has there been fruitful cooperation between graphic designers and psychologists. This, he suggests, is because the traditional objectives and methods of both groups are not sufficiently oriented towards the communication of information. He argues that a user-centred approach is needed which would draw from both the intuitive problem-solving skills of designers and the methodologies of psychologists.

In the article, Waller provides a good description of the problems facing an information designer who wishes to learn from studying the results of psychology research. Psychologists often talk of a spectrum from pure to applied research. Pure research is concerned with the investigation of fundamental and relatively abstract aspects of human perception and cognition and, as such, it is often isolated from a practical context and often speculative and exploratory in nature. Applied research uses the same scientific methods to tackle real-world problems more or less directly. Even so, the 'applied' research is often of dubious practical value.

A great deal of the research psychology which is published appears at first sight to be directly addressing an issue of central interest to the information designer. Closer examination shows, however, that it has quite a different purpose. For example, numerous studies on human memory have used strings of letters or numbers as 'stimulus material' for experimental purposes, but the use of typographical material is quite incidental to the main focus of the study. Similarly much work has used illustrations to investigate the role of mental imagery in comprehension, but it is not always the researcher's intention to say anything about the illustrations themselves.

Experiments can be evaluated primarily on their reliability and their validity. Reliability refers to the accuracy and stability of measurements and results. Validity refers to the extent to which the controlled laboratory situation simulates the theoretical model being tested. This has, in turn, led to the concept of 'ecological validity'. Ecological validity refers to the extent to which the controlled laboratory situation represents the real world which the theory reflects and to which the result might be applied.

Furthermore, there is a problem with the generalisability of a large proportion of applied research. So, although it may examine a real-world problem, the results are not, on the whole, generalisible to other contexts. This may be through the choice of research subjects, often college students, or through the choice of materials studied— often single sentences or short passages of fiction.

Waller (1984)

Robert Waller. 'Designing a government form: a case study'.
Information Design Journal 4(1), 1984, 36-57.

An account of research on a prototype postal claim form for
unemployed people claiming Supplementary Benefit. See Lefrere
(1983).

Waller and others (1982)

Robert Waller, Paul Lefrere and Michael Macdonald Ross. 'Do you need
that second colour?'
IEEE Transactions on Professional Communication 25(2), 1982, 80-85.

This paper offers guidance to inform decisions about the use of a
second colour in texts. This guidance is based partly on research
evidence (almost all of which pre-dates 1979) and partly on a study
undertaken by the authors on Open University textbooks.

The authors identify a number situations where a second colour may
be used to advantage:

- Highlighting individual words.

- Highlighting a block of text.

- Presenting a parallel discourse (eg notes in the margin).

- Distinguishing between similar features in a graphic which have
  different functions (eg caption lines from a diagram).

- Highlighting certain parts of an illustration.

- Colour coding of quantities where colour shades are used to
  indicate magnitude.

At the same time, the authors point to some important constraints.
There is a need, for example, to think about which colours are most
easily seen. This is a function of the contrast between ink and paper
and between the first and second colours. The designer also needs to
be aware of the lighting conditions under which the document is
typically likely to be used, and to consider the difficulties of people
with defective colour vision.

There may be further technical problems resulting from the use of a second colour: for example, two sets of proofs will be needed, and the limitations of the cheaper printing and photocopying techniques. They conclude that 'a second colour is only one of a range of graphic factors which must be used with an integrity and consistency of meaning, and with full regard to the users' needs and context'.

Walmsley and others (1981)

SA Walmsley, KM Scott and R Lehrer. 'Effects of document simplification on the reading comprehension of the elderly'.
Journal of Reading Behaviour 13(3), 1981, 237-248.

Four leaflets describing the provision of social services were tested on 52 readers over the age of 60. Each leaflet was tested in three versions:

- The original document.

- A version simplified to meet the requirements of the Dale-Chall readability formula.

- A version simplified subjectively by skilled writers.

The subjects were tested to judge their level of comprehension of each of the texts. This showed that simplification to the requirements of the Dale-Chall readability formula had no effect on comprehension. Simplification through subjective rewriting improved the level of comprehension of only the longest of the four documents.

The researchers conclude that the 'readability' of a document is a very poor indicator of its comprehensibility for elderly people and that simplifying the language of the documents may not be sufficient to improve comprehension. Using a readability measure as a guide to compilation will almost certainly lead to an over-estimate of the number of subjects expected to understand the document.

The study also showed that the subjects consistently rated the subjective versions of the documents easier to read than the original or the objective versions. However, as in other studies, it was found that these views did not correlate with levels of comprehension. Subjective assessments about how well a document will be understood are a poor predictor of actual performance. However, as Patricia Wright points out (see Wright 1980), making a subjective judgment about the difficulty of a document may act as a deterrent to its being read at all.

Walter (1985)

Gerard G Walter. 'Estimating the vocabulary size of the disadvantaged reader'.
IEEE Transactions on Professional Communication 28(4), 1985, 21-25.

This paper describes a vocabulary test in multiple-choice response format, which was administered to two groups: 277 hearing students aged between 9 and 14 years, and 438 hearing-impaired students aged between 10 and 19. The test consisted of sentences with a word omitted, and the subject was required to supply the correct word from a list of five options. The words omitted from the sentence were a stratified random sample of the words in the Word Frequency Book (American Heritage Publishing Co., 1973) and ranged between the 100th most frequently occurring word in printed English to the 25,743rd most frequent.

The results supported the hypothesis that the less often a word appears in print, the less likely it is to be known by a reader. Walter also showed that pre-lingually deaf students are likely to know far fewer printed words than their hearing peers. Whilst hearing subjects knew 63 per cent of the words up to the 24,000th most frequent word, hearing-impaired subjects knew 62 per cent of words only up to the 2,000th most frequently occurring word.

On the basis of the study, the author concludes that a test based on the Word Frequency Book may have some value in assessing the potential readability of the text. It does, however, have limitations. It does not evaluate the ability to comprehend function words, such as articles, auxiliary verbs, conjunctions, prepositions and pronouns. It also fails to estimate a person's knowledge of second or third meanings of words.

Warder and England (1981)

John Warder and Judith England. *Social security research: Rayner forms study.*
Social and Community Planning Research for the Department of Health and Social Security, 1981.

This study was commissioned by the Department of Health and Social Security as part of a wide-ranging review of administrative forms requested by Sir Derek Rayner. The aim of the study was to identify the origin of the difficulties caused by a small number of forms and leaflets relating to National Insurance, and to suggest ways in which they might be overcome. To do this 56 depth interviews were held, studying four forms and two leaflets.

The results showed that, generally, people were unable to understand either the content of particular sections or the need for specific items of information. Explanatory leaflets did not help with this understanding. Where people could not understand a form or leaflet they treated it as unimportant and irrelevant.

It seems that the initial impact of a form or leaflet (its layout, print size, and design) can act as a strong disincentive to it being read and used at all.

Wheildon (1984)

Colin Wheildon. *Communicating, or just making pretty shapes: a study of the validity – or otherwise – of some elements of typographic design.* Newspaper Advertising Bureau of Australia, 1984.

A very practical study which set out to identify the typographical elements which 'not only do not encourage reading, but actually discourage the reader by throwing unnecessary distractions in his or her path, thereby interrupting reading rhythm'. Wheildon carried out the study because he was not satisfied that previous research, with its heavy reliance on the laboratory testing of students, provided any useful findings to inform design practice.

In this study, Wheildon used 224 people who were given several pages of magazine text which was varied to test six design parameters: the positional relationship of headlines to text; serif versus sans-serif type;

the use of unjustified text; the use of spot colour in headlines; lower case as opposed to upper case for headlines, and the ease with which italic type is read. After reading the text, participants were asked questions in order to test their comprehension. The results are described below for each of the main experimental parameters.

Position of headlines
Wheildon established that the eye does move down the page diagonally from top left to bottom right. Illustrations can be used to attract the eye to the top right and bottom left corners. Comprehension scores for text which took account of this were markedly higher, indicating that the best place for a headline is at the top of the page, beginning at the left-hand margin.

Serif versus sans serif
A similar form of test was carried out and the serif type scored much higher for comprehensibility. Most readers found it difficult to hold their concentration when reading the sans serif text.

Justified or unjustified text
Wheildon tested totally justified text, text with a ragged right-hand margin, and text with a ragged left-hand margin and concluded that unjustified setting should be avoided since it can impair comprehension significantly.

Spot colour in headlines
Here he found a paradox. Colour, particularly high chroma colours, initially attract the reader's attention to the page, but then seem to interfere with the reading process. Wheildon concluded that 'this is not a recommendation that a "black" ban be placed on spot colour. Used judiciously and sparingly, it can be a most compelling and useful feature. But great care should be taken that the colour does not get in the way of the message'.

Lower case or upper case for headlines
The author concluded that capital letter headlines are less legible than lower case. Kerning, or closing up the gap between letters, reduces comprehension levels.

Wheildon (1986)

Colin Wheildon. *Any colour as long as it's black.*
Unpublished research in typescript, 1986.

This is a follow-up study to that conducted by the author during the period 1982-84 (see Wheildon 1984) and uses the same 224 adult subjects to evaluate the comprehensibility of texts printed in and on colours.

Participants were asked to read single-page articles printed on white paper in a range of colours, including black, and then on tinted paper. Their levels of comprehension of the texts were then measured. The layout and type employed were in a format that the previous research had shown to offer minimal distraction for the reader. Throughout the study participants were assigned to either an experimental group or a control group. Those in the control group always read identical matter printed in black. The results are described below for each of the main experimental parameters.

Text printed in colour
Text printed in colours (purple, French blue, olive green, warm red, and cyan) yielded a considerably lower level of comprehension than text printed black on white. Comprehension increased the closer the colour was to black.

At the conclusion of each test on a coloured text, participants were asked for general comments on the presentation. The results showed that the coloured type was more difficult to read. However, on being shown pages printed in black and in cyan, 90 per cent said they found the black page more boring. Even so, all readers said they would prefer to read black type.

Text on tinted ground
A second series of tests was conducted into the comprehensibility and acceptability of text printed on tinted grounds. These showed that black text printed on a light (10 per cent) tint had both a high level of comprehensibility and was attractive to readers. Not only were colours and their tints extremely difficult to comprehend, they were also unattractive to the reader.

Black on not-so-black
Increasing the shade strength of the background beyond 10 per cent
significantly reduced levels of comprehension. Readers also
commented that they experienced more difficulty in discerning
the words.

Reverse printing
Reversing the print so that the text was white on black dramatically
reduced the levels of comprehension. This was slightly less the case
when sans serif type was used, but even so the comprehension levels
remained low.

Bold type
Text printed in bold type led to reduced levels of comprehension and
readers frequently complained that it caused fatigue.

It would seem, then, that for maximum comprehension text should
be printed in black on white paper. Printing black on a 10 per cent
coloured tint, however, affected comprehension only marginally,
whilst readers considered it to be a great deal more attractive. Other
devices such as the use of bold or reverse printing adversely affect
both comprehension and reader acceptability.

Italic type
While readers commented that italic type caused an initial reaction
because it was unusual in such volume, the comprehension level was
identical to ordinary type.

Other findings
- 30 per cent found type set wider than 60 characters hard to read and
  a further 22 per cent said they would not read wide-set type.
- 87 per cent found narrow-set type—less than 20 characters—hard to
  read.
- 78 per cent found cross headings useful.
- Only 7 per cent found typeset in capitals easy to read.
- 81 per cent found special screening effects on illustrations to be
  annoying.

Wilbur and Goodhart (1985)

Ronnie Wilbur and William C Goodhart. Comprehension of indefinite pronouns and quantifiers by hearing-impaired students.
Applied Psycholinguistics 6, 1985, 417-434.

Wilbur and Goodhart focus on the difficulties caused by indefinite pronouns and quantifiers in the case of deaf students. The authors make a number of theoretical predictions based on previous linguistic research. Firstly that 'some' would be the easiest of the quantifiers to learn, followed in turn by 'no' 'any', 'all', and finally that 'each' and 'every' would be of equal difficulty. Secondly there would be a parallel order of development for indefinite pronouns containing these quantifiers. Evidence from previous developmental studies of children with normal hearing aged between two and seven years of age supports these theoretical predictions. However, they were not confirmed in experiments with deaf students.

One hundred and seventy eight profoundly deaf students, aged between seven and 23 years were grouped into eight reading levels. They were then presented with specially designed test booklets, each page of which was a complete comic strip using bubbles for speakers and boxes for the narrator. All vocabulary was kept to first grade level or below. Blanks were left in sentences and the subjects were instructed to complete the blanks, selecting from four possible responses. In all, 24 of the sentences contained indefinite pronouns, while 14 contained quantifiers. Overall, indefinite pronouns were found to be easier than quantifiers. There was also a significant improvement with both as reading levels improved. The authors conclude by drawing out the lessons for teaching profoundly hearing-impaired children.

Wilbur and others (1983)

Ronnie Wilbur, Wendy Goodhart and Elizabeth Montandon.
Comprehension of nine syntactic structures by hearing-impaired students.
Volta Review 85, 1983, 328-345.

This study was undertaken as part of a larger investigation into various aspects of captioning television programmes for deaf people.

Using a comic book format, 187 hearing-impaired students were presented with nine previously uninvestigated syntactic structures. These included: 'why' questions; conditionals; non-locative prepositions; indefinite pronouns; quantifiers; modal verbs; elliptical constructions; reciprocal pronouns; and comparative constructions. A total of 125 items were constructed to test the nine syntactic structures. They were reproduced as sentences in speech bubbles, which the students were required to complete from a choice of four possible alternatives (such as 'I can't see ... anything / nothing / all / nobody).

The results of the tests were analysed both for all students by the reading ability level (from one to eight) of the student.

The overall finding, not surprisingly, was that performance improves as the reading level increases. The results of the study also provide general guidelines to the relative difficulty of the various structures— overall, 'why' questions were the easiest.

Wilhite (1989)

Stephen C Wilhite. Headings as memory facilitators: the importance of prior knowledge.
Journal of Educational Psychology 81(1), 1989, 115-117.

Ninety-four college students were given a 4,840-word passage to read, with headings either present or absent. The students were selected from two groups: those with a high degree of prior subject knowledge and those with lay knowledge only.

The beneficial effects of headings on memory recall were shown to be limited to students with existing knowledge, suggesting that headings somehow activate relevant prior knowledge in these readers. Wilhite warns that these results should be interpreted with caution—the only type of performance measured was recognition memory. It is conceivable that low-pre-existing-knowledge readers still benefit from the presence of headings in other ways, such as facilitating search tasks.

Worthen and Valcarce (1985)

Blaine R Worthen and Rebecca W Valcarce. 'Relative effectiveness of personalized and form covering in initial and follow-up mail surveys'. *Psychological Reports* 57(3), 1985, 735-744.

This paper reports the findings of a research project which aimed to determine whether or not personalised covering letters yield higher response rates than form letters.

A questionnaire about college courses was sent to 1,000 school teachers in Utah. Half the questionnaires were sent out with a personalised covering letter, the remainder with a form letter. Follow up letters to non-respondents were similarly divided, so that half of them received a personalised reminder. No statistically significant differences were found in the relative effectiveness of personalised or form letters in either the initial or follow-up mailings.

The results of this study have been further analysed by Ashton Trice (see Trice 1986).

Wright (1979a)

Patricia Wright. *Communicating with the public.* Central Office of Information, 1979.

In 1979 the Central Office of Information commissioned Patricia Wright to undertake a review of research findings which were relevant to the design and writing of leaflets. Her report covers many aspects of information design and brings together the results of a number of research studies that are not otherwise covered in this review.

Posters and leaflet covers
The main factors affecting the legibility of a poster or the title of a leaflet at a distance are the typeface and the colours used. There are two opposing considerations affecting the choice of typeface. The larger the letters the easier they can be seen; but upper case letters take up more horizontal space than lower case. So the key factor to consider for lettering a leaflet title is the length of the line in relation to the width of the leaflet. If the title is short, capital letters are easier to see. If the title is long, then lower case is preferable. An additional

consideration is that short titles are more easily remembered than long ones.

The most significant factor affecting the impact of different colours is contrast. There should be the greatest possible contrast between print and background. When reading at a distance, there is a slight advantage in having light print set against a dark background.

When reference numbers are used on the covers of leaflets, they can be made easier to remember by introducing mnemonics into the alphabetic parts of the code. When three or more digits are used in a number they should be grouped into just two or three digits. If both digits and letters are used they should be kept in two separate groups. If this is not possible, a pattern of changes from letters to digits, such as CB2 EF3 is easier to remember than random changes such as CB2 3EF.

Language of the text
A number of different types of words cause problems. Unfamiliar words present particular difficulties. Obviously if people do not know the meaning of a word in a sentence they will have trouble understanding the whole sentence. Even where an unfamiliar word is understood correctly, however, people will still have greater difficulty understanding the sentence than they would if it used only familiar words.

A rough guide to the familiarity of words is their length. In general the words that people are most familiar with are the short ones. It is therefore better to use several short words than one long one.

Words that are derived from verbs cause problems. Research suggests that people find it easier to handle simple word forms than longer ones. Compare:

- The department will give consideration to a proposal for a reduction in energy consumption.

- The department will consider a proposal to reduce the amount of energy consumed.

Prefixes and suffixes also cause difficulties. It is often possible to use a shorter alternatives, such as *sad* for *unhappy*.

People have more difficulty with negative words - *decrease, forget, omit, under, less* - than with their opposites - *increase, remember, include, above, more*. Similarly, people find comparisons like *bigger, heavier, taller* more easy to understand than the opposite terms - *smaller, lighter, shorter, less*.

Problems arise with the use of the word *not*. In part this is because it is a negative word. But it can also make a sentence ambiguous:

> To qualify you should not be over 65 and in full-time employment.

Generally speaking it is best to avoid using the word *not* except when it is being used to emphasise a point as in *the benefit is not means-tested*.

Certain types of phrase cause people difficulty. Problems arise where a number of qualifiers are used together, as in the phrase *industrial injuries compensation review tribunal*. Verb tenses cause problems. There is a confusion between the future tense and its modification as a command. The distinctions between 'will' and 'shall' or between 'might' and 'may' escape many people. 'Must' is a safer way of expressing a command than 'should'. People also have problems with passive verbs, so an active tense is preferable.

Care needs to be exercised when constructing sentences. People understand sentences joined by 'and' more easily than those joined by 'but'. The word 'or' is more difficult still. Even more difficult are link words implying causal relationships like 'because'. Where sentences contain more than one clause, they are better understood if the main clause comes first, followed by the subordinate clauses.

While long sentences are difficult to understand, the fault lies in the way the ideas are inter-related, not in the length itself. To reduce the impact of this problem, writers should take care when shortening sentences. Ambiguity can be introduced by omitting short function words like 'the', 'to' or 'with'.

People expect that the important information will appear at the beginning or the end of a paragraph rather than in the middle.

Presentation of the text
Wright found that little was known about the ways in which people navigate their way around forms and leaflets. Readers were helped if

breaks in the text corresponded with breaks between pages or between columns.

She also found that little was known about the effect of headings other than readers preferred them to solid blocks of text. At the time when she was writing, there was no research evidence to suggest where a heading is best located.

There was research to suggest that the optimum line length is one that is long enough to get seven or eight words to a line. The maximum recommended line length was 55 characters. Longer lines needed more space between them.

Lower case vertical typefaces are easiest to read. The 'x' height should be between 2mm and 4mm, corresponding to a point size of between 6 and 12. Type that is smaller or larger than this slows the reader down. Proportional spacing aids reading, as does an unjustified or ragged right margin. Using capitals or italics for more than just a couple of words slows readers down and too many typographical variations is confusing.

Colour should be used with care. The research suggested that a minimum contrast of 30 per cent was necessary for easy reading. Yellow on white will seldom achieve this, orange on white is borderline.

Supplements to the text
Text can be supplemented in a number of ways. When using tables, space should be used to guide the reader's eye from one set of figures to another. Items within columns should be grouped and vertical spacing introduced to create groups of five items or less. People appeared to find complex tables difficult to use.

Graphs should be used to illustrate a single point. If two or more curves are shown, they should be labelled directly rather than explained in a key.

Wright found that much of the research into illustrations and pictorial material was misleading as it was carried out in areas where the findings could not be applied directly to public documents, such as children's picture books and toilet doors.

Notes and explanations, like illustrations, are best located in the text close to the material to which they refer. When itemising notes or other material use arabic numerals as they are easier to understand than roman ones or alphabetical sequences.

Wright (1979b)

Patricia Wright. 'The quality control of document design'.
Information Design Journal 1(1), 1979, 33-42.

In order to assess the effectiveness of a public document it is necessary to determine what should be said (content), how it should be said (presentation), and whether the information can be adequately used by the reader (usability). These three factors are at the heart of a discussion of quality control proposed by the author.

For each of the factors, Wright looks at the pros and cons of four behaviourial research methodologies: field studies; interviews; surveys; and laboratory experiments. The results can be summaried as follows:

Research techniques	Three quality control checks		
	Content	Presentation	Usability
Field studies	●	●	
Interviews	●		●
Surveys	●	●	
Laboratory experiments		●	●

Content
It is important to realise at the outset that there can be a mismatch between what the writer wants to write, and what the reader wants to know or needs to be told. Observational field studies will indicate who reads the document, and they may show how the document is encountered. This will have implications for the title of the design of the cover. It will also indicate compatibility requirements—with other information the user may have or with the systems that will be used to process the document. In-depth interviews can provide valuable information on readers' pre-suppositions and conceptual confusions. They can indicate where such assumptions or confusions need to be explicitly corrected in the text. Surveys—of people and documents—

are particularly useful for finding out if special or technical terms are understood.

Presentation

Information from observational field studies which indicates how the text is used, may, for example, influence how the material is presented. There are, however, problems in using field studies to investigate information pamphlet presentation since the study is likely to alter the behaviour of the subjects. Laboratory experiments can give an indication of the comparative performance of different methods of presentation but the results may not be generalisable. Similarly it is possible to carry out a literature survey to investigate the comparative performance of different methods of presentation. The problems here arise with finding relevant research, interpreting and applying research results and integrating them with other, practical factors.

Usability

Non-behaviourial evaluations can be a very inexpensive way of improving a document. The two main methods are critical appraisal and readability tests. Critical appraisal by 'good' writers who are not experts in the subject matter of the document. This will indicate incomprehensible jargon, unstated assumptions, as well as difficult sentence construction and ease of use of the document. Readability formulas are perhaps one of the most widely used means of testing documents. As they become incorporated into computerised text editing systems they become easier and quicker to apply. However it is widely accepted, even by the people who have devised such formulas, that their value is primarily diagnostic and that they have severe limitations when it comes to pinpointing precise difficulties that would arise from the document in use. There are, in addition, a number of behaviourial techniques for evaluating the usability of a document. Field studies of a draft version are impractical for most documents. Testing of pilot forms and leaflet has been undertaken with some success. Interviews can be useful—especially if subjects are given a case study to provide a specific context for the interpretation of the document. These will be useful in identifying particular trouble spots. Laboratory tests can be undertaken of draft documents to assess the performance of the document.

Wright (1980)

Patricia Wright. Textual literacy: an outline sketch of psychological research on reading and writing. In: P Kolers and others (eds), *Processing of Visible Language II,*
Plenum Press, 1980, 517-535.

In this paper, Wright outlines the main lines of psychological research into reading and writing, identifying some issues that have been overlooked. These include for reading:

- Different types of reading.

- Perception of letters.

- Reading of words.

- Reading sentences.

- Reading paragraphs.

And for writing:

- Conceptual approach.

- Selection of the appropriate presentation option.

- Evaluation of the communication.

Wright's outline shows that there are various kinds of reading and that literacy comprises many different skills, associated with both reading and writing. She suggests that one of the deficiencies in the research is in the general assumption that the meaning lies entirely within the text whereas, in reality, readers go far beyond the text in deriving their interpretation.

Wright (1981)

Patricia Wright. 'Informed design for forms'.
Information Design Journal 2(3/4), 1981, 151-178.

A review of the theory underlying form design and the practical lessons suggested by the research evidence. Wright identifies two contrasting approaches: investigations which focus on issues raised by specific forms (action research) and investigations which try to develop a more general understanding of the ways people interact with written material. These approaches, in turn, fall into two further categories: those which aim to determine the functional relationship between design and performance; and those which investigate the underlying cognitive processes (perception, attention, memory, language and decision-making). The author then considers whether it is possible to take action on, and generalise from, the findings of the different schools of research.

Wright then reviews the research that relates specifically to form design. This covers the overall structure; legibility; questions and answers; and adjuncts to the text. Based on this review, Wright presents the following heuristic for form design.

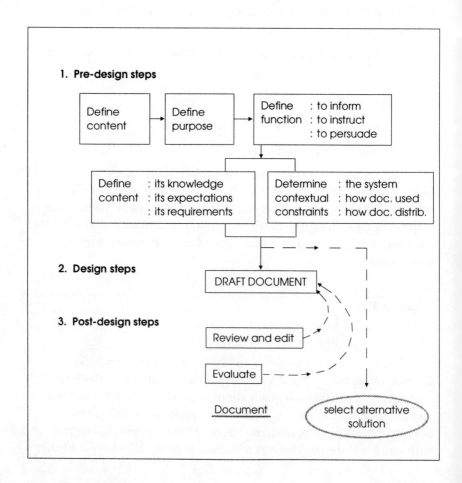

Wright (1982)

Patricia Wright. A user-oriented approach to the design of tables and flowcharts. In: David H Jonassen (ed.), *The technology of text: principles for structuring, designing, and displaying text.*
Educational Technology Publications, New Jersey, 1982, 317-340.

This contribution is a review of research relating to information design issues associated with tables and flowcharts. Wright concludes that it is not possible to distil the research findings into a neat list of guidelines. There are, however, some general principles which might be helpful for designers bear in mind:

- Ease of use depends on more than legibility and layout—in particular it requires that the designer should be aware of how readers interact with printed materials.

- Eliminating redundancy can be a false economy—it may save space, but it can often mean that users have more problems using the table.

- Designers should provide the users of tables and flowcharts with a decision structure.

- Space should be used to help readers perceive the functional groupings within the material.

Wright (1985)

Patricia Wright. Editing: policies and processes. In: Thomas Duffy and Robert Waller (eds), *Designing usable texts.*
Academic Press, 1985.

After reviewing some of the earlier research, Wright reports on the findings of five small investigations, each of which relates to an editing process.

Experiment 1: People's global assessment of text
Forty two adult volunteers were given texts and asked to give them marks out of ten for comprehensibility, content, and style. Six texts were assessed: three written accounts of how to play the game draughts, and three accounts of snakes and ladders. The results showed a considerable degree of agreement about what constitutes a good text and which texts are deficient. At the same time, however,

there were marked differences of opinion among people when they are making global assessments of a text.

Experiment 2: Global assessment of forms
Fifty nine people were each asked to assess five local authority forms. Both the methodology used and the results are of general interest.

Several techniques were used for obtaining a judgement about the relative merits of the forms. First, each form was divided into small sections which were then numbered (for instance, a question, a paragraph of notes, or a column heading). Each person was asked to go through the form and decide how easy they thought each numbered section would be for an applicant to understand. These decisions were recorded on an answer sheet by circling a number between 1 (very easy) and 6 (very difficult) for each of the listed items. Subjects were then asked to assess various design and presentation factors, including the printing, adequacy of the answer space, and ease of understanding the instructions. They indicated their assessment by ticking one of six multiple-choice alternative statements in answer to an assessment question. For example, 'Sometimes statements, words or questions are printed in a way that makes it uncomfortable or difficult to read. Please tick the statement below that comes closest to your own opinion of the printing on this form.'

Finally, the volunteers were asked to make an overall judgement about the design of the form. Here they were told, 'Pretend that you are judging a contest for forms designers, how many marks out of 20 would you give the designer of this form? You should take into account the way in which the questions were phrased as well as the general layout of the form'. The results suggested a higher degree of consistency among the 'editors' than had been apparent in the first experiment, although this consistency fell as the forms became poorer. There was, however, a subgroup who had trouble detecting the inadequacy of specific elements of the form and who were also out of step with the remainder of the group when making global assessments of the various specific aspects of the form. This experiment demonstrated that people's ratings of the elements within a form (and presumably other texts) can be used to identify possible trouble-spots.

By averaging the ratings given to the individual numbered elements of the form, it was possible to identify where revision was necessary.

Experiment 3: Detailed revision of a text
This followed up the second experiment by attempting to identify whether people are poor editors because they do not know what to look for or because they do not recognise where their knowledge should be applied. To do this 31 volunteers were given a text to revise, together with a sheet headed 'Suggestions for improving text'. A further 28 volunteers were given just the text. Within the text were three typographic errors and eight aspects of sentence style, such as the use of passives, which previous research has shown are likely to cause comprehension difficulties.

The groups did not differ in their ability to detect typographic errors. There was, however, a marginally significant difference in the number of corrections made to the intended lapses in style. The groups also differed with respect to the total number of changes they made to the text. These findings seem to be consistent with the view that some editors may lack certain knowledge. When they are given this knowledge in the form of guidelines, they seem to be able to apply it to the text. The precise nature of the changes made to the text were analyzed in detail. These showed significant differences between the two groups, suggesting that people are very willing to adapt the way in which they edit. However, the guidelines seemed to have a more general effect of increasing the number of changes made to the text. So it seems that guidelines do not necessarily operate by supplying knowledge that editors are lacking.

Experiment 4: The relation between preference for linguistic styles and comprehension
Since the earlier experiment been inconclusive, further work was needed to pursue the problem of whether poor editorial performance is due to lack of knowledge or lack of awareness about where to apply this knowledge. Forty nine volunteers were presented with 36 pairs of typewritten sentences which illustrated six sentence styles:

- Sentences with or without nominalisations.
- Sentences with or without relative clauses.

- Sentences with or without adverbial clauses.
- Sentences with or without passive verbs.
- Sentences with or without stacked adjectives.
- 'Garden path' or convoluted sentences.

For each pair, the 'editors' were asked to indicate their preference on a five-category analogue scale. One end of the scale was labelled 'Sentence (a) very much easier' and the other end 'Sentence (b) very much easier'. The mid-point was labelled 'No difference'.

In a second part of the study another 46 people were asked to read each of the sentences when it was projected as a photographic transparency of white typescript against a blue background. A number of nonsense sentences were added to the original set. In order to measure comprehension time for each sentence people were asked to press a button to indicate whether or not they thought it made sense. The results of both parts were as follows.

Nominalisations Twice as many people preferred the verb form as preferred the nominalisation. The sentences containing the verb forms were also read more quickly. Within this overall finding there was, however, variation between the 6 sentences illustrating this point. Some nominalisations, such as reduction and investment, seem to function as lexical terms in their own right.

Relative clauses Here three times as many people preferred the longer sentence containing the relative clause, compared with the two sentence version. The relative clause sentence was also read slightly more quickly.

Adverbial clauses People were presented with three versions of each sentence. The words within the sentence were the same, only the position of the adverbial clause was altered.

Two-thirds of people preferred the adverbial clause to be in the middle of the sentence. In contrast, sentences where the adverbial clause came either early or in the middle were read significantly faster than those where the adverbial clause came at the end.

The author concludes that, as this experiment reduced the recognition problem for editors, the people taking part in the study, may have lacked specific knowledge to help them edit texts.

Experiment 5: 'Correct' style as seen by amateur and professional writers
In the final experiment, Wright compares her results using amateur editors to those obtained in an earlier study using professional technical writers. Forty three people were given a series of eleven expressions in current vernacular usage, such as split infinitives. They were asked to indicate whether they thought each expression was correct, with a tick, or incorrect, with a cross. A further 49 people were asked to suggest alternative wording for any sentence with which they felt unhappy. For many expressions, the general public were much more willing to accept current vernacular usage than were the technical writers. There seemed to be no systematic relationship between a person's age and the tendency to reject certain forms of linguistic expression.

General conclusions
A number of interesting points emerged from this research. It seems that lack of knowledge may not easily be remedied by written guidelines (Experiment 3). Preferences for styles of language may not correspond to the styles that readers find easier to understand (Experiment 4). Above all, it seems that there are considerable differences among people both in the number and the nature of their editorial decisions (Experiments 1 and 2).

Finally, there is some evidence to suggest that the editorial decisions of professional writers are different from those of the general public (Experiment 5).

Wright (1988)

Patricia Wright. 'Functional literacy: reading and writing at work'. *Ergonomics* 31(3), 1988, 265-290.

A paper that considers the phrase 'functional literacy', a convenient term which is used to refer to the information design and information management skills needed in contemporary working life. Research findings alone are insufficient to improve the quality of written materials in the workplace. Wright suggests that readers and writers need to have:

- Search skills for finding information.
- Comprehension skills for interpreting information.
- Inference, reasoning and problem solving skills to apply that information.
- The ability to deal with information systems rather than simply with information.

As well as considering written information, Wright examines the impact of new information technologies on writing and information design. Rather than offer guidelines to help people with information design, she suggests an heuristic for drawing attention to potential trouble spots that may arise when information materials are used. This heuristic invites information designers to ask themselves three categories of questions concerning:

- What readers may do and know before encountering the information, the questions that they will formulate and how they will approach finding the information.
- What happens during the encounter – what comprehension processes are involved and what might help or hinder them.
- What happens after the encounter – how users use their newly acquired knowledge.

Using a hospital signing system as an example of a poor piece of information design that pays little attention to the needs of the users, Wright goes on to show how the application of her suggested heuristic could help to define a more effective and useful system of signs.

Wright emphasises the importance of functional literacy in the modern workplace by pointing to the high costs associated with poor information design and inadequate training. The concept of literacy—and its social consequences—has changed across time and cultures. We think of 'reading' as a leisure activity and few professional organisations give heed to the information design and information management skills needed in the modern workplace.

Wright and Hull (1986)

Patricia Wright and A J Hull. Answering questions about negative conditionals.

Journal of Memory and Language 25, 1986, 691-709.

In most respects the two negative conditionals 'if not' and 'unless' are very similar. The main difference lies in the explicitness of the negation.

Wright and Hull investigated whether readers process the two terms in a similar way. To do this they carried out two complex series of experiments. In both series, 32 adults were presented with two successive sentences on a VDU screen. They were then asked a question which required them to integrate the information from both sentences. For example. Sentence 1 – 'The team would lodge an objection if the referee did not start the game'. Sentence 2 – 'The referee did start the game'. Question – 'Did the team lodge the objection?'.

Each group of two sentences and question was produced in 16 variant forms in which the variables included clause order and the use of 'unless' and 'if not'.

The results suggest that the two terms are processed quite differently, and that 'if not' is processed more accurately than 'unless'. Several possible reasons may underlie this difference: for example, readers may be responding to the fact that the negation is more explicit in 'if not' than in 'unless'. Another possibility is that 'if not' is simply easier to process than 'unless'. A third possibility, and one that was tentatively supported by the research, was that the difference was simply the result of differences in common usage. The other significant finding from this research is that the order of the main and subordinate, conditional clauses did not affect the performance for 'if not' sentences. It was, however, better if subsequent information referred to the condition rather than the action. That is, in the example above, if the second sentence and question were

    'The referee did start the game'

    'Did the team lodge the objection?'
rather than

    'The team lodged the objection'

'Did the referee start the game?'

Wright and Hull (1988)

Patricia Wright and AJ Hull. Reading to do: creating contingent action plans.
British Journal of Psychology 78(2), 1988, 187-211.

This paper reports further work into the use of negative conditionals. The research develops from that reported in Wright and Hull 1986. They carried out three studies to explore the use of 'if', 'if not' and 'unless' and to test the effect of the sequence of the action and condition statements in an instruction.

The studies used volunteers who were asked to follow instructions containing negative conditionals, such as 'Press the button unless the item is cold' or 'Do not tick X unless a daisy is a flower'. They found that statements using 'if' were followed more accurately than those using 'if not' and that 'if not' instructions were followed more accurately than those using 'unless'.

The results also showed that mentioning the action before the condition had no effect on accuracy when the instruction used a negative conditional. However, where the instruction began with an 'if' statement followed by a condition then an action, levels of accuracy were higher than for instructions where the 'if' statement was followed by the action then the condition.

The research findings show that negatives are more of a problem when it is the action that is negated than when the condition is negated. And that condition—action instructions are easier to follow than action—condition instructions. They suggest that this is because the order of the instruction links with the sequence that people apply the action plans: they check the contingency then select the appropriate action.

Wright And Wilcox (1979)

Patricia Wright and P Wilcox. When two 'no's' nearly make a 'yes': a study of conditional imperatives. In: P A Kolers, M Wrolstad and H Bouma (eds), *Processing of visible language VI*, Plenum, 1979, 413-430.

A series of laboratory experiments was carried out to test the effects of negative elements in sentences. In the first experiment, four types of sentences were used:

- No negative ('Only press if the letter is P').

- One negative in the main clause ('Do not press if the letter is P').

- One negative in the subordinate clause ('Press unless the letter is P').

- Two negatives ('Do not press unless the letter is P').

Adult volunteers were given these instructions either visually or aurally. In each case the latency and errors of responses were recorded.

In the second series of experiments, subjects were required to give binary responses to binary stimuli. That is subjects were given two buttons to press in response to instructions such as 'Do not press the right-hand button unless the picture is a square'. The same four constructions were used for the instructions, but this time subjects were only given the instructions visually. It was found that:

- Performance was always better for instructions without negatives.

- Performance with instructions having two negatives is not necessarily worse and may even be significantly better than those with only one negative since the readers could reframe them as a positive instruction.

- Double negatives are more difficult in situations requiring a binary response, than in the cases of a single choice.

Nevertheless, the authors caution against generalising from these results. They argue that there is a 'readily apparent need to explore performance across a range of situations before developing theories about the processes mediating comprehension'.

Wydick (1985)

Richard Wydick. *Plain English for lawyers.*
Carolina Academic Press, 1985.

A very useful set of information design guidelines that contains much of the usual advice on writing, but presented in a highly approachable manner. Although written specifically for practising lawyers, the book is applicable in many other situations.

Yuill and others (1989)

Nicola Yuill, Jane Oakhill and Alan Parkin. 'Working memory, comprehension ability and the resolution of text anomaly'.
British Journal of Psychology 80(4), 1989, 351-361.

Recent research into reading comprehension suggests that successful comprehension depends on having an efficient working memory—in other words, a system to store and process information temporarily. This research study investigated possible deficits in working memory in 7 and 8 year olds who were good at reading but relatively poor at comprehension.

In the first experiment—a test of working memory—poor comprehenders performed generally less well than good comprehenders, especially on the more difficult tasks. In the second experiment, both groups were subjected to a test designed to explore the relationship between working memory and text comprehension. Poor comprehenders were less able to resolve anomalies in children's stories when certain key information was presented several sentences away from the actual anomaly.

These findings lend support to the hypothesis that text processing is influenced by working memory demands and that reading comprehension in children is related to the efficiency of a general (non-linguistic) working memory system.

Zwaga (1989)

Hans J G Zwaga. Predicting the public's comprehension of graphic symbols. In: E D Megaw (ed.), *Contemporary Ergonomics 1989,* Taylor & Francis, 1989, 430-435.

The use of graphic symbols on signs has expanded rapidly in applications where information needs to be presented in language-independent ways. In 1972, the International Standardisation Organisation (ISO) began work on the standardisation of public information symbols (see International Standards Organisation 1984). The ISO developed and adopted a standardisation procedure based on two principles. First, that the standardisation procedures should be applied to a description of the image contents of a symbol—not to the symbol itself. Secondly, that objective proof should be gathered to ensure that particular symbol designs are actually comprehensible to potential users.

Zwaga shows that it is possible to identify good and bad symbols at an early stage of development, and thereby predict their acceptability with the public, by means of a simple estimation test.